DATE DUE		

AIR POWER

OTHER BOOKS BY BILL GILBERT

The Seasons: Ten Memorable Years in Baseball, and in America

Ship of Miracles: A Korean War Rescue

Babe Ruth: Major League Dad, with Julia Ruth Stevens

The Duke of Flatbush, with baseball Hall of Famer Duke Snider

Over Here, Over There: The Andrews Sisters and the USO Stars in World War II, with Maxene Andrews

They Also Served: Baseball and the Home Front, 1941–1945

How to Talk to Anyone, Anytime, Anywhere, with talk-show host Larry King

Real Grass, Real Heroes: Baseball's Historic 1941 Season, with baseball All-Star Dom DiMaggio

Now Pitching: Bob Feller, with baseball Hall of Famer Bob Feller

The Truth of the Matter, with Bert Lance

This City, This Man: The Cookingham Era in Kansas City

Five O'Clock Lightning: Ruth, Gehrig, DiMaggio, Mantle and the Glory Years of the NY Yankees, with baseball All-Star Tommy Henrich

All These Mornings, with *Washington Post* columnist Shirley Povich

They Call Me The Big E, with basketball Hall of Famer Elvin Hayes

Keep Off My Turf, with football All-Pro Mike Curtis

A Coach for All Seasons, with basketball Hall of Famer Morgan Wootten

From Orphans to Champions, also with basketball Hall of Famer Morgan Wootten

High School Basketball: How to Be a Winner in Every Way, with Coach Joe Gallagher.

Municipal Public Relations, with selected coauthors

The 500 Home Run Club: Baseball's 16 Greatest Home Run Hitters from Babe Ruth toMark McGwire, with Bob Allen

AIR POWER

HEROES AND HEROISM IN AMERICAN FLIGHT MISSIONS, 1916 TO TODAY

BILL GILBERT

CITADEL PRESS
Kensington Publishing Corp.
www.kensingtonbooks.com

To the brave men who flew these missions,
Especially those who didn't come back

CITADEL PRESS BOOKS are published by

Kensington Publishing Corp.
850 Third Avenue
New York, NY 10022

Copyright © 2003 Bill Gilbert

All Kensington titles, imprints, and distributed lines are available at special quantity discounts for bulk purchases for sales promotions, premiums, fund-raising, educational, or institutional use. Special book excerpts or customized printings can also be created to fit specific needs. For details, write or phone the office of the Kensington special sales manager: Kensington Publishing Corp., 850 Third Avenue, New York, NY 10022, attn: Special Sales Department; phone 1-800-221-2647.

CITADEL PRESS and the Citadel logo are Reg. U.S. Pat. & TM Off.

First printing: September 2003

10 9 8 7 6 5 4 3 2 1

Printed in the United States of America

Designed by Leonard Telesca

Library of Congress Control Number: 2003103990

ISBN 0-8065-2479-0

Contents

Salutes

Any author who seeks to write a book about the most dramatic missions in the history of the United States Air Force, some of them before World War I, will need help from knowledgeable and professional experts—and plenty of it. It was my great fortune to have such assistance from aviation experts, historians, researchers, commanding generals, and the pilots who made these missions some of the greatest chapters in the Air Force story, from the pursuit of Pancho Villa in 1916 to the Gulf War in 1991.

I am pleased to single them out here, with my gratitude and respect:

Bob Shuman, senior editor of Citadel Press.

Jeremie Ruby-Strauss, senior editor of Citadel Press.

Jenna Bagnini, production editor of Citadel Press.

Brigadier General Paul W. Tibbets, pilot of the *Enola Gay*, the plane that dropped the first atomic bomb in the history of the world on Hiroshima in 1945.

Gerry Newhouse, president/publisher of Mid Coast Marketing in Columbus, Ohio.

Colonel C. V. Glines, curator of the Jimmy Doolittle Museum in Dallas, Texas.

Colonel Ken Herman, a pilot who flew 190 missions during the Berlin Airlift.

Lieutenant Gail Halvorsen, the "Candy Bomber" who brought happiness to so many children in Berlin during the airlift.

Major Robert W. Sternfels, a B-24 pilot in a historic bombing mission over Romania in World War II.

Ted Fusaro, the personnel sergeant for the Maintenance and Supply Group of the Air Force's 58th Fighter-Bomber Wing in the Korean War.

Robert F. Dorr, author of seventy books on the Air Force and airplanes and collector of 250,000 photos showing Air Force missions, personnel, and planes.

Richard P. Hallion, former chief historian of the Air Force.

Four other senior military historians for the Air Force—Herman Wolk, Wayne Thompson, Roger Miller, and Tom Y'blood.

Lieutenant Colonel Steve Kirkpatrick, a B-52 bomber pilot in the Gulf War.

John T. Correll, retired editor of *Air Force Magazine,* the official journal of the Air Force Association.

Pearlie Draughan, librarian for *Air Force Magazine.*

Lynn Gamma, chief archivist of the Air Force Historical Research Agency at Maxwell Air Force Base in Montgomery, Alabama.

Yvonne Kincaid, a reference historian at the Air Force History Office at Bolling Air Force Base in Washington, D.C.

Airman First Class Ryan Hansen of the public affairs staff of the 2nd Bomb Wing at Barksdale Air Force Base, Louisiana.

— Bill Gilbert

Introduction: Eleven Stories and Their Heroes

This book is actually eleven books—eleven stories of the most dramatic missions flown by the men of the United States Air Force in the twentieth century, from flights over Mexico in 1916 to the bombing raids in the desert during America's high-tech Persian Gulf War against Iraq in 1991.

The book tells the stories of the men who flew our historic flights over Tokyo, Ploesti, the Himalayan Mountains, and Hiroshima in World War II and the sustained, fifteen-month drama of the Berlin Airlift in 1948, plus vital missions in Korea, Vietnam, the Gulf War of 1991, and "Gulf War II" in 2003. They were selected because they cover the history of airpower in its dazzling development throughout the twentieth century and into the twenty-first, and its role in the history—civil as well as military—of this nation and all nations during those decades and beyond.

Not all of the stories took place during a shooting war. The Berlin Airlift was conducted during the "Cold War" in 1948, but, as you will see, it was just as dramatic and just as critical to the peace and freedom of America and the rest of the world as the wartime missions that also unfold on these pages.

This book describes three heroic missions in aviation's infancy that remain relatively unknown—the "Mexican Punitive Expedition" to capture the revolutionary-bandit-murderer Pancho Villa in 1916; the St. Mihiel offensive—history's first air war—that led to victory by the Allies over Germany in World War I; and the flight of the *Question Mark* over Los Angeles for six days in 1929, which paved the way for in-flight refueling of long-range bombers in the wars that followed.

As I have done in other books, I submitted my text to experts for their review to ensure its accuracy and completeness and to obtain a consensus on which missions to cover, especially since many of these missions were flown so long ago. Before the manuscript became this book, it was reviewed by many of the people mentioned in the list of "Salutes" above—the pilots who flew these missions, the senior officers who planned them, four military historians of the Air Force, the former chief Air Force historian, the curator of the Jimmy Doolittle Museum in Dallas, plus the authors of many books about these missions.

The stories on these pages are told not by the author of this book alone but also by the courageous pilots and crew members who flew these flights and the men like Billy Mitchell, Curtis LeMay, Bob Sternfels, Paul Tibbets, and others who conceived the missions and commanded them.

This book is a salute to them on behalf of today's 275 million Americans, who owe their freedom to these heroes.

Bill Gilbert
Washington, D.C.
January 15, 2003

PART 1

The Hunt for Pancho Villa

★ 1 ★

"Crazy Birdmen"

Less than thirteen years after the Wright Brothers flew their biplane at Kitty Hawk, North Carolina, and eleven years before Charles Lindbergh became the first person to make a solo flight non-stop across the Atlantic Ocean, American air power was being born, not in the United States but in the skies over Mexico.

It began with political unrest south of the border, in Mexico, which led to serious border disturbances and jeopardized relations between the United States and Mexico. On February 22, 1913, General Victoriano Huerta seized control of the Mexican government after the president, Francisco Madero, was assassinated. At that time, the U.S. Army's Signal Corps, still the agency that housed the fledgling American air arm, had a total of eleven airplanes, eight of them stationed in College Park, Maryland.

In response to the assassination of the Mexican president, Madero's supporters threatened civil war. The American president, Woodrow Wilson, who took office ten days after Huerta seized Mexico's government, adopted a policy of "watchful waiting." The United States withheld recognition of the Huerta government because it had installed itself by force instead of through a democratic process.

Relations between the two nations worsened, and the United States occupied the Mexican port city of Vera Cruz. A war seemed inevitable until President Huerta resigned and General Venustiano Carranza assumed the presidency. Pancho Villa, a

3

Mexican revolutionary and bandit, tried to overthrow Carranza in 1916 by attempting to seize most of northern Mexico, but he failed.

At the same time, World War I, which had started in 1914, was spreading across the European continent and threatening to involve American forces. Major General Benjamin Foulois, in his 1968 autobiography *From the Wright Brothers to the Astronauts,* written with Air Force colonel C. V. Glines, recalled that the Army submitted a budget request in 1916 to Secretary of War Lindley M. Garrison for the Aviation Section of the Signal Corps. The request was for slightly more than one million dollars. In sharp contrast, Germany appropriated $45 million for air power development, Russia proposed to spend $22.5 million, France $12.8 million, Austria $3 million, and England $1.08 million.

Despite the meager amount compared to some other countries, Secretary Garrison slashed the Army's request by more than half and included only four hundred thousand dollars for American military aviation in the budget he submitted to Congress. At that time, according to General Foulois, who was then a captain, the nation's military air strength consisted of 29 officers, 155 men, and a dozen planes.

Foulois was one of those pioneers. He became a pilot in 1909, when fliers, he said, "were regarded as fit inmates for insane asylums." He had ample reason to make this statement. In that year, with little more than a handful of pilots in the United States and Europe, thirty-two of them were killed in plane crashes. Even the Speaker of the House of Representatives, Joe Cannon, had his doubts about the future of flying.

Cannon, in fact, got his first sight of an airplane in the sky on July 30, 1909, at Fort Myer, Virginia. He told someone nearby, "You can't convince me that that thing will fly." After the plane made it into the air, he conceded, "Well, it's flying—but you can't make me believe it will stay up."

The plane made it all the way to Alexandria, turned around, and flew back to Fort Myer. In that flight, the plane's pilot and his partner established three world records—they flew at the almost unbelievable speed of forty-two and a half miles an hour, their round trip covered ten miles, and they reached the dizzying altitude of four hundred feet.

The plane's pilot was none other than Orville Wright, who was demonstrating his invention to officers of the U.S. Army in the hope that they would buy one. The other man in the plane, serving as an observer for the Army, was Foulois.

Foulois writes in his memoirs that he submitted a report on the test flight giving the plane a satisfactory performance rating. The Wrights' plane had already satisfied the Army on at least one important count: It was small and light enough to be transported by horse and wagon. After reading Foulois's report, the Army paid the Wright brothers twenty-five thousand dollars for their plane, plus a five-thousand-dollar bonus. As Foulois wrote, "Now all the new air service needed was a pilot. As it turned out, I was to be it."

Foulois received his pilot training in 1909 from the Wright brothers themselves at College Park, Maryland, where the Army kept its only airplane at that time. Foulois, only five feet, six inches tall, was dwarfed by the new "aeroplane." He joined two other pioneer aviators, Lieutenants Frederic Humphreys and Frank Lahm, in what passed for a training course and logged fifty-four minutes with Wilbur Wright.

Humphreys and Lahm had already started their training when Foulois was assigned to join them, so at the completion of their schooling, Foulois was told by General James Allen, the Army's chief signal officer, to take Aeroplane Number 1 to Fort Sam Houston, Texas, where the weather was better for flying. General Allen told the young officer, "Your orders are simple, Lieutenant: You are to evaluate the airplane. Just take plenty of spare parts—and teach yourself to fly." He did, with the help of occasional letters from the Wright brothers. Foulois said later that he spent considerable time at Fort Sam Houston "writing to Orville Wright, asking him how to execute basic maneuvers, how to avoid basic disasters—in short, how to fly an airplane. As far as I know, I am the only pilot in history who learned to fly by correspondence."

To pay for the spare parts caused by the frequent crashes in those trailblazing days, Foulois was given a maintenance budget of $150 for one year. It was the first for the American Air Force. It wasn't enough, however. By the time Foulois bought various materials and parts for new wings, rudders, an elevator, and a propeller, he had spent three hundred dollars out of his own pocket to keep the new Air Force in the air.

Army Aeroplane No. 1, the plane in which he was following General Allen's orders to "teach yourself to fly," was the "pusher" type of plane, pushed by two chain-driven propellers behind the pilot that were powered by one four-cylinder engine with twenty-five horsepower. One historian later described the plane as "a collection of bamboo poles, more or less indefinitely attached to a gasoline engine."

Before Foulois could fly Army Aeroplane No. 1, he had to unpack it. It arrived in San Antonio in seventeen wooden cases. Eight enlisted men reassembled the plate under the watchful eye of Lieutenant Foulois. The unpacking and reassembling took place on the fort's parade ground, and as the men worked, veteran members of the U.S. cavalry mocked them with needling remarks like, "What are you making, boys—a kite?" They called Foulois and his workers "crazy birdmen."

Despite their taunts, the members of the cavalry at Fort Sam proved helpful. Foulis said they "even aided us as we improvised our way into the wild blue yonder. A blacksmith lent his forge and skill to help us fabricate parts. A tailor helped us sew linen for wing, elevator, and rudder surfaces. A plumber secured pipe fittings to fuel lines."

After his course of self-instruction, Foulois made his first four solo flights on March 2, 1910, for a total of less than an hour in the air. He achieved a record that surely has never been equaled by any pilot: He made his first takeoff, first solo flight, first landing, and first crash on the same day.

On his last landing, Foulois was almost thrown out of the plane because of turbulence. Aeroplane No. 1 ended up in the shop for ten days. As a result of that experience, Foulois took action to make sure he wouldn't come close to being thrown out of any more planes. The saddle maker of a field artillery unit modified a trunk strap to hold Foulois in his seat. Together they invented the seat belt.

The experience served to remind him what Orville Wright had taught him: "Coming down is the most critical part of flying."

Meanwhile, interest in aviation was growing, stimulated by a continuing series of record-setting achievements that sparked the public's imagination. In August 1911, the first "long cross-country flight" was announced, when the Army was invited to send two airplanes from College Park to the annual encampment of the District of Columbia National Guard near Frederick, Maryland, a distance of forty-two miles. One plane piloted by Lieutenants Thomas Milling and Roy Kirtland had to make a forced landing near Kensington, Maryland, a Washington suburb, because of engine failure. The two pilots in the other plane, Captain Charles Chandler and Lieutenant Henry H. "Hap" Arnold, a future chief of staff of the Air Force, became lost on the return flight to College Park and landed to ask directions from a farmer. In trying to take off again, they crashed. They had to take a train home.

Arnold set an altitude record for military planes when he reached 3,260 feet on a local flight from College Park, a mark that he topped eleven days later when he reached an altitude of 4,167 feet.

Aware of the growing interest in aviation, Congress appropriated funds for fiscal year 1912 that led to the establishment of the nation's first flying school at College Park plus the purchase of five planes and the appointment of two students to learn to fly them.

Another dimension of aviation—its potential for military uses—was also coming in for attention. A former Coast Artillery officer, Riley Scott, invented a bombsight in 1911 and brought it to College Park for testing. During the tests, Scott lay prone on the lower wing of his plane with the sight, which weighed sixty-four pounds, on the leading edge. Bombs weighing eighteen pounds each were dropped within ten feet of a target that measured four feet by five feet.

As 1911 ended, recognition was growing that future military

planning would have to include planes with longer flying range and a capacity for carrying heavier loads if they were to support troops on the ground. It was widely accepted by that point that airplanes had two military purposes: aerial reconnaissance and the ability to fly senior ground officers to various locations quickly. "Even though bombs had been dropped and guns fired from planes," Benny Foulois wrote in 1968, "no one took these efforts as giving any promise that the airplane could ever become an offensive weapon."

Foulois, who went on to serve in the Spanish-American War, the aerial pursuit of Pancho Villa, and World War I, and who became one of America's most famous air generals, almost never got to serve in anything but that first war. In October 1911, he fainted at the breakfast table and was rushed to Walter Reed Army Medical Center in Washington. The diagnosis: acute appendicitis. After successful surgery, a nurse told him his heart had stopped beating twice during the operation. The doctors saved his life each time by applying artificial respiration.

She told him, "Lieutenant Foulois, there's only one reason you're alive. When your name was called out at the Pearly Gates, you were refused admittance, and when your name was called out at the devil's door, you were turned down again. They wouldn't have you in either place."

A medic at Walter Reed confirmed the nurse's story by pointing out a window later and saying to Foulois, "See that building there, Lieutenant? That's the hospital morgue. We had a locker all reserved for you in there for the first ten days." Washington's newspapers ran major articles about the famous flier's critical condition. One published what Foulois later called "an advanced obituary" under a headline that read:

NATION'S FOREMOST AIRMAN
NOT EXPECTED TO LIVE

Foulois may well have been the first strong military advocate for air power, ahead of the famed Billy Mitchell, a point that Foulois discussed willingly, even eagerly, in his book. While attending the Army's Signal School at Fort Leavenworth, Kansas, in 1907, Foulois wrote a thesis with a title that obscured the importance of its subject: *The Tactical and Strategical Value of Dirigible Balloons and Aerodynamical Flying Machines.*

He wrote that Germany and France were the leading nations in "aerial accomplishments," with England closing the gap. He made a prediction, bold for the time, that, "In all future warfare, we can expect to see engagements in the air between hostile aerial fleets"—airplanes actually fighting in the air.

Noting the progress already made by Germany, France, and England in the military applications of air power, Foulois wrote, "Such activity on the part of these powers makes it imperative that we take a like interest if we do not wish to be outclassed in army equipment."

Then, in a statement by the young officer that provided a remarkably accurate look into the future, Foulois wrote:

> Our geographical position has saved us from numerous difficulties in the past, but it is hardly possible that we can expect to be unmolested in the future, with such means of transport and communications as are available at the present day.

In his autobiography, Foulois was candid about these farsighted predictions and the role played by Billy Mitchell in voicing the same concerns beginning a few years later. He pointed out that his thesis was dated December 1, 1907, and was relayed to the staff of the chief signal officer for study. "I make a point of this," he said in his book,

> because many years later the world was to give credit to a brother officer of mine named Billy Mitchell for being the first military man to foresee the future of the airplane as a weapon of war. With all due respect to Mitchell, neither he nor his worshippers can document that claim. As far as I know, I was the first military man in modern history to predict the future military uses of the airplane and predict them accurately.

He added out that Mitchell wrote in 1913 that aviation was a reconnaissance device and "the offensive value of this thing has yet to be proved."

In a footnote in his autobiography with Colonel Glines, General Foulois was even more blunt. "A zealous and jealous man by nature," he said of Mitchell, "it was inevitable that the two of us would clash someday. We did, and he attacked me viciously many times in print." Foulois said he was making his comments about Mitchell in his book "in the interest of historical accuracy."

On the night of March 9, 1916, Pancho Villa led a band of invaders across the U.S.-Mexican border into the town of Columbus, New Mexico, where his raiders killed seventeen Americans before they were driven off by members of the U.S. 13th Cavalry.

President Wilson wasted no time in retaliating. He abandoned his policy of "watchful waiting" the next day and ordered a "punitive expedition" of U.S. Army forces into Mexico to find Villa and his men and bring them to justice. The expedition was under the command of Brigadier General John J. Pershing. The assignment soon made Pershing an international celebrity, helping to qualify him for his leadership role in World War I the next year as the acclaimed "Black Jack."

The American response to Villa's border excursions consisted of twelve-thousand soldiers under Pershing's command. One of the key units in his force was the 1st Aero Squadron, which arrived in Columbus on March 19, 1916, composed of eleven pilot-officers, eighty-four enlisted men, and one civilian mechanic. That unit grew to become the United States Air Force. Wilson's new secretary of war, Newton Baker, ordered Pershing to "make all practical use of the aeroplanes at San Antonio, Texas, for observation" and to "telegraph for whatever reinforcements or material you need."

In his autobiography with Colonel Glines, Foulois said:

> While I wondered what was going to happen, I mentally planned what I would do if the 1st Aero Squadron were

ordered to help Pershing. During the three days after Villa's raid, I made it a point to talk to all of my men individually to find out what problems they were having both on and off the job. I checked over the eight planes, ten trucks, and one automobile assigned. I looked at maps of Mexico and memorized names of towns, rivers, mountains, their elevations and distances between major points. I reviewed the airplane maintenance problems we had and inventoried the stocks of spare parts, gasoline, and personal equipment for the men.

Foulois didn't like what he learned. "The answers to my self-asked questions were disturbing," he wrote:

We might be able to last thirty days, I told myself, but after that we would probably be in deep trouble for parts. The sand and heat in the daytime and the cold of Mexican nights would probably take enough of a toll on parts, planes and men. To add a requirement to fly many missions in support of ground troops would put a severe strain on the squadron. I gritted my teeth, drove my men to distraction with my questions about their personal readiness to go into the field, and watched the newspapers.

The 1st Aero Squadron received orders at noon on March 12, 1916, to proceed by train to Columbus. Foulois was ready.

I reacted automatically, as if I had been practicing, and I guess I had. Within four hours, the squadron's complete equipment was packed and ready to go. The next morning, we flew the planes to the Fort Sam drill grounds, where they were disassembled and loaded on flatcars. Shortly after midnight, we left San Antonio and arrived at Columbus about thirty hours later.

The expectation was that the 1st Aero Squadron would be employed for observation of Pancho Villa's forces and the advanced parties of the U.S. expedition to find him, to carry mail and dispatches, and for aerial photography. Before leaving San Antonio, however, Foulois requested a Scott bombsight, plus bombs and machine guns, which were starting to be used on the war planes of Germany and France in the war in Europe.

"I never received sight, bombs, or guns," Foulois said. "The reason was simple: They weren't to be had."

Members of the 1st Aero Squadron began flying reconnaissance missions to locate their own troops as well as those of Villa. If their missions were not as dramatic as those that followed in the wars of the twentieth century, they were dangerous and heroic in their own way and their own time. The pilots and crew members, after all, were flying what amounted to operational missions only one decade after the airplane itself had first been flown successfully.

The initial flight was piloted by Foulois with his deputy, Captain Townsend Dodd. They flew thirty miles into Mexico, the first aerial reconnaissance flight by U.S. military aircraft ever made over foreign territory. "Although we had a negative report to make to General Pershing," Foulois said, "this fact alone was significant for it meant that there were no Mexican rebels within a day's march of the head or flanks of his infantry and cavalry columns."

A report by Foulois, then a young captain in the Army's Signal Corps who became a major general and chief of the Air Corps in 1931, described the harrowing nature of some of history's first wartime flights. In his thorough way, Foulois, who became known as "the Little General" and "General Benny" as he rose to the top of America's military air service, wrote that the first American wartime air casualty occurred when Lieutenant T. S. Bowen, flying in "whirlwinds and terrific vertical currents of air," crashed while attempting to land. "The plane was completely wrecked," Foulois said in his report, "but Lieutenant Bowen escaped with a broken nose and minor injuries."

The pioneering missions included flying in severe weather in those years before instruments were invented—a time also marked by engine failures, defective propellers, plane crashes, forced landings, and construction defects.

Foulois reported that the 1st Aero Squadron had hardly been

in any condition to fight a war, a "punitive expedition," or anything else. He said his squadron had eight old, low-powered Curtiss planes that were unsuitable for flying long distances. The ground equipment available to him consisted of "ten trucks, one automobile and a few spare parts," according to his coauthor, Colonel Glines, in *Air Force Magazine,* the journal of the Air Force Association.

In his report, Captain Foulois said, "All officers thoroughly appreciated the fact that motor failure while flying through mountainous canyons and over rugged mountains would invariably result in death." He added, "They also realized that, in the event of a forced landing, even if safely made, there was every possible risk of being taken prisoner by an enemy whose ideas of the laws of war might not be on a par with those of our own country."

Five of the first eight planes used in the pioneering aerial operation were wrecked. Another, damaged in a forced landing, was abandoned. The result was that on April 20, with the operation only one month old, only two airplanes remained, and both of them were considered unsafe for continued service. They were flown back to New Mexico and destroyed.

The overall operation to find Pancho Villa and force him to stay on his side of the border failed, partly because the American forces were ordered to avoid using the Mexican railroads for transportation in their pursuit. The troops were withdrawn in 1917.

In his 1968 autobiography, General Foulois offered a unique view of the Mexican Punitive Expedition. "As I read of Villa's attack and subsequent withdrawal across the border," he wrote, "I realized for the first time in my life that I was visualizing the raid from an airman's point of view." He said that in his mind he could picture the location, the raid itself and other elements of the expedition "as though I were hovering above the scene. In short, I realized that I was thinking about a ground battle from the vantage point of the sky."

General Foulois continued,

> It is this third-dimensional point of view of ground events that sets the airman apart from his earth-bound

colleagues. Experienced pilots always have it. Only rarely is anyone whose life is tied to the ground so gifted that he can truly assess military situations with the omni-science of the flier. This difference has long separated the men of the air from their counterparts in the Army and Navy.

Foulois criticized Wilson's conduct of the Mexican Punitive Expedition. "Historians have concluded that President Woodrow Wilson's overall policy regarding Mexico was both ineffective and unsuccessful," he wrote in 1968. "His military policy must be considered likewise. His dispatching of the punitive expedition without adequate backing, while assigning to it a most difficult mission, was an improper application of military persuasive force."

From March 15 to August 15, the men of the 1st Aero Squadron flew 540 missions, logging a total of 345 hours and 43 minutes of flying time, all of this shortly after the flight of the Wright brothers. The total distance of their flights amounted to 19,553 miles, a figure that could be imagined only by the most farsighted visionaries of that era.

In a special report dated August 28, 1916, on the operations of the 1st Aero Squadron during the expedition, Captain Foulois described the hardships endured by these first combat pilots. "All officer pilots on duty with the Squadron during its active service in Mexico were constantly exposed to personal risk and physical suffering." Because the planes were not big enough to carry heavy loads, "it was impossible to carry even sufficient food, water, or clothing on many of the reconnaissance flights. During their flights, the pilots were frequently caught in snow, rain, and hail storms which, because of their inadequate clothing, invariably caused excessive suffering."

Pilots were forced to land in the Mexican desert and other hostile country fifty to seventy miles from their American posts. In such cases, the pilots abandoned their planes or destroyed them, then set out on foot through desert country and mountains until arriving in an exhausted condition at an American camp.

Hostility from the surrounding population was another hazard for the American fliers. On a a flight to Chihuhua to meet with the U.S. Consul, local citizens confronted Foulois after he landed. "A number of townspeople had seen us circling south of the city," he wrote, "and came running toward the field we selected." He said four men "waved rifles at us excitedly when we landed."

As his pilot took off again, Foulis said, "I immediately started walking briskly toward the city and tried to ignore the group shouting and shaking their fists at the departing plane. Four shots were fired, but Lieutenant Dargue got away. . . . I shouted at the crowd to divert their attention." Foulois added that the four men "wheeled and leveled their rifles at me. I was defenseless except for a Colt .45, which was no match for four Winchester rifles. There was nothing I could do but put my hands up and pray. I did both."

For what it was worth, Foulois was about to make history. He was thrown into a jail cell. "An iron door clanged shut behind me," he said, "and I became the first American aviator ever to become a prisoner of war."

The military governor, a General Gutierrez, described by Foulois as an "affable" man, intervened and negotiated his release.

The role of air power in the hunt for Pancho Villa was not lost on Secretary of War Newton Baker. In a hearing on Capitol Hill, he said:

> The men in the Aviation Corps have been almost exclusively comparatively young men, very young men, indeed, and they have been engaged in an art desperate, daredevil, hazardous indeed, so that they have an attitude toward life and toward themselves that men have who are engaged in an especially hazardous service. Being fliers, they have had rather a disposition to chafe at the restraint and discipline which was made for more normal kinds of service, feeling that they were not adapted to the regulations and restrictions of men who were not engaged in so unusual an occupation. In other words, they had an impatience at being controlled by men who did not themselves know the business in

which they were engaged. I do not want to be understood to criticize these young men. They are pioneering for the Army and the United States and their exploits are superb. The net result of it all is that I am going to reorganize the entire Aviation Section.

It was one of the early steps that led to the establishment of the Air Force as a separate branch of the U.S. armed forces under the Unification Act, which was signed into law by President Truman more than forty years later, in 1948.

Despite the harsh conditions and constant dangers endured by Captain Foulois and his men, plus his strong criticism of Wilson's conduct of the Mexican Punitive Expedition, Foulois took a positive view of the hunt for Pancho Villa. "Although Pershing failed to capture Villa," Foulois wrote, "the activities of the American troops in Mexico and along the border were not wasted effort. The dispersal of his band by the penetration of American forces deep into Villa's territory put an end to serious border incidents."

Foulois was also optimistic in assessing the role and effectiveness of air power in future wars. He said the experience and knowledge gained by the pilots and the military planners during the expedition would accelerate the development of the Army's "aviation service." That acceleration was ordered one year and one month later, in the first major air war in the history of the world.

PART 2

The St. Mihiel Offensive of World War I

★ 2 ★

"Be an American Eagle!"

Even before the American expedition into Mexico in 1916, the world was witnessing the arrival of air power as a means of fighting wars, maybe the most destructive means ever devised by mankind. In September 1915, with the Wright brothers' achievement only twelve years in the background, the people of London were shocked witnesses to what warring nations could do with airplanes. Their city was bombed by the German Air Force in that second year of World War I. The raid caused two and a half million dollars in damage.

Immediately after, lighting restrictions were imposed on the people of London, an effect of war never experienced before. In that same year, the British government published posters showing silhouettes of German and British warplanes to help citizens recognize whether approaching planes were friend or foe. In large, bold, underlined capital letters, the posters carried the grim heading:

PUBLIC WARNING

The posters offer a rare insight into the effect of the new weapons of war on the people of the world. Not only had they never experienced anything like this before, but they hadn't even imagined that conditions like these could exist in their lives.

Nevertheless, with parts of the message in bold type, the posters told Londoners:

> The public are advised to familiarize themselves with the appearance of British and German Airships and Aeroplanes so that they may not be alarmed by British aircraft and may take shelter if German aircraft appear. **Should hostile aircraft be seen,** take shelter **immediately** in the nearest available house, preferably in the basement, and remain there until the aircraft have left the vicinity. Do not stand about in crowds **and do not touch unexploded bombs.**

When the United States entered World War I by declaring war on Germany on April 5, 1917, America was alarmingly unprepared for an air war. General Foulois wrote in 1968, "It is almost impossible to realize now the utter unpreparedness of the United States in April, 1917. Germany had entered the war with nearly 1,000 airplanes, France with about 300, and England with about 250. We not only had less than 100, but ours were already obsolete and not a single one was suitable for combat."

Recruiting posters showing fierce-looking American eagles in the skies with biplanes—presumably ours—in their midst called on America's young men to:

JOIN THE ARMY AIR SERVICE—BE AN AMERICAN EAGLE!

By 1918, the last year of the war, American air strength had been bolstered considerably, and a young Army colonel in the Signal Corps, the first home of today's Air Force, was assigned the responsibility of supporting an attack by the U.S. First Army against the St. Mihiel "salient"—the military term for the battle line that projects farthest toward the enemy. The Germans had held such a salient on the Western Front since 1914. It was a V-shaped part of the German line that ran some thirty-five miles across its base and fifteen miles up to its apex.

Since 1914, the Germans had resisted all attempts by the French to break their salient. In September of that year, the Germans had captured St. Mihiel during an attempt to envelop the fortress of Verdun. They failed to take the fortress, and the salient remained relatively quiet. This calm was achieved in part because the rising terrain made the salient easy for the Germans to defend, even though it was too narrow for them to use as a launch point for an offensive campaign.

Over the next four years, the Germans fortified the region with trenches, barbed wire, and concrete pillboxes in the front line. Behind that line was a second line of the same kinds of barricades. In the unlikely event that the Allied forces could break through the first line and then the second, they would encounter a third barricade—the Hindenburg Line, a series of heavily wired trenches and sturdy dugouts equipped with German armament. As if all this weren't enough, the salient was defended by eight divisions of ground troops.

In March 1918, the German army unleashed its last great offensive on the Western Front, and many observers thought Germany was close to winning the war. The Allied commander, General Pershing, was forced to separate his American fighting forces so various units could come to the aid of French and British forces in May and June during the Battle of Château Thierry.

This led to a battle of a different sort, according to Walter J. Boyne, the former director of the National Air and Space Museum in Washington, a retired Air Force colonel and an author. Writing in *Air Force Magazine* in February 2000, Colonel Boyne said, "Because they thought a precedent had been set, Pershing's British and French counterparts were taken aback when he insisted that the American Army fight the next battle as a unit and under his command. Pershing's demand provoked a pointed argument with Field Marshal Ferdinand Foch, the Allied Supreme Commander in Chief," but Pershing won that battle within the war.

Two months later, Pershing combined his sixteen divisions into the U.S. 1st Army, supplemented by a corps of soldiers from the French Army, and then pledged that his fighting forces would break the German salient at St. Mihiel. The American Expeditionary Forces—now indelibly written into history books as the AEF—was assigned the mission of breaking through the St. Mihiel salient, with the U.S. Infantry being supported by American air power. The commander of the air campaign was a thirty-nine-year-old colonel named Billy Mitchell.

Despite the German stronghold at St. Mihiel, Pershing agreed to pinch off the salient as the first step in a series of Allied counteroffensives designed to stop the Germans and win the war, if he could. This was to be done through a coordinated attack by ground and air. Walter Boyne pointed out in his magazine article, "He was not an airman, but Pershing believed that control of the air was necessary . . . ."

The engagement that followed became the greatest air battle of World War I, with Mitchell and almost fifteen hundred planes under his command fighting against five hundred German planes in an engagement that lasted four days. The Americans did not fly alone. Pilots and planes from England, France, Italy, and Portugal teamed up with the U.S. airmen to execute the Allied strike. The objective was to force the German army out of its salient, breaking battle lines as part of a larger strategy to puncture the German lines at various points and wipe out the German Army along the Western Front.

Lieutenant Colonel George M. Lauderbaugh of the Airpower Research Institute wrote that another objective of the mission was to gather information about the enemy's whereabouts and apparent intentions. That required observation by the Allied pilots, but therein lay a serious risk: Closer air observation could lead the German defenders to think something might be in the works, so secrecy had to be one of the orders of the day. "Phony patrols, false movements and communications, construction of dummy airdromes and a host of other methods were employed to maintain secrecy," Lauderbaugh wrote.

Mitchell, as always when in command, was a hands-on leader. "On-scene observers," Lauderbaugh said, "remember Mitchell as being everywhere, seemingly at the same time. He was frequently in the air, checking the progress of plans. He would drop in on airfields and chat with crews. His boundless energy enabled him to review the volumes of orders that went out and the reports that came back in."

In all, Mitchell would be commanding an airborne force of ninety-nine squadrons. The French and Italian commanders agreed to place their air units under Mitchell's command. The British agreed to cooperate, but they retained command of their bombers. Mitchell thus commanded twenty-six American squadrons, sixty-one French, three Italian, and nine British. It would be a test for all proponents of air power, including Mitchell, their most vocal advocate—the man who had said, "Men will someday wage war in the sky."

Considering the sorry state of American air power, or the lack of it, at the beginning of the war, it was remarkable that the mission could be attempted at all. General Pershing said after the war, "At the start of the war, no American air unit had received combat training." The two flying fields operated by the Army had only fifty-five trainers. Pershing continued, "Fifty-one were obsolete, and the other four were obsolescent." No plane flown by the Allies in World War I was manufactured in the United States.

In addition, the Allied airmen faced a strong German air force. The Germans may not have been quite as strong as Mitchell wanted people to believe. "His estimate was for effect," Colonel Boyne wrote. "He had intelligence reports showing that the enemy had 150 pursuit aircraft, 120 reconnaissance aircraft and 25 'battle airplanes' (the kind used for ground attacks) available."

Mitchell's command was composed of 1,481 planes, the largest airborne force ever formed for one combat operation. His aerial fleet consisted of 366 observation plans, 323 bombers, ninety-one night bombers, and 701 pursuit planes. The unit also included twenty-one balloon companies, fifteen of them American.

In retrospect, the prospects for success at St. Mihiel were far brighter than anyone had any way of knowing at the time. The reason: the leaders involved. With General Pershing in command of all Allied forces, the responsibility for coordinating the movements of the ground troops with the air attack into the overall offensive was conceived and supervised by George C. Marshall.

Pershing's staff also included Brigadier General Douglas MacArthur and Colonel George S. Patton Jr. The assault from the air was planned and executed by Billy Mitchell. One of the pilots who contributed to the victory became an air hero in both world wars, Captain Eddie Rickenbacker. With an all-star lineup like that, it is clear now that success was assured.

Lauderbaugh pointed out that "Mitchell understood the airplane made war three-dimensional." This understanding, plus his driving personality, gave the Allied airmen the leadership and the force needed to overcome the German superiority.

"The plans were incredibly detailed," Colonel Boyne wrote in *Air Force Magazine:*

> They laid out exactly how the army observation corps, bombardment and pursuit units were to operate. These instructions included everything from orders for daily procedures, to how formations would be flown, to the exact format of the mission reports, and the chain of command through which they would be forwarded. There were even explicit instructions on how pilots and observers were to conduct themselves in case of capture.

During the buildup period before the raid to shatter the St. Mihiel salient, pursuit planes were kept in the air over each airfield twenty-four hours a day so enemy pilots would not spot the dramatic increase in Allied planes on the ground.

At the same time, the Allied pilots were doing some spotting, too. "The front was photographed daily," Boyne reported, "with photo-interpreters checking to see where artillery was emplaced, the condition of the trenches, and other near-term events. Sorties [individual missions] were also flown deep behind enemy lines, photographing and observing traffic on roads and railways, checking the activity at ammunition dumps, and establishing targets for both day and night bombardment operations."

One of the leaders of that third dimension called air power, Eddie Rickenbacker, arrived at Mitchell's headquarters on September 11, 1918, the night before the start of the mission. It was set for

0500 hours—five o'clock in the morning—the next day. The air strike would be accompanied by a ground attack of three hundred thousand troops under the command of General Pershing. Three hours later, 110,000 French troops joined the American ground force.

Rickenbacker became the highest-ranking American "ace" of World War I, with twenty-six "victories"—planes shot down—to his credit, a number that could have been even higher if he had not been grounded for two months with an ear infection. In remembering his excitement the night before what became known as the St. Mihiel offensive, Rickenbacker still had trouble containing his enthusiasm:

> Precisely at five o'clock, I was awakened by the thundering of thousands of colossal guns. It was September 12, 1918. The St. Mihiel Drive was on! Leaping out of bed, I put my head outside the tent. We had received orders to be over the lines at daybreak in large formations. It was an exciting moment in my life as I realized that the great American attack upon which so many hopes had been fastened was actually on. I suppose every American in the world wanted to be in that great attack. The very sound of the guns thrilled one and filled one with excitement. The good reputation of America seemed bound up in the outcome of that attack.

The guns Rickenbacker was hearing were the American artillery, which began softening up enemy resistance with a barrage that started in rain, high winds, and fog at 1 A.M.

The "good reputation of America" was in jeopardy even before the St. Mihiel Offensive began. Six bombers patrolling in bad weather before the attack became disoriented and accidentally flew over the German lines. They ran out of fuel and eventually were captured. In other mistakes, orders arrived after deadlines; balloons to support the mission became tangled in telephone lines hung up by the Signal Corps; rainy French weather turned the grass and dirt runways into mud; some pilots found targets difficult to spot because of cloudy conditions.

Accompanied by a fellow pilot, Reed Chambers, in another "aeroplane," Rickenbacker flew into "the very heart of the St. Mihiel salient." The two encountered a column of enemy soldiers mounted on horseback. "I sprinkled a few bullets over the leading teams," Rickenbacker remembered. "Horses fell right and left. One driver leaped from his seat and started running for the ditch. Halfway across the road he threw up his arms and rolled over upon his face. He had stepped full in front of my stream of machine-gun bullets!"

Rickenbacker continued, "The whole column was thrown into the wildest confusion. Horses plunged and broke away. Some were killed and fell in their tracks. Most of the drivers and gunners had taken to the trees before we reached them."

When Rickenbacker and Chambers returned, they reported their success. "This was evidently splendid news and exactly what G.H.Q. [General Headquarters] had been anxious to know," Rickenbacker wrote, "for they questioned us closely upon this subject, inquiring whether or not we were convinced that the Germans were actually quitting St. Mihiel."

While Rickenbacker and Chambers were doing their part, five hundred other pilots strafed and bombed the Germans along the Western Front. Another thousand planes headed deeper into enemy territory to sever and bomb supply lines, and disrupt communications.

While Pershing watched from an abandoned fort high on a hill overlooking a part of the salient, the roads out of it became clogged with German soldiers. Even the foggy, rainy weather could not stop the Allied aerial offensive. Restrictions normally imposed during bad weather were relaxed so the flights could continue. Pilots reported their successes with convincing evidence—enemy balloons destroyed, aircraft shot out of the air, and roads drilled to pieces by bullets from the Allied planes.

On the first day of the air offensive, Americans flew 390 sorties and dropped 14,300 pounds of bombs. As the Allied bombing continued from the air and the ground forces moved into the salient relentlessly and almost unopposed, victory became apparent.

By the night of September 16, the Americans had flown 2,469 sorties, fought 145 aerial duels with enemy pilots, and dropped 44,118 pounds of bombs. Allied pilots claimed to have shot down fifty-two enemy planes, although most of these claims were not confirmed. The cost to the Allies was twenty planes lost, at least forty crew members killed in action, and another sixteen captured.

The offensive became a success in only four days, with the outcome already obvious on the second day—Pershing's fifty-eighth birthday. After four years, the German salient had been broken, a major strategic victory for the Allies.

The victory produced fifteen thousand German prisoners of war while also recapturing two hundred square miles of French territory. One American "doughboy"—the nickname for American fighting men in that war—said, "We had to press forward so fast we could not keep track of the prisoners, but gave them a kick in the back and sent them on their way."

The Air Force history of the St. Mihiel Offensive said:

> Despite handicaps of weather and inexperience, the Air Service contributed all in its power to the success of this St. Mihiel operation. The staff was kept informed of developments practically hourly by clear and intelligible reports. The hostile air forces were beaten back whenever they could be attacked, the rear areas were watched, photographed and bombed. Our airplanes participating in the battle, by the material damage and confusion which they caused, helped to increase the total prisoners.

Colonel Boyne pointed out, "There would be other battles . . . and more casualties as well, but St. Mihiel had established the Air Service as a fighting command, willing to take losses to learn its job and able to take on both aerial combat and ground attack duties."

General Foulois singled out Lieutenant Frank Luke of the 27th Aero Squadron as "the American air hero that emerged from the St. Mihiel operation." In his autobiography, General Foulois said Lieutenant Luke "has become a legend." The lieutenant, for whom Luke Air Force Base in Phoenix is named, predicted to his colleagues that he would shoot down two German balloons behind enemy lines at precisely 7:03 and 7:07 P.M. on September 16. He made good on his boast, prompting General Foulois to compare Luke's feat to "Babe Ruth pointing out where he would hit a home run." Two days later, Luke shot down two more balloons and three enemy planes, all within the space of twenty minutes.

The victory in the air during the St. Mihiel offensive was the breakthrough the Allies needed, and the first major victory in the air in the history of the American "aviation" forces. General Foulois, despite his differences with Billy Mitchell over the years, wrote,

> The accomplishments of Mitchell and his staff during the operation were exemplary. The unit under his command was unique in air warfare because it was the first time that air units of all the Allies . . . had banded together in a common effort. It also marked the largest concentration of aviation placed under the command of one man [Pershing] up to this time.

Foulois said the secret to Mitchell's success at St. Mihiel "lay in the massing of the 1,476 planes before the battle without the Germans finding out about it." Pershing was so thrilled with the victory that he generously rewarded his officers and men in various ways. Mitchell, for example, was promoted to brigadier general after Foulois endorsed the recommendation. Later, Foulois wrote candidly, "In all fairness, I thought Mitchell had certainly carried out a tremendous operation in spite of his inability to get along with people. On October 1, Mitchell pinned on the star he had obviously wanted for so long."

One month and eleven days later, Germany surrendered.

Billy Mitchell, however, began fighting his own war, one that did not end until his death in 1936. He never stopped preaching his gospel of air power, and he didn't care whose feathers he ruffled. To his superiors in the military and their superiors in Congress, Mitchell was the farsighted but strident voice of the future.

Unlike those whose view of planes in combat was limited to reconnaissance flights, Mitchell now saw far greater value. "The airplane," he said, "is an offensive weapon, not a defensive weapon. Air power, properly organized, will make it possible to attack and to continue to attack, even though the enemy is on the offensive. We have been using the airplane improperly. . . . The sky itself is too large to defend. . . ."

In those same years following World War I, Mitchell also warned that Germany posed a serious menace to the security of the free world. In 1920, the same year that Adolf Hitler helped organize the National Socialist German Workers' party—the Nazis—Mitchell warned bluntly, "German militarism endangers the world."

When Mitchell continued to speak out, accusing the War Department and the Navy of criminal negligence, his superior officers brought court-martial proceedings against him. He was convicted in 1925 of defying his senior officers, and suspended for five years. Rather than serve out the suspension, he resigned from the Army, but not before sounding a chilling alarm about what he saw in the future: "Japan may unleash a war in the Pacific. She could attack America by striking first at Hawaii, some fine Sunday morning."

Sixteen years later, Japan attacked America by striking first at Hawaii, on a "fine Sunday morning."

PART 3

The
Question Mark

★ 3 ★

150 Hours, 40 Minutes, 14 Seconds

Only two years after Charles Lindbergh electrified the world by becoming the first person to fly solo across the Atlantic Ocean nonstop, four pilots in the Army's Air Service also won worldwide acclaim for an aviation achievement of their own. After Billy Mitchell, Benny Foulois, and others demonstrated the military applications of air power in combat, members of the Air Service, which was still a part of the Army's Signal Corps, grew anxious to demonstrate its potential in a dramatic peacetime exhibition.

Of the four pilots, three of them were destined to become generals and World War II leaders—Major Ira Eaker, Lieutenant Elwood "Pete" Quesada, and Captain Carl "Tooey" Spaatz, who became the first chief of staff of the Air Force almost twenty years later. They were selected, with a fourth pilot, Lieutenant Harry Halverson, to fly a plane as long as they could without stopping.

The mission was the brainchild of Eaker, who conceived the idea as an experiment to determine whether planes could travel unimaginably long distances through a technique called in-flight refueling, pumping more gasoline into a plane while it was still in the air so it could continue heading toward its destination—its target in wartime—without taking time to land. It was the latest attempt to pioneer the cause of this new phenomenon called aviation. Its leaders and their political bosses, including the members of Congress and other leaders in other nations, would be watching around the world.

The party of pioneers also included a crew chief, Sergeant Roy Hooe. The five men would be flying in a plane appropriately called the *Question Mark,* because no one knew how long it would stay up.

The men were attempting to break the record for staying aloft, set in 1923 by two lieutenants, Lowell Smith and John Richter, in the air above Rockwell Field, California. In 1928, a young officer, Ross G. Hoyt, later a brigadier general, received orders to participate in an "air-to-air" refueling endurance flight as the pilot of one of two refueling planes.

The pilots of the *Question Mark* and the two support planes trained for their mission in practice flights in the area around Bolling Field in Washington, D.C., testing equipment in both daytime and night flights. At the same time, they were demonstrating the feasibility of air-to-air refueling to Secretary of War Dwight Davis, Assistant Secretary of War for Aviation F. Trubee Davison, and Major General James E. Fechet, chief of the Air Corps.

In mid-December, the men headed for their mission, and getting there was a mission in itself. They had to fly across the country, no easy achievement in those days, to Rockwell Field in San Diego, which had been chosen as the test site because of its clear weather during the winter months—a decision that was to prove debatable after their arrival.

The *Question Mark* and "Refueling Airplane No. 1," which became known as RP #1, took off from Bolling on December 18. Along the way, the pilots would learn about each other's habits. As one example, Eaker said later that Quesada, a Roman Catholic, knelt beside his hotel bed in Atlanta on the first night of the flight west and said his prayers. Eaker remembered, "He did not allow our presence to prevent him from showing his religious teaching and conviction. I know this courage in the youngster impressed all of us very much."

The attempt to break the endurance record was eventful even before the group reached California. As Ross Hoyt, the pilot, remembered forty-five years later, "The flight was routine until we reached Shreveport, Louisiana, on December 20." He continued in an *Air Force Magazine* article dated January 1974, "There it was found that the field was too soft, due to the heavy rains, for the *Question Mark* to take off with a full load of fuel." Instead, RP #1 headed for Love Field in Dallas ahead of the *Question Mark* to fill its tanks there and refuel the *Question Mark* over Dallas.

"Speed gradually increased" as RP #1 attempted to fly from Shreveport, Hoyt said, "and about halfway down the field the tail came up. We lifted off, barely clearing the high-tension lines at the end of the field, climbed up, delivered 250 gallons of fuel, and continued on. . . ."

Their arrival in San Diego was another eventful chapter in their story, with the endurance mission almost coming to an untimely end before it even got started. Major Spaatz wrote in the log of the *Question Mark* on January 3:

> Arrived Rockwell Field at 11:00 A.M. at 4,000 feet. Field covered with clouds. In urgent need of gas. Just a few gallons left. Went beneath the clouds. Cross Rockwell Field at 300 feet altitude. . . . Climbed back through clouds.

Spaatz made a later entry in the log reporting that "Rockwell Field showed keen judgment in picking us up promptly and getting fuel to us just as we were about to use up our last few gallons."

Ross Hoyt said, "Fortunately, RP #1 was fully serviced and its crew on alert so that we could take off immediately, climb up to the *Question Mark* and replenish its rapidly dwindling fuel supply. The prompt action no doubt saved the midair refueling endurance flight from an untimely end before the world record had been broken."

The pioneers, in their leather helmets and goggles, took off from Metropolitan Airport in Van Nuys, California, near Los Angeles, at 0726 hours (7:26 A.M.) on New Year's Day 1929. The *Question Mark* was a three-engine Fokker C-2A, which was lifted into the air by three two-hundred-horsepower engines. The aircraft was forty-eight feet, four inches long, with a wingspan of seventy-four feet, two inches. Spaatz was the mission commander, but all four pilots took their turns at the controls. A refueling plane was only twelve feet above the *Question Mark* and slightly ahead of it.

Less than an hour later, at 0815 hours, the tanker lowered a hose toward the *Question Mark*. Spaatz reached up and grabbed it and began pouring a hundred gallons of gasoline into his experimental craft. In that primitive and dangerous time, the pilot of the refueling plane said, "Lieutenants Woodring and Strickland lowered the hose from the fuselage, and Major Spaatz fit it into the funnel. My only signals came from Woodring by a rope attached to my arm. One long pull meant slow up, two pulls, speed up. A constant jiggle meant the refueling was over."

On the next day, the refueling was not the only interesting thing going on. As the men aboard the *Question Mark* continued to refuel periodically in the second day of their nonstop flying, they circled over the Los Angeles area. When they looked down, they saw the football teams from the University of California and Georgia Tech playing each other in the Rose Bowl below.

For the next four days, the *Question Mark* flew up and down the California coast from San Diego to Los Angeles, improvising in every phase of the operation. There was no radio in either the *Question Mark* or the refueling plane, so communications were makeshift. The pilots and crew members communicated between the two planes by hand signals, writing on a blackboard, or dropping a note to the ground. At night they used flashlights to blink their messages from one plane to the other. Those on the refueling plane provided oil for the *Question Mark* plus food, water, and supplies for the occupants by lowering the items on a rope. When the Pacific coast fog thickened, which happened more than once, they had no instruments to aid their flying. The invention of flying instruments still lay in the future. Hoyt wrote the following in *Air Force Magazine*:

> Night refueling placed a heavy burden on the pilot and crew of the refueling airplane, both from a physical and piloting standpoint. There were frequent interruptions of rest during the night. We always took off with heavy

loads and often had to fly and land in fog and dust during the hours of darkness, without instruments or blind-landing equipment. We shared an intense feeling of responsibility for the success of the undertaking.

When each support plane landed after another refueling, the men responsible for carrying out the process "would be exhausted and drenched with perspiration," Hoyt remembered. "In the cramped quarters of the refueling compartment, they had to remove their parachutes. This increased the hazards in case of collision or fire, which could have occurred during any one of the refueling contacts."

The final refueling of the *Question Mark* took place at 1:50 P.M. on January 7, 1929. By that time, the two support planes had made a total of forty-three takeoffs and landings, by day and night. The *Question Mark* itself touched down at 2:07 P.M. on January 7. With necessity proving the mother of invention once again, its pilots had set a world endurance record. The *Question Mark* flew 7,360 miles and stayed aloft for 150 hours, 40 minutes, and 14 seconds. The plane's average speed was seventy miles an hour. During those perilous hours, the men in the *Question Mark* were able to bring aboard 5,660 gallons of gas, 245 gallons of oil, seventeen meals, plus water, batteries, and other supplies weighing a total of almost forty tons. Some of the provisions included ham and eggs, steak, ice cream, hot coffee, newspapers, fan mail, and fresh towels.

The fan mail was a happy surprise to Spaatz. On the fifth day he wrote, "We are pleased with the mail we are getting, especially Lieutenant Quesada, who is kept busy answering fan letters." In a letter to his mother, Quesada said, "We are going strong. . . . No trouble at all. . . ." Speaking of Charles Lindbergh and his transoceanic flight of 1927, Quesada told his mother, "Now I will have something to bounce off Lindy whenever he boasts too much about that little hop he made."

Spaatz wrote in his report on the mission that mechanical restrictions "rather than the condition of man is the only limiting factor in sustained flight. After the first day or so, the longest period any man slept was four hours. No one got on another's nerves. In cramped quarters, with parachutes on, we knocked each other about, but there was always a smile."

When they landed, the members of the *Question Mark* were met by a mob of reporters and two thousand enthusiastic fans. Congress approved a resolution of congratulations, and President Calvin Coolidge awarded the pilots the Distinguished Flying Cross, a rare honor in peacetime. Still, when the planes landed back at Bolling Field on January 20, the crew members of the *Question Mark* received their medals not from President Coolidge himself but from the War Department, the forerunner of today's Defense Department. The pilots and crews on the refueling planes received no medals, only letters of commendation from the chief of the Air Corps.

In his 1974 magazine article, General Hoyt took a strong stand in behalf of his colleagues on the two refueling planes, protesting that everyone on the mission should have received the Distinguished Flying Cross, not just those on the *Question Mark*. "When considering the early refueling flights," he said, "where the success of the operation was so dependent on the refuelers who delivered the requisites for keeping the refueled airplane in flight, the refueled and the refueler should be treated as a unit."

He continued, "Those pioneering flights of both airplanes—refueled and refueler—hold a special and secure position in the advancement of the capabilities of the United States Air Force. They are special with respect to both place and time. They are not only historical; their value to national security lives today and will continue to live."

Thirty-five years after the achievement of the *Question Mark* and its refueling planes, General Hoyt received a letter from the chief of staff of the Air Force, General Curtis LeMay:

Dear General Hoyt:

On the 35th anniversary of the flight of the *Question Mark,* I send best wishes both personally and on behalf of the United States Air Force.

Although few recognized the long-range impact in 1929, it was certainly the first glimmer of light leading to the development of the KC-135 and today's sophisticated refueling techniques.

You have left to the Air Force a heritage of which you may well be proud.

Sincerely,
Curtis E. LeMay
Chief of Staff

In 1976, twelve years after receiving LeMay's letter and forty-seven years after their achievement, the two surviving members of the refueling crews, General Hoyt and Joseph G. Hopkins, were awarded the Distinguished Flying Cross by one of LeMay's successors as chief of staff, David Jones, in a red-white-and-blue ceremony at the Pentagon.

PART 4

Doolittle's Raid Over Tokyo

★ 4 ★

When Americans Cheered Again

Listen, my children, and you shall hear
Of the midnight ride of Paul Revere.
'Twas the eighteenth of April . . .
— Henry Wadsworth Longfellow

One hundred sixty-seven years after Paul Revere's ride, another historic ride took place on April 18. It happened in 1942. The rider in this story was a former stunt man who pulled the biggest "stunt" since Pearl Harbor when he led a flight of bombers in a mission over Tokyo, something the people of Japan believed was impossible. Japan's leaders had told their citizens that America would not be able to bomb the island nation on the other side of the Pacific because it was too far away from the United States.

When the impossible suddenly happened, the Japanese people were stunned, confused, and worried. And their military leaders were forced to make a move that cost them dearly for the rest of the war: They felt compelled to transfer troops and armament from key locations in the Pacific, where they were intended to be instrumental in the Japanese conquests, back to the homeland to protect the island nation.

The Japanese leaders hadn't anticipated one way of overcoming that distance between their nation and America: an aircraft carrier.

Back home, the result was a resounding psychological victory that lifted America's spirits, electrified the whole world, and put a smile back on the faces of the United States and all of her allies. After four months of shock and discouragement, starting with Pearl Harbor and extending to humiliating defeats along a string of islands with names like Wake Island, Guam, and Bataan, and

43

with the fall of the Philippine Islands only days away, Americans began to believe that victory was possible after all.

It could be argued that the American war with Japan started a full ten years before the Japanese attack on Pearl Harbor, eight years before Adolf Hitler's tanks and troops invaded Poland, and two years before Hitler even came to power.

The seeds for the war in the Pacific were planted even before any of these other events, in 1918, when Japan's rulers adopted an "Imperial Defense Policy" that identified the United States as potentially the nation's biggest enemy. Three years later, an author named Hector E. Bywater, the Far East correspondent for the *London Daily Telegraph,* wrote the nonfiction *Seapower in the Pacific,* following it in 1925 with *The Great Pacific War,* a novel.

In this novel, Bywater described a fictitious attack by the Japanese against the American Asiatic Fleet at Pearl Harbor, accompanied by other attacks against Guam and the Philippine Islands. Both books were translated at Japan's Naval War College. They were used by the students there as textbooks and discussed at length in seminars at the college. One particularly interested reader of Bywater's books was Isoroku Yamamoto, the future mastermind of Japan's strategy to conquer China and the islands in the Pacific Ocean and convert them into Japanese possessions.

Author Carroll V. Glines, in his book *The Doolittle Raid: America's Daring First Strike Against Japan,* wrote in 1991:

> Encouraged by Yamamoto, who was promoted to admiral and placed in command of the Combined Japanese Fleet in 1939, other Japanese militarists became obsessed with the thought of defeating a powerful enemy like America. All Japanese high-ranking officers who occupied leading positions in the navy for two decades avidly and openly discussed the possibility of war against America.

In 1931, Japan, demonstrating a growing attitude of expansion under its ambitious military leaders, invaded Manchuria, then a province of China, and established a puppet state called Manchukuo. In 1937, units of the Japanese Army swept through other portions of China and captured principal cities including Nanking, the nation's former capital, where its troops burned much of the city in what is still called "the rape of Nanking."

Author Glines reported,

> Dr. Ricardo Rivera Schreiber, the Peruvian envoy in Tokyo, learned that the Japanese were indeed planning to make a "surprise attack on Pearl Harbor" and reported it on January 27, 1941, to a top staff member at the American embassy. Passed through State Department channels, the report ended up in U.S. Navy headquarters in Washington.

The response to the State Department from the Navy's intelligence analysts was revealed by John Toland in his 1970 book, *The Rising Sun:* "Based on known data regarding the present disposition and employment of Japanese naval and army forces, no move against Pearl Harbor appears imminent or planned for the foreseeable future."

At the same time, Admiral Yamamoto, who had lived in the United States as a student at Harvard and as a naval attaché in Washington, was developing his basic plan for attacking Pearl. On November 4, 1941, he approved Combined Fleet Top Secret Order Number 1, a 151-page document that covered his strategy not only for attacking Pearl Harbor but also for launching assaults against Malaya, the Philippines, Guam, Wake Island, and Hong Kong, all as part of "Operation Z."

Two days later he set the date for "Y-Day"—December 7.

By 0600 hours (6 A.M.) on Sunday, December 7, there were twenty-eight U.S. Navy warships anchored at Pearl Harbor—eight battleships, seventeen destroyers, and three airplane tenders—plus smaller ships, but no aircraft carriers. The Japanese air attack was massive—135 dive-bombers, 104 high-altitude bombers, eighty-one fighter planes, and forty torpedo bombers.

Their attack lasted a relatively brief period of time, one hour and forty-five minutes, but caused a crippling degree of damage to the American fleet:

- Eighteen ships sunk or seriously damaged, including seven battleships.
- Twenty-nine naval planes destroyed and thirty-nine damaged badly.
- Severe damage to U.S. Navy and Army Air Forces installations.
- A total of 2,403 American military personnel and civilians killed.

The Japanese lost twenty-nine airplanes, five midget submarines and a large one, fifty-five airmen, and nine submariners.

The devastation to the American fleet in the Pacific and the American morale around the world had been carried out under the leadership of Commander Mitsuo Fuchida, who directed the attack from his aircraft carrier in the Pacific. Years later, the man whose forces crippled the American Navy and killed so many Americans was destined to meet an American in Japan, a man who had been a bombardier in the Pacific during World War II. In another of the ironies of wars and their aftermath, the meeting was to change Fuchida's life.

Only four months after Pearl Harbor, the Japanese leaders, who had been feeling supremely confident after the smashing success of their sneak attack, were forced to scramble and rearrange their defenses to protect the island nation that they had long thought was invulnerable to an enemy attack by air. They pulled back some of the men, equipment, and supplies that were being employed in their string of successes in the Pacific and stationed them closer to the mainland in case of any more American attacks from the air. In doing so, they proved that the American raid over Tokyo was more than simply a morale booster. It had an impact on Japanese planning for the rest of the war.

The man who made it happen was a former stunt flier named Jimmy Doolittle, a lieutenant colonel who had been a career officer in the U.S. Army Air Corps. And the man who started things in motion was his boss, President Franklin Delano Roosevelt. Immediately after Pearl Harbor, FDR asked his military chiefs to develop a way to strike back at the Japanese homeland. A Navy captain, Francis Low, wondered if it would be possible to attack Japan with bombers flying from an aircraft carrier, something never done before. If so, Low, who was not a pilot but a submarine officer, thought the mission should be flown by Army planes instead of those assigned to the Navy because the Army planes had greater range, including the B-25, which had a range of twelve hundred miles. Carriers would have been forced to take the Navy planes, with their shorter range, closer to the Japanese mainland, exposing the carriers and the planes to gunfire from enemy shore defenses and attack from the air.

The B-25, a new fast bomber that was manufactured beginning in the late 1930s, became the weapon of choice because of its other advantages. First, it was small enough to squeeze a fleet of such planes onto a carrier—fifty-two feet, eleven inches long, with a wingspan of sixty-seven feet, seven inches. It was big enough to carry a sufficient payload of bombs but was easy to handle. Powered by two seventeen-hundred-horsepower engines, it had a cruising speed of 230 miles an hour and a maximum speed of 275. With the manufacture of new cars halted after the 1942 automobile year, America's factories were retooled to turn out planes, ships, and tanks. By the end of the war, the American genius for responding to crises had produced more than ninety-eight hundred B-25s. The new bomber, named the Mitchell B-25 for Billy Mitchell, was a perfect fit in Low's scheme.

Captain Low submitted his idea to his boss, the chief of naval operations, Admiral Ernest King, who liked the proposal and turned to another officer on his staff, Captain Donald B. "Wu" Duncan, to develop a specific plan to execute Low's idea. Duncan, a 1917 graduate of the Naval Academy, was King's air operations officer and a man admired for his knowledge of carrier aviation. He completed his plan in five days and wrote it out in longhand. King then forwarded the plan to the chief of the Army Air Corps, General Henry "Hap" Arnold. In turn, Arnold called on Doolittle to determine if such an idea could succeed.

In assigning Doolittle to conduct the analysis, General Arnold was tapping the right man. Doolittle, a veteran of World War I who did not see action, had been a flight instructor who then set a variety of aviation records from 1917 to 1930 while also gaining publicity and support for what was now being called "the Air Corps," still a part of the Army.

Doolittle had teamed up with General Billy Mitchell in demonstrations in the 1920s when they bombed and sank captured German ships from World War I, proving that airplanes were capable of sinking ships with bombs dropped from the air, something else that had never been done before. He became a stunt flier and a test pilot as well. He set speed records and won the "Big Three" of the air races—the Schneider Cup, the Bendix Trophy, and the Thompson Trophy. He also found time to earn a degree as a doctor of aeronautical science from the Massachusetts Institute of Technology. By the time of the attack on Pearl Harbor, he was one of the most famous pilots in the world, with as much celebrity status as Mitchell, Rickenbacker, and others, in addition to being one of the most experienced and most educated.

After his participation in these early successes proving the value of airplanes as instruments of war, Doolittle retired from the Army and became an executive with the Shell Oil Company. As the war clouds darkened and Hitler stormed his way across Europe beginning in 1939, while Japan continued to make military threats in the Pacific, Doolittle left Shell and returned to active duty with the Army in 1940.

Two days after being asked by General Arnold for his opinion on whether an air attack from a carrier was a feasible idea, Doolittle gave Arnold his answer. He said the mission could be accomplished with B-25 bombers. As it developed to include more specifics, the plan for the raid called for an afternoon takeoff, allowing the planes to be flying over Japan at night. With that timing, the incendiary bombs from their first planes would illuminate the sky and give the following planes sufficient lighting to attack Tokyo while the first wave would strike military and industrial targets in Yokohama, Osaka-Kobe, and Nagoya at dawn. It would be a one-way mission, with the planes heading for safe haven in China after their attack. Doolittle's estimate of the raid's chances for success: 50 percent.

For their return flight, the bombers would pick up a radio signal from Chuchow in China, two hundred miles south of Shanghai. After landing there and refueling, they would be able to fly another eight hundred miles to Chunking, China's wartime capital.

In a television interview in 1980, Doolittle said, "We were to go bomb our targets, turn in a southerly direction, get out to sea as quickly as possible, and, after being out of sight of land, turn and take a westerly course to China." Their fuel supply was expected to be adequate, but just barely. That factor became even more critical as the operation unfolded, making the raid far more dangerous than had been anticipated.

Doolittle's answer to General Arnold that such a mission was feasible was put to a test on February 2, 1942, when two lieutenants, John Fitzgerald and James McCarthy, climbed into two B-25s and successfully took off from the deck of a new carrier, the USS *Hornet*, commanded by Captain Marc Mitscher. The successful test prompted Arnold to give the green light to the mission to bomb Tokyo, something that seemed beyond the wildest hopes of Americans in those first days of 1942 as they continued to reel from the terrible news still coming from the Pacific. As the man responsible for the mission, Arnold chose Doolittle. After the war, he said Doolittle was "a man who could impart his spirit to others."

Doolittle recruited twenty-four plane crews, 140 men who were pilots, navigators, bombardiers, and engineer-gunners. All of them were volunteers from two of the first B-25 units, the 17th Bombardment Group and its associated 89th Reconnaissance Squadron. Pilots and crew members were told only that they were volunteering for an extremely dangerous mission overseas. None knew exactly what the mission was.

"I found out what B-25 unit had the most experience," Doolittle said, "and then went to that organization and called for volunteers and the entire group, including the group commander, volunteered."

Doolittle met with his men for the first time at Eglin Field in the panhandle region of Florida on March 1, 1942. During interviews with C. V. Glines in 1962 and 1963, they recalled Doolittle's opening remarks to them at that first meeting:

> My name's Doolittle. I've been put in charge of the project that you men have volunteered for. It's a tough one and it will be the most dangerous thing any of you have ever done. Any man can drop out and nothing will ever be said about it. The operation must be made up entirely of volunteers. If anyone wants to bow out, he can do so right now.

No one did.

Then Doolittle emphasized the need for the tightest level of security:

> The lives of many men are going to depend on how well you keep this project to yourselves. Not only your lives but the lives of hundreds of others will be endangered because there are a lot of people working on this thing. Don't start any rumors and don't pass any along. If anybody outside this project gets nosy, get his name and give it to me. The FBI will find out all about him.

Doolitle also told his volunteers, "The main job for the pilots is to learn how to get the B-25 off the ground in the shortest possible distance with heavy loads. We've got about three weeks, maybe less. Remember, if anyone wants to drop out, he can. No questions asked. That's all for now."

They trained for ten weeks at Eglin, practicing short-field take-offs. One pilot, Jack Sims, said, "We practiced over and over, ramming the engines at full throttle, taking off at 65 miles per hour in a 500-foot run. It could be done, as long as an engine didn't skip a beat."

By late March, the volunteers were ready for their secret mission, after Doolittle reduced the number of pilots and crews to sixteen. The volunteers still had not been told what the mission was, its exact purpose, their destination, or that they would be taking off from an aircraft carrier.

Doolittle had to do more than supervise the training of his crews. He had to make extensive revisions to the planes because of the unique nature of the flight. The gun turrets on the planes' bellies were removed. In their place, tanks holding sixty gallons of fuel were installed to increase the chances that the pilots and crews would be able to make it to safety in China after bombing Tokyo. The B-25 did not come equipped with rear guns, so one of the bombardiers, Captain C. Ross Greening, came up with the idea of painting a collection of broomsticks black and mounting them in the back of the planes in the hope that the Japanese would think they were real guns and would not attack the American planes from the rear. Doolittle approved the idea.

The Norden bombsight, the state-of-the-art device that was giving American bombardiers more accuracy than ever, was removed in favor of a less accurate but also less secret bombsight so the Norden would not fall into enemy hands. That decision was made easier because American air officers knew that the B-25s would be flying at low levels, and the Norden was more effective at higher altitudes. The substitute bombsight was also the rigged brainchild of Greening. The cost of the device would have no impact on the budget for the operation—each one cost twenty cents.

As the third week of March ended, Navy captain Donald Duncan sent a wire from Honolulu to the top officer in the Navy, Admiral Ernest King in Washington:

TELL JIMMY TO GET ON HIS HORSE

King called General Arnold, who then relayed the message to Doolittle at Eglin. All the officers involved recognized the message. It was the coded sentence they had been waiting for, the go-ahead to launch the operation. The date was March 23.

Doolittle assembled his men and told them:

> Today's the day we move out. I'm going to tell you one
> more time what I've been harping on ever since we
> came to Eglin. Don't tell *any*one what we were doing
> down here. Even if you think you've guessed what our
> mission is, just keep in mind that the lives of your bud-
> dies depend on your not breathing a word about this to
> another soul.

Under the operational plan developed by Doolittle and his
staff, the Navy was assigned the responsibility for taking the
planes and their crews through enemy waters to within five hundred miles of Japan. The volunteers still did not know their destination, although some of them thought they could make a good
guess.

At the beginning of April, Doolittle's volunteers were transported toward Japan in Task Force 16, composed of fifteen ships—
seven under Mitscher's command and eight more assigned to
Admiral William "Bull" Halsey, the commander in chief of Allied
naval forces in the South Pacific. Two submarines, the USS *Thresher*
and the USS *Trout,* escorted the rest of the task force.

On April 2, as their voyage was just getting under way, Captain
Mitscher got on the *Hornet*'s loudspeaker system and announced,
"This force is bound for Tokyo." A loud cheer went up from everyone on board. The airmen and the sailors all wanted to fight back
against the enemy. Now they were getting that chance.

★ 5 ★

"Army Pilots, Man Your Planes!"

The commanders of the ships in Task Force 16 were sailing under orders that any ship spotted from then on should be considered the enemy and sunk on sight. Those orders became a factor early in the mission. As they sailed, Doolittle remained mindful of the contingency provisions that he had included in his plan. Allowing for the very real possibility that the task force might be intercepted by Japanese planes, Doolittle said that in such a case, the B-25s "would immediately leave the decks." If the task force was within range of Tokyo, he said the planes "would go ahead and bomb Tokyo, even though they would run out of gasoline shortly thereafter. That was the worst thing we could think of. And if we were not in range of Tokyo, we would go back to Midway. If we were not in range of either Tokyo or Midway, we would permit our aeroplanes to be pushed overboard so the decks could be cleared for the use of the carrier's own aircraft," which were stored below the flight deck.

The days behind them since December 7 had brought nothing but bad news to the American people as the Japanese aggressor forces stormed their way across the Pacific islands in their renewed attempt to expand the size of their empire and acquire new national resources, including additional supplies of oil.

At the time of the Japanese attack against Pearl Harbor, the German Army, after occupying France, Poland, and the Scandinavian countries and then failing to bomb England into submission, became bogged down in Russia. Hitler, ignoring the history lesson learned by Napoleon more than a hundred years before, insanely invaded Russia on a two-thousand-mile front in a massive attack on June 22, 1941. By the time the U.S.-Japanese war began in the Pacific in December, the German Army was attempting to launch a counteroffensive after its second drive toward Moscow was repulsed.

At the same time, the Japanese were sweeping their way across the Pacific virtually unchecked. After Pearl Harbor, they attacked the Philippines repeatedly and fiercely and quickly captured islands and peninsulas that most Americans had never heard of, but whose names quickly became household words—Wake Island, Guam, Bataan. Manila, declared an open city and therefore supposedly protected from attack by either nation, was nevertheless bombed brutally by Japanese planes three days after Christmas. On January 2, the Japanese Army occupied the city. On the same day, General Douglas MacArthur, the American Army commander in the Pacific, ordered his troops to dig in on Bataan.

The Japanese maintained their momentum in the Pacific and also attempted to rattle America's nerves even more when a submarine shelled an oil refinery off the coast of California near Santa Barbara.

On March 11, President Roosevelt ordered MacArthur to leave the Philippines and establish a new headquarters in Australia to take command of all Allied forces in the southwest Pacific from that location. That was when MacArthur was asked what his withdrawal to Australia meant for the people left behind in the Philippines, and he gave his classic answer: "I shall return."

As Doolittle and his raiders prepared for their surprise attack against Japan, the American forces continued to reel under the repeated blows from the enemy. On April 9, Bataan fell. Immediately, one of the cruelest chapters in American military history began to unfold—the Bataan Death March, when Japanese soldiers ordered twelve thousand Americans and sixty thousand Filipinos on a doomed march in which ten thousand died.

It was against this backdrop of staggering losses, one after another lasting for four months, that Jimmy Doolittle and his men entered the final hours of the first leg of their journey aboard the carrier *Hornet.*

Early on the morning of April 18, an American patrol plane flying above the task force spotted a Japanese fishing boat. The officers on the *Hornet* and the other ships did not know that Japan had fifty fishing vessels, maybe more, in a line that stretched hundreds of miles from the coast of Japan as an early-warning system. Each of the "fishing" boats was actually a picket ship that maintained radio contact with Japanese Navy officers.

The pilot in the American plane alerted the *Hornet* that he was sure he had been seen. This surprise development forced Halsey's hand. He ordered the Japanese boat sunk. Another ship in the Allied task force, the USS *Nashville,* carried out the order. Then Halsey quickly sent a message from his ship to the *Hornet:*

> **Launch planes. . . . To Col. Doolittle and gallant command, good luck and God bless you.**

The public-address system aboard the *Hornet* blared out the command, "Army pilots, man your planes!" They were still about 650 miles from Japan instead of the 450 called for in the plan.

The planes of Task Force 16 took off thirty hours ahead of schedule, heading into a wind of thirty knots and low clouds. Doolittle led the mission; he had previously worn down General Arnold's concerns about Doolittle's age—forty-five. As the flight deck pitched up and down in the rough seas, Doolittle took off first, at 0820 hours. All eyes were glued on his plane. Doolittle waved to the captain of the *Hornet,* Mitscher, who returned the wave with a military salute.

One of the other pilots, Captain Ted Lawson, later wrote a best-selling book, *Thirty Seconds Over Tokyo,* in which he said, "We watched him like hawks, wondering what the wind would do to him, and whether we could get off in that little run to the bow. If he couldn't, we couldn't." Lawson said Doolittle made it off the *Hornet* "with yards to spare."

As Doolittle successfully piloted his way off the end of the flight deck and skimmed over the waters toward the sky, he was followed by the other fifteen planes making up the band of "Doolittle's Raiders." The mission was beginning a day earlier than planned because of the Japanese "fishing boat" and the fear that its skipper had enough time to radio Japan before his ship was sunk by the American guns. Under Doolittle's planning, the Chinese would make certain that previously designated airfields would be ready to receive the American bombers after their mission.

When all sixteen B-25s became airborne, taking off within five minutes of each other, the ships of Task Force 16 reversed course and headed back toward Pearl Harbor, their home port. Meanwhile, Doolittle's Raiders continued toward Tokyo, flying at a reduced airspeed of 150 miles an hour, 80 miles an hour below the B-25's normal cruising speed and 125 miles an hour below its maximum speed, to conserve fuel.

As they flew, the first of several lucky breaks occurred. The Japanese government staged an air-raid drill that morning. It was a Saturday, and when the drill ended around noon the people of Tokyo went about their usual Saturday business of shopping or going places. The feeling of safety and invulnerability espoused over Radio Tokyo in the four months since Pearl Harbor continued that day, even as sixteen B-25s droned toward the capital.

People on the outskirts of Tokyo were shocked shortly after noon to spot airplanes—dark green ones, obviously not of the Japanese Air Force. They had white stars painted on them instead of the red Japanese sun. They were flying low—so low that some of the Japanese on the beaches waved up to them. A French journalist said later, "I heard a rugged, powerful sound of airplane engines. A raid at high noon! Explosions. I spotted a dark airplane traveling very fast, at rooftop level."

Japanese fighter planes scrambled to the sky. From the ground, anti-aircraft bursts sought out the American fliers, who had climbed to fifteen hundred feet to avoid being hit by fragments from their own bombs. They dropped their first bombs, with the bombardiers using their twenty-cent bombsights to strike their targets—

oil refineries, factories, supply depots, and other strategic points. Then, with their mission accomplished, they headed for the East China Sea and the safety they hoped to find in China, leaving the people of Tokyo in a state of panic below.

The planes were already running low on fuel. A second lucky break came to their aid—a tailwind. The prevailing winds in that part of the world almost always blew from China toward Japan, but not on this day. The wind began to blow toward China, aiding the crews considerably in their efforts to reach safety instead of having to ditch their planes at sea.

Even with that tailwind, however, the needles on the gas gauges in the cockpits were perilously close to empty. The pilots knew what they had to do: keep flying until they ran out of fuel, then bail out or ditch the plane in the sea. Eleven of the sixteen crews bailed out, including Doolittle's. At nine-thirty that evening, he put his plane on automatic pilot and ordered his crew to bail out. Then he did the same.

The pilots and crew members of fifteen of the planes either bailed out and ditched their planes near the China coast or crash-landed. Eleven crewmen were injured, three were killed, and eight who landed in Japanese-held territory were captured. Three of these were executed by a firing squad in October after being held in a prison camp and tortured. A fourth died of malnutrition a year later.

Only one of the planes was able to make a safe landing at an airfield. Captain Edward J. York, piloting Plane Number 8, made it to Vladivostock, in Russian territory, and landed at a small military field. The Russians took the Americans into custody and treated them harshly until they were able to escape through Iran more than a year later.

Lieutenant Horace "Sally" Crouch was a twenty-one-year-old navigator-bombardier from Columbia, South Carolina, on Plane Number 10, which bombed a Tokyo steel mill. His plane ran into Japanese fighters and heavy flak—anti-aircraft fire from the ground—on the flight toward China, and Crouch's crew shot down two of the planes. Flying through a heavy storm, the crew members, headed by Lieutenant Richard Joyce and his copilot, J. R.

Stork, were forced to bail out over the coast of China, where they were rescued by Chinese guerrillas near Chuchow and led to safety.

Today Crouch, who survived the war and became a math teacher at Columbia High School, has explained his survival in a simply stated expression of faith. In an interview in 2002, he said, "I believe the good Lord took a commanding interest in our mission." He added, "There were eighty mortals on that mission, and one immortal—the good Lord."

Doolittle and his crew crash-landed in darkness on a mountaintop in China. Doolittle; his copilot, Lieutenant Richard Cole; his navigator, Lieutenant Henry Potter; his bombardier, Staff Sergeant Fred Braemer; and his engineer-gunner, Staff Sergeant Paul Leonard, were all rescued by Chinese peasants and guerrillas.

The second B-25, piloted by Lieutenant Travis Hoover and his copilot, Lieutenant William Fitzhugh, followed Doolittle to Tokyo and then toward China. They lost sight of Doolittle's plane in the gathering darkness over China and crash-landed into a rice paddy. Lieutenant Hoover and the rest of the crew set fire to the plane and were then rescued, also by Chinese guerrillas.

The only fatality during the flight was Corporal Leland Faktor, the engineer-gunner on Plane Number 3. After bombing a factory and a dock area, Corporal Faktor's B-25, piloted by Lieutenant Robert Gray and Lieutenant Jacob Manch, was running out of fuel just as they arrived over the coast of China. Lieutenant Gray ordered everyone to bail out. Corporal Faktor was killed during his jump. The other four members of the crew made the jump safely. Corporal Faktor was buried by the Chinese.

Later, Doolittle went back to his plane to examine the wreckage, accompanied by Sergeant Leonard. When Leonard asked Doolittle what might become of him, Doolittle answered, "Well, I guess they'll send me to Leavenworth"—the federal prison in Kansas.

While he worked his way to safety in China, Doolittle was haunted by a feeling of failure. As reports of the fates of the other crews reached him, Doolittle, usually upbeat and a positive thinker, felt that he had failed his men, even though he believed the raid had been a success. He was unaware that news of the raid was greeted wildly by the American public as the first victory of the war in the Pacific.

The *New York Times* ran a page one banner line that proclaimed:

JAPAN REPORTS TOKYO, YOKOHAMA BOMBED BY 'ENEMY PLANES' IN DAYLIGHT

American papers quoted a broadcast from the official voice of the Japanese government, one that confirmed the attack but also gave the people of Japan a heavy dose of wartime propaganda:

> Enemy bombers appeared over Tokyo for the first time in the current war, inflicting damage on schools and hospitals. The raid occurred shortly past noon on Saturday (Tokyo time).
>
> Invading planes failed to cause any damage on military establishments, although casualties in the schools and hospitals were as yet unknown.
>
> This inhuman attack on these cultural establishments and on residential districts is causing widespread indignation among the populace.

Another Japanese broadcast, with more propaganda, said:

> Just after noon on the 18th, the first enemy planes appeared over the city of Tokyo. A number of bombs were dropped. The enemy planes did not attempt to hit military establishments and only inflicted damage on grammar schools, hospitals and cultural establishments.
>
> These planes were repulsed by a heavy barrage from our defense guns. The previous training of the Tokyo populace for air raid defense was put into immediate practice. I wish to reveal that our losses were exceedingly light.

Despite Colonel Doolittle's fears that his mission would be considered a failure and he would be the target of harsh reaction and even a prison sentence at Leavenworth, exactly the opposite occurred. The American people were jubilant at both this first American victory in the war against Japan and the proof that their bombers could reach the supposedly safe empire.

An editorial in the *New York Times* was typical of countless others in America's newspapers. The *Times* said the dramatic raid "serves unmistakable notice on the Mikado's warlords that they must begin to pay the price of the treacherous act of December 7 which plunged the island empire into war with the United States."

The *Times* continued: ". . . now there is increasing evidence that the tide is turning." The paper concluded, "The important thing is that the capability of carrying the war to Japan has been demonstrated while we are still far from having reached the maximum of our offensive strength."

The *Columbus Dispatch* told its readers:

U.S. WARPLANES RAIN BOMBS ON LEADING CITIES OF JAP EMPIRE

Three days after the mission, General Arnold received a message in Washington from Doolittle, who was still somewhere in China. The message said:

> *Mission to bomb Tokyo has been accomplished. On entering China, we ran into bad weather and it is feared that all planes crashed. Up to the present, five fliers are safe.*

President Roosevelt held a press conference on April 21 and confirmed that American planes had bombed Japan. When a reporter asked him where the planes came from, FDR had a ready answer. Calling on a remote location in the Himalayan valley mentioned in James Hilton's classic novel *Lost Horizon,* the president said, "They came from our new secret base in Shangri-la."

Some of the pilots and crews from the mission were ordered back to the United States. Others were reassigned to posts in the

China-Burma-India (C-B-I) Theater. Those they left behind, the people of East China, paid a heavy price for rescuing the American airmen. Fifty-three Japanese battalions fought their way through China's Chekiang province, where most of the Doolittle Raiders had landed, and punished the Chinese in a ferocious three-month campaign of revenge carried out by murders, rapes and fires. The bloodbath began with more than six hundred air raids against the towns and villages of East China to weaken any possible resistance by the Chinese people or their army. On April 28, ten days after the B-25s bombed Tokyo, the word went out to Japan's "China Expeditionary Forces." They were ordered to "thwart the enemy's plans to carry out air raids on the homeland of Japan from the Chekiang Province area."

When Generalissimo Chiang Kai-shek, China's leader, learned of the bloodbath, he sent a bluntly worded message to Washington by cable on April 30. He told his American allies, "After they had been caught unawares by the falling of American bombs on Tokyo, Japanese troops attacked the coastal areas of China where many of the American flyers had landed." He described just how vicious the retaliation by the Japanese was. Then, for emphasis, he told them a second time in the same paragraph.

"These Japanese troops," he said, "slaughtered every man, woman and child in those areas—let me repeat—these Japanese troops slaughtered every man, woman and child in those areas. . . ."

General Claire Chennault, who had been the aviation adviser to the Chinese government before the war and founded the legendary "Flying Tigers," a squadron of fighter planes, confirmed Chiang's description of the horror. He reported that the villages that the Americans had traveled through after reaching China were burned to the ground, with every member of the village murdered on the spot.

In his 1949 book *Way of a Fighter,* Chennault wrote, "One sizable city was razed for no other reason than the sentiment displayed by its citizens in filling up Jap bomb craters on the nearby airfields. A quarter-million Chinese soldiers and civilians were killed in the three-month campaign."

A magistrate in China submitted a report on the revenge to

General Joseph Stilwell, the commander of U.S. ground troops in the China Burma India Theater. The report documented what Chiang Kai-shek and General Chennault and others also reported. The magistrate's report, which became part of the record in the War Crimes Trials held in Shanghai in 1946, described the case of First Lieutenant Dean E. Hallmark, the twenty-seven-year-old pilot from the town of Robert Lee, Texas, and his crew on Plane Number 6. It said the plane made a forced landing in the sea off the coast of China at about 6 P.M. on April 18. The report continued:

> Yang Shib-diao, the village alderman, heard it and went out to see when he saw three foreigners trudging on the road wet with water and in great distress. He knew at once that they had swam in the sea and tried to find out their trouble. But owing to the language barrier Yang could not get anything that would help. Thereupon, both tried to draw pictures of flags in the sand with their fingers from which Alderman Yang understood that the survivors were American pilots who after bombing Tokyo had dropped on the sea. He found out also that the other two members of the crew who could not swim were drowned in the sea. Seeing the importance of the matter Alderman Yang led the American members to his home where he gave them such comforts as were available.
>
> On the following morning Yang led by a secret path the American pilots to the Magistrate's Office under an escort of some ten inhabitants hoping to save them out of danger. But unfortunately the puppet troops heard it and told the enemy about it. On arriving at Paishawan some forty to fifty enemy troops suddenly came and took them up.
>
> The American pilots were sent to Macyang but the Chinese inhabitants were ordered to stand in a row when all of them were machine-gunned by the enemy. After killing the local inhabitants the enemy then went into Chiachsi to search for more. Whilst in Chiachsi Village they committed many atrocities killing and robbing the inhabitants. Alderman Yang though escaped

death at first died of shock afterwards when his home and those of many other local inhabitants were robbed and destroyed by the enemy.

On the morning of May 1, however, an enemy vessel arrived covered by an airplane which hovered over Numenchiao. The enemy then picked up the wrecked plane from the sea and carried it away. The bodies of the two American Pilots who had been drowned floated for sometime on the sea but were afterwards picked up by Alderman Yang and buried at Shatow, Chiachsi. Stone tablets were set up at the tombs.

We are sorry that what we had done toward saving the American Pilots was very little and at the same time our hearts burn with rage for the cruel deeds of the enemy who killed our inhabitants.

In a bitter irony, the Americans had given many of their life-saving Chinese friends tokens of their appreciation—their parachutes, gloves, coins. The Reverend Charles L. Meeus, a missionary who was born in Belgium but became a Chinese citizen, said later, "Little did the Doolittle men realize that those same little gifts which they gave their rescuers in grateful acknowledgment of their hospitality . . . would a few weeks later become the telltale evidence of their presence and lead to the torture and death of their friends." The added irony was that many of the Chinese civilians who were killed for helping the Doolittle Raiders had never heard of the raid on Tokyo.

Doolittle was one of the American fliers sent back to the United States. At the same time, he was promoted. On orders from Roosevelt, his superior officers skipped him over the rank of full colonel and jumped him instead from lieutenant colonel to brigadier general.

On May 19, one month and one day after his raid over Tokyo, General Marshall and General Arnold picked up General Doolittle in Washington and told him they were going to the White House. When Marshall and Arnold told Doolittle he was going to be presented the Medal of Honor by President Roosevelt, he protested. One account of their conversation says that Doolittle told his two superiors, "Well, I don't think I earned the Medal of Honor. The medal was given when one chap lost his life saving somebody else's life. So I don't think I earned it."

Marshall said simply, "I think you earned it."

To which Doolittle answered with military obedience, "Yes, sir."

Despite Doolittle's protests that he didn't deserve it, President Roosevelt pinned the nation's highest award for bravery on the chest of his uniform, making him the first airman to receive the award in World War II. A month later, Arnold awarded the Distinguished Flying Cross to every man who had returned to the United States. The rest received theirs on their return.

By the end of the war, sixty-one of the original eighty men on the mission survived.

Admiral Halsey joined in the acclaim for the men of the Doolittle Raid. In his series in *Air Force Magazine,* "Valor," contributing editor John L. Frisbee said Halsey called the mission "one of the most courageous deeds in military history."

Japan reported that fifty people were killed in the raid over Tokyo, and another 250 were wounded. Ninety buildings were destroyed.

Eight Americans from two of the planes were captured by the Japanese after the mission and made prisoners of war in Shanghai. Two others from the same two planes were drowned in their crashes. The eight who survived were tortured and developed dysentery and beriberi from the subhuman living conditions in their prison. Three were given a "trial" four months later, on August 28. Without being told what the charges were against them, the three—Lieutenants Dean E. Hallmark and W. G. Farrow, both pilots, and Sergeant H. A. Spatz, an engineer-gunner—were declared guilty. On October 14, they were told they would be executed the next day. At 4:30 P.M. on October 15, they were taken by truck to a cemetery and shot to death.

The other five prisoners whose lives were spared were moved to Nanking in April 1943, one year after their attack on Tokyo.

Lieutenant R. J. Meder, the copilot of Plane Number 6, died there. The remaining four—Lieutenants Chase J. Nielsen, Robert L. Hite, and George Barr, along with Corporal Jacob D. DeShazer—managed to keep themselves alive, drawing strength from frequent readings from a tattered and worn copy of the Bible. Receiving only slightly better treatment than they did before Meder died, they survived until August 1945, the month the war ended after Colonel Paul Tibbets and his crew dropped history's first atomic bomb on Hiroshima.

After the war, four Japanese officers were tried for their war crimes against the eight Doolittle Raiders and found guilty. Three of them were sentenced to hard labor for five years. The fourth was sentenced to nine years.

★ 6 ★

The Eighty Heroes

The eighty men in those sixteen planes have been forever since regarded as American heroes because of their bravery and the role they played in restoring America's morale so dramatically, while also alarming Japan's leaders and her people. The men and their fates were:

THE LEAD PLANE

PILOT—Lieutenant Colonel James Harold Doolittle, 45, of Alameda, California.
COPILOT—Lieutenant Richard E. Cole, 26, of Dayton, Ohio.
NAVIGATOR—Lieutenant Henry A. Potter, 23, of Pierre, South Dakota.
BOMBARDIER—Staff Sergeant Fred Anthony Braemer, 25, of Seattle, Washington.
ENGINEER-GUNNER—Staff Sergeant Paul John Leonard, 29, of Roswell, New Mexico.

The lead plane arrived over Tokyo at 1:30 P.M. It dropped incendiary bombs on a factory complex and then braved anti-aircraft fire to head back to sea, reaching the coast of China at dusk. Doolittle and his crew bailed out and were rescued by Chinese guerrillas and peasants in the countryside. The Chinese knew that Japanese soldiers were patrolling the area and would take harsh actions against them if they aided the Americans and were found out. They knew there was a good chance the Japanese would kill them, but they aided the Doolittle crew anyway, providing them with shelter and other help.

PLANE 2

PILOT—Lieutenant Travis Hoover, 24, of Melrose, New Mexico.
COPILOT—Lieutenant William N. Fitzhugh, 26, of Temple, Texas.
NAVIGATOR—Lieutenant Carl Richard Wildner, 26, of Holyoke, Massachusetts.
BOMBARDIER—Lieutenant Richard Ewing Miller, 26, of Fort Wayne, Indiana.
ENGINEER-GUNNER—Staff Sergeant Douglas V. Radney, 25, of Mineola, Texas.

Plane 2 arrived over Tokyo shortly after Doolittle's lead plane and also bombed a factory, from only nine hundred feet. Like Doolittle and his crew, the five men on Plane 2 were also bound for the Chinese coast in the darkness that began to envelop the coast. Hoover crash-landed his B-25 into a rice paddy and set it on fire so it would not be of any value to the enemy. All five men were rescued by Chinese guerrillas.

PLANE 3

PILOT—Lieutenant Robert Manning Gray, 22, of Killeen, Texas.
COPILOT—Lieutenant Jacob Earle Manch, 23, of Staunton, Virginia.
NAVIGATOR—Lieutenant Charles J. Ozuk, 26, of Vesta Heights, Pennsylvania.
BOMBARDIER—Sergeant Aden Earl Jones, 21, of Flint, Michigan.
ENGINEER-GUNNER—Corporal Leland D. Faktor, 20, of Plymouth, Iowa.

Plane 3 also bombed a factory, plus a dock in the harbor. With the Japanese air defenses now alerted because of the arrival of the first two bombers over Tokyo, the crew members of Plane 3 had to fight off enemy fighter planes and increasingly heavy amounts of anti-aircraft fire as they headed toward the sea. As the plane approached China, the fuel gauge on the B-25 showed that the tank was almost empty. Lieutenant Gray ordered everyone to bail out. Corporal Faktor became the first fatality of the mission when he was killed in the jump. The other four members of the crew landed safely and were reunited with other members of the raid, including Doolittle, when they made it safely to Chunking.

PLANE 4

PILOT—Lieutenant Everett Holstrom, 25, of Cottage Grove, Oregon.

COPILOT—Lieutenant Lucian Nevelson Youngblood, 23, of Pampa, Texas.

NAVIGATOR—Lieutenant Harry C. McCool, 23, of La Junta, Colorado.

BOMBARDIER—Sergeant Robert J. Stephens, 27, of Hobart, Oklahoma.

ENGINEER-GUNNER—Corporal Bert M. Jordan, 22, of Covington, Oklahoma.

Plane 4 was the first to encounter serious difficulties on the mission. It developed a fuel leak in one of the wing tanks and was then attacked by Japanese fighter planes. Holstrom decided to unload his bombs while still at sea, before reaching his target, planning to then head for safety in China. On their flight toward the mainland, they flew into rain and darkness. All five members of the crew bailed out as soon as the plane reached the coast. They were rescued by the Chinese.

PLANE 5

PILOT—Captain David M. Jones, 28, of Marshfield, Oregon.

COPILOT—Lieutenant Ross R. Wilder, 25, of Taylor, Texas.

NAVIGATOR—Lieutenant Eugene Francis McGurl, 25, of Belmont, Massachusetts.

BOMBARDIER—Lieutenant D. V. Truelove, 22, of Clermont, Georgia.

ENGINEER-GUNNER—Sergeant Joseph W. Manske, 21, of Gowanda, New York.

Unfortunately for the five men aboard Plane 5, its tanks were not completely filled because of a fueling error, so they were thirty gallons shy of capacity when they took off from the *Hornet*. This mistake was compounded when the plane strayed off course, causing it to arrive over Tokyo's docks later than planned. Bombardier Truelove quickly dropped his bombs, and Captain Jones headed for China, only to encounter the darkness and rain that were plaguing the other crews. All five members of this crew became separated from each other and were not reunited until daybreak. After their reunion, they also were reunited with some of the other crews from the mission. With help from the Chinese again, the crews reached Chunking and safety on April 29, eleven days after their mission over Tokyo.

PLANE 6

PILOT—Lieutenant Dean E. Hallmark, 27, of Robert Lee, Texas.
COPILOT—Lieutenant Robert John Meder, 24, of Cleveland, Ohio.
NAVIGATOR—Lieutenant Chase J. Nielsen, 25, of Hyrum, Utah.
BOMBARDIER—Sergeant William Dieter, 29, of Vail, Iowa.
ENGINEER-GUNNER—Sergeant Donald E. Fitzmaurice, 23, of Lincoln, Nebraska.

The crews had received special training in low-level bombing for the mission, so Lieutenant Hallmark skimmed his way over the Pacific Ocean in what pilots call "hedge-hopping." At its low altitude, the plane encountered heavy anti-aircraft fire on reaching the Japanese coast. After bombing its target, Plane 6 ran out of fuel before reaching China and crashed into the sea. Although his plane was only a few miles from shore, it took Hallmark several hours to make it to land. The next morning, he was told by the Chinese that they had recovered the bodies of Fitzmaurice and Dieter after they were washed up onto the beach. After the two victims were buried, the remaining three crew members were hidden by Chinese soldiers, but then they were betrayed by a Chinese officer and turned over to a Japanese patrol. Following Lieutenant Hallmark's execution, the other two members of his crew were imprisoned and tortured for the rest of the war.

PLANE 7

PILOT—Lieutenant Ted W. Lawson, 25, of Fresno, California.
COPILOT—Lieutenant Dean Davenport, 23, of Spokane, Washington.
NAVIGATOR—Lieutenant Charles L. McClure, 25, of St. Louis, Missouri.
BOMBARDIER—Lieutenant Robert S. Clever, 27, of Portland, Oregon.
ENGINEER-GUNNER—Sergeant David J. Thatcher, 20, of Bridger, Montana.

Plane 7 also bombed a factory complex, this one in Tokyo Bay, then headed toward China while running low on fuel. When pilot Lawson concluded that he could not reach the coast of China, he attempted a landing on the beach, then ditched his plane at sea. A Chinese fishing boat picked them up the next day. Lawson injured his leg severely, but good luck came his way later when he was reunited with a member of the crew of Plane 15, Lieutenant Robert White—"Doc" White." White was a physician who volunteered for the Tokyo raid and trained as a gunner to win a spot on Plane 15. He operated on Lawson and saved his life.

PLANE 8

PILOT—Captain Edward J. York, 29, of Batavia, New York.
COPILOT—Lieutenant Robert G. Emmens, 29, of Medford, Oregon.
NAVIGATOR-BOMBARDIER—Lieutenant Nolan Anderson Herndon, 23, of Greenville, Texas.
ENGINEER—Lieutenant Theodore H. Laban, 27, of Kenosha, Wisconsin.
GUNNER—Sergeant David W. Pohl, 20, of Boston, Massachusetts.

Like too many of the others, this plane experienced fuel problems during the flight. Before reaching their target, Captain York decided to head for Russian territory after they bombed the first factory he saw in Tokyo. The five made it safely to Russian territory. Even though Russia was an ally of the United States in the war, it was not yet at war with Japan—so the Russian troops captured the Americans and held them as prisoners for the rest of the war.

PLANE 9

PILOT—Lieutenant Harold Francis Watson, 26, of Buffalo, New York.
COPILOT—Lieutenant James N. Parker, 22, of Houston, Texas.
NAVIGATOR—Lieutenant Thomas Carson Griffin, 24, of Green Bay, Wisconsin.
BOMBARDIER—Sergeant Wayne Max Bissell, 20, of Walker, Minnesota.
ENGINEER-GUNNER—Technical Sergeant Eldred V. Scott, 34, of Atlanta, Georgia.

This plane bombed the Tokyo Gas & Electric Company. Its crew members were also forced to bail out in the rain and darkness because they ran out of fuel. They landed apart from each other but were found by the Chinese individually. Watson was injured in the landing, suffering a broken shoulder.

PLANE 10

PILOT—Lieutenant Richard Outcalt Joyce, 22, of Lincoln, Nebraska.
COPILOT—Lieutenant J. Royden Stork, 25, of Frost, Minnesota.
NAVIGATOR-BOMBARDIER—Lieutenant Horace Ellis Crouch, 23, Columbia, South Carolina.
GUNNER—Staff Sergeant Edwin Weston Horton Jr., 26, of North Eastham, Massachusetts.
ENGINEER—Sergeant George E. Larkin Jr., 23, of New Haven, Kentucky.

Plane 10 bombed a steel mill in Tokyo but then encountered heavy anti-aircraft fire from the ground and resistance from Japanese fighter planes as its crew began to head back to sea. The five airmen managed to make it safely out of the Tokyo area and even shot down two fighter planes on the way. The flight became even more eventful when they, too, were forced to bail out over the coast of China. They were quickly rescued by the Chinese.

PLANE 11

PILOT—Captain Charles Ross Greening, 27, of Carroll, Iowa.

CO-PILOT—Lieutenant Kenneth E. Reddy, 21, of Bowie, Texas.

NAVIGATOR—Lieutenant Frank Albert Kappeler, 28, of San Francisco, California.

BOMBARDIER—Staff Sergeant William L. Birch, 24, of Galexico, California.

ENGINEER-GUNNER—Sergeant Melvin J. Gardner, 21, of Mesa, Arizona.

This plane bombed a factory between Tokyo and Yokohama despite heavy flak. Japanese fighter planes caught up with them as they began to head toward China, but Sergeant Gardner, manning the top turret guns, shot down two of the enemy planes. This crew also had to bail out at night over China when the plane ran out of fuel. The five members were among the lucky ones. They were rescued by the Chinese.

PLANE 12

PILOT—Lieutenant William M. Bower, 25, of Ravenna, Ohio.

COPILOT—Lieutenant Thadd Harrison Blanton, 23, of Archer City, Texas.

NAVIGATOR—Lieutenant William R. Pound Jr., 23, of Milford, Utah.

BOMBARDIER—Technical Sergeant Waldo J. Bither, 35, of Houlton, Maine.

ENGINEER-GUNNER—Staff Sergeant Omer Adelard Duquette, 26, of West Warwick, Rhode Island.

Plane 12 bombed an oil refinery in Yokohama and also strafed a power station. The members of this plane's crew were forced to bail out as they reached China, too, not because they were running out of fuel like the rest but because of heavy fog. The Chinese guerrillas hid them in the countryside for several days while Japanese soldiers patrolled the area. Eventually they were guided toward the other raid crews and reunited with them.

PLANE 13

PILOT—Lieutenant Edgar F. McElroy, 30, of Ennis, Texas.

COPILOT—Lieutenant Richard A. Knobloch, 23, of Milwaukee, Wisconsin.

NAVIGATOR—Lieutenant Clayton J. Campbell, 25, of St. Maries, Idaho.

BOMBARDIER—Sergeant Robert C. Bourgeois, 24, of Lecompte, Louisiana.

ENGINEER-GUNNER—Sergeant Adam Ray Williams, 22, of Gastonia, North Carolina.

Plane 13 bombed ships and docks in Tokyo Bay. The five on board made it to the Chinese coast at 10 P.M. before their plane's fuel tank reached empty and they bailed out. The Chinese hid them until they were led to the other crews later.

PLANE 14

PILOT—Major John A. Hilger, 36, of Sherman, Texas.

COPILOT—Lieutenant Jack A. Sims, 23, of Kalamazoo, Michigan.

NAVIGATOR-BOMBARDIER—Lieutenant James Herbert Macia, 25, of Tombstone, Arizona.

ENGINEER-GUNNER—Staff Sergeant Jacob Eierman, 29, of Baltimore, Maryland.

RADIO GUNNER—Staff Sergeant Edwin V. Bain, 24, Greensboro, North Carolina.

Major Hilger flew to Nagoya and struck military targets, then guided his plane toward China. After the members of this crew also were forced to bail out, they were hidden by Chinese farmers until they could be reunited safely with the crews from the other fifteen planes on the mission.

PLANE 15

PILOT—Lieutenant Donald G. Smith, 24, of Oldham, South Dakota.

COPILOT—Lieutenant Griffith Paul Williams, 21, of Chicago, Illinois.

NAVIGATOR-BOMBARDIER—Lieutenant Howard Albert Sessler, 24, of Boston, Massachusetts.

ENGINEER-GUNNER—Sergeant Edward Joseph Saylor, 22, of Brusett, Montana.

GUNNER AND SURGEON—Lieutenant Thomas Robert "Doc" White, 33, of Haiku, Hawaii.

Lieutenant Smith's assignment was to bomb an industrial complex in Kobe. After carrying out his mission, he headed his B-25 toward China but had to make a crash landing into the sea just before reaching the coast. All five crew members parachuted to safety. After they survived, "Doc" White treated Captain Ted Lawson and is credited by author C. V. Glines and others with saving Lawson's life. White also treated others who were wounded in their crash landings or their parachute jumps.

PLANE 16

PILOT—Lieutenant William G. Farrow, 23, of Darlington, South Carolina.

COPILOT—Lieutenant Robert L. Hite, 22, of Odell, Texas.

NAVIGATOR—Lieutenant George Barr of Brooklyn, New York, who turned 25 twelve days before the raid.

BOMBARDIER—Corporal Jacob DeShazer, 29, of West Stayton, Oregon.

ENGINEER-GUNNER—Sergeant Harold A. Spatz, 20, of Lebo, Kansas.

Plane 16 also reached its target and dropped its bombs successfully, but unlike the other crews, its members were not as fortunate after they, too, were forced to make a crash landing in China. They were captured by Japanese soldiers and were tortured before the enemy executed Lieutenant Farrow and Sergeant Spatz, along with Lieutenant Hallmark.

Corporal DeShazer, the bombardier, was a native of West Stayton, Oregon, and was thirty-two years old when the war ended. In his prison camp on August 9, 1945, the day the second atomic bomb was dropped, this time on Nagasaki, DeShazer heard a voice telling him, "Start praying." He said the voice told him to pray for peace.

He began to pray at seven o'clock that morning. He recalled after the war that seven hours later, at two o'clock that same day, "The Holy Spirit told me, 'You don't have to pray anymore. The victory is won.'"

At the same time, the same voice told DeShazer, "You are called to go and teach the Japanese people wherever I send you." Ten days later, a Japanese guard at the prison camp opened the cell door and said, "The war is over. You can go home now."

DeShazer, emaciated after forty months as a prisoner of war and with seventy-five huge boils covering his body at one time, went home and enrolled as a seminarian at Seattle Pacific College. He completed his education in 1948 and then went back to Japan to preach the Gospel as a Free Methodist missionary. Except for a sabbatical leave to earn his master's degree at Asbury Theological Seminary in 1958, he stayed in Japan until he retired.

In April 1950, the former prisoner of the Japanese converted Mitsuo Fuchida to Christianity—the man who almost nine years earlier had led the attack on Pearl Harbor.

In an intelligence report in 1945, Jimmy Doolittle—who by then had risen to the three-star rank of lieutenant general—wrote a report on the Tokyo raid. He described what he considered the purpose of his historic mission and his evaluation of its results:

It was hoped that the damage done would be both material and psychological. Material damage was to be the destruction of specific targets with ensuing confusion and retardation of production. The psychological results, it was hoped, would be the recalling of combat equipment and other theaters for home defense, the development of a fear complex in Japan, improved relationships with our Allies, and a favorable reaction in the American people.

In 1980, Doolittle said again that the raid over Tokyo was intended to provide a morale boost for the Americans on the home front as their first good news of the war, but there were two other results. He confirmed the view that the raid "caused the Japanese to question their warlords." And from a tactical point of view, he said, "The raid caused the retention of aircraft in Japan for the defense of the home islands when we had no intention of hitting them again seriously in the near future. Those airplanes would have been much more effective in the South Pacific, where the war was going on."

By the time General Doolittle died in 1993 at the age of ninety-six, he had reached a level of respect and affection that stood in stark contrast to his fears in those first days after his raid over Tokyo when he thought he might be sent to prison as a failure. One of the most telling tributes came from his own men, the veterans of the raid. They issued a salute to him as part of his burial ceremony in the rolling green hills of Arlington National Cemetery in Northern Virginia, just outside Washington, D.C. His men said of their leader:

He was an uncommon man whose foresight, integrity, courage and intellect are unmatched in the annals of aviation. He was a man of wisdom and wit, compassion and concern. His extraordinary feats in an airplane were matched by his ability to command men from the smallest units, such as the 79 of us who participated with him in our raid on Japan, to the 8th Air Force, the largest aerial fighting force in history. He was a patriot in the fullest sense of the word.

Senator Barry Goldwater of Arizona, a major general in the Air Force Reserve, said, "We lost the finest man I've ever known in my life."

Those Doolittle Raiders whose health still allows them to do so meet again every April 18, on the anniversary of their history-making, morale-boosting, tide-turning raid over Tokyo. To commemorate their dramatic achievement, eighty silver goblets, each inscribed with the name of one of the Raiders and on permanent display at the Air Force Academy in Colorado Springs, Colorado, are flown to the reunion.

In a private ceremony, the survivors lift their cups as a toast to their departed members, whose goblets were turned upside down after their deaths. The cups of any who have died since the last reunion are then also turned upside down. When the last member of Doolittle's Raiders has passed away, his goblet will be turned upside down, in a final salute to eighty American men who, in those darkest and most terrifying first months after Pearl Harbor, gave their countrymen something to cheer about—and America's enemy in the Pacific something to think about.

PART 5

Conquering the Himalayas

★ 7 ★

"Flying the Hump"

In the same month that Japan attacked Pearl Harbor, it also attacked Burma and quickly closed the Burma Road. This had been called "China's lifeline to the outside world"—the chief supply route into China from the United States and Great Britain. The Japanese coveted Burma's rich supplies of oil, tin, and rice.

By the time of the Pearl Harbor attack, war was nothing new to the Chinese people. They had been suffering at the hands of the Japanese Army for ten years, with many of them killed in bombing raids by planes flying from Manchuria.

Plans were begun immediately after Pearl Harbor to start an "air bridge"—a way to fly supplies and equipment to the Chinese Army while also doing something else: keeping parts of Japan's army and equipment tied down in Burma and China so they would be unable to help their colleagues in their war in the Pacific against the Allies. American pilots and crews would accomplish this by flying for five hundred miles over the snowcapped Himalayan Mountains, whose name means "house of snow" in the Sanskrit language of that region. The Himalayas featured some of the tallest mountain peaks in the world, forcing the American pilots to fly at altitudes as high as twenty-two thousand feet. In the lingo of the war in that region, these men would "fly the Hump," often in the face of the feared "Zeroes"—Japan's respected fighter planes.

They accomplished one of the most remarkable records in the history of military aviation. In December 1942, U.S. pilots airlifted 1,226 tons of supplies into China over the Hump. One year later, they carried ten times that amount, 12,641 tons. They reached their peak in July 1945, one month before the end of the war, with a total of 71,045 tons. On August 1, they made 1,118 flights in one twenty-four-hour period, airlifting 5,327 tons into China.

That the continuing mission was a success is reflected in the box score for the operation after the three-year operation ended:

- Flights over the Himalayas: 167,285.
- Amount of cargo: 721,000 tons.
- Number of pilots: 3,026.

The high price of that success is reflected in other numbers:

- Number of planes lost: More than six hundred.
- Number of pilots and crew members lost: Over one thousand.

The same American ingenuity that produced the dramatically good news of Doolittle's Raid over Tokyo produced this triumph in the skies over that part of the world, but it wasn't a bombing mission, and it wasn't a single mission. Instead, it was a series of flights that lasted almost the entire war, from 1942 to 1945, and became a major factor in the defeat of Japan.

It was one of those "they-said-it-couldn't-be-done-but-we-did-it" stories.

As soon as the United States and Japan began fighting each other after the attack on Pearl Harbor, the need to keep China in the war and aiding the Allied fight became critical. The Allied leaders knew that the Chinese Army could keep Japan's forces tied down on the mainland—troops who could have been used effectively by the Japanese in fighting against the Americans in the island campaigns. The Chinese could also provide bases for the American airborne forces from which they could attack Japan.

The idea of supporting the Chinese Army in its fight against units of the Japanese Army did not meet with unanimous agreement at the outset. President Roosevelt, a strong supporter of China, backed the idea, but Churchill was less enthusiastic. The British leader said later,

> I had found the extraordinary significance of China in American minds, even at the top, strangely out of proportion. . . . I told the President how much I felt American opinion overestimated the contributions which China could make to the general war. He differed strongly. There were 500 million people in China. What would happen if this enormous population developed in the same way as Japan had done in the last century and got hold of modern weapons? I replied I was speaking of the present war, which was quite enough to go on with for the time being.

China's leader, Chiang Kai-shek, strongly favored keeping his troops in China supplied in their own war against the Japanese and thus supported the idea of an airlift over the Himalayas. He argued that "Burma is the key to the whole campaign in Asia. After the enemy has been cleared out of Burma, his next stand would be in North China and, finally, in Manchuria."

Supporting his position was the chief of the Chinese Air Force—his wife, Madame Chiang Kai-shek, named to that position by her husband, thus becoming the only woman commander of a national air force anywhere in the world. Madame Chiang was even more than that. She was a powerful influence on her husband's thinking in the affairs of China and its position in Asian affairs. The former May-ling Soong, she was the daughter of Charlie Soong, a wealthy publisher, missionary, and revolutionist who was able to send his daughter to America's Wellesley College, where she learned to speak English flawlessly.

She became a supporter of a strong Chinese air force after watching an air show in 1933 performed by the first graduates of an American-operated flight school in Hangchow, China. Enthusiastic at what she saw, she remarked to those around her, "This is what China needs—what China must have. Thousands more like these boys—and thousands of airplanes for them to fly and fight with." That enthusiasm and strong belief in air power helped prompt her husband to appoint her commander of the Chinese Air Force several years later.

Churchill remained unenthusiastic about the idea of an airlift over the Himalayas, and so did the American Naval leaders involved, Admirals King and Chester Nimitz, commander in chief of the U.S. Pacific Fleet. Both of them favored the use of sea power in dealing with the Japanese presence in that part of Asia. Chiang won the battle for Roosevelt's support, however, and plans for an airlift over Burma were put into motion.

At the time of Pearl Harbor, there already was an American air unit in China, the fabled Flying Tigers, under the command of General Claire Chennault, which had been formed with the strong encouragement of Madame Chiang Kai-shek. They needed to be supplied, too, along with whatever additional aviation personnel, planes, and equipment would be arriving in China to support the American air effort.

The Japanese, of course, knew this as well. In March 1942, only three months after Pearl Harbor, they shut down the Burma Road, the only overland supply route from northern India through Burma and into China, and destroyed it. The only other way to continue supplying the growing number of Allied forces there was through the air, but the Himalayas, the highest mountain range in the world, were in the way.

The distance was not a problem—five hundred miles—but the dangers involved were a serious threat to the ability to fly over what American pilots called the Hump. The official Air Force history described the challenge presented by the rugged range, saying that the land near a major American base was ninety feet above sea level but "the mountain wall surrounding the valley rises quickly to 10,000 feet and higher." At their crest, this part of the Himalayas reached sixteen thousand feet into the sky—more than three miles.

The Air Force history told the story of one pilot's experience:

> Flying eastward out of the valley, the pilot first topped the Patkai Range, then passed over the Chindwin River Valley, bounded on the east by a 14,000-foot ridge, the Kumon Mountains. He then crossed a series of 14,000–16,000-foot ridges separated by the valleys of the West Irrawaddy, East Irrawaddy, Salween and Mekong Rivers. The main "Hump," which gave its name to the whole awesome mountainous mass and to the air route which crossed it, was the Santsung Range, often 15,000 feet high, between the Salween and Mekong Rivers.

Adding to the challenge presented by the Hump were the difficulties encountered by pilots of the U.S. 10th Air Force in northern India, who were struggling to get their cargo planes to safe altitudes. They had heavy loads plus the strong turbulence, thunderstorms, and icing conditions all associated with flying over an imposing, towering mountain range. Nor were all the challenges in the air. Heat and humidity were oppressive on the ground. The weather conditions were compounded by the monsoon season, the six-month period when two hundred inches of rain fell on the air bases in India and Burma where the planes flying to China were based.

Another Hump pilot, Winton R. Close, who was destined to become a major general, remembered his own experiences with the weather. "We were constantly on the verge of losing control of the aircraft," he wrote. "We could never get the aircraft completely under control." He said that at times four or five bombs were torn loose from their shackles and "disappeared through the closed bomb bay doors."

C. V. Glines, the respected author of thirty books on aviation and military subjects and curator of the Doolittle Library at the University of Texas at Dallas, wrote in *Air Force Magazine,* "If the U.S. was to conquer such obstacles, it would have to build an organization to ensure the smooth flow of planes, people and supplies. The seeds of such an organization already existed. On May 29, 1941 . . . the U.S. Army had created the Air Corps Ferrying Command. Out of this small organization grew the U.S. Air Transport Command of Major General Harold L. George."

After the Japanese cut off ground access to China by closing the Burma Road, American officials developed plans to send five thousand tons of supplies a month over the Hump and into China to help keep Japan bogged down in fighting there, reducing its ability to continue sweeping across the South Pacific after a series of victories at Guam, Bataan, Corregidor, and the Philippines.

American C-46 and C-47 cargo planes, the workhorses of the U.S. air cargo fleet at the start of the war, began to deliver small amounts of supplies in July 1942. After additional airfields were constructed, more pilots were trained, and more planes were ferried to the China Burma India Theater, the operation increased dramatically in size and volume.

The C-46 was almost twenty thousand pounds heavier than the C-47 at fifty-one thousand pounds and was powered by two engines, stronger than the C-47s at two thousand horsepower each. Both planes had a cruising speed of 175 miles an hour. One veteran Hump pilot, Otha C. Spencer, was an enthusiastic fan of the C-46. "I liked the C-46," he wrote in his 1992 book about his experiences, *Flying the Hump.* "It had the best engines in the world. If you can't have faith in your airplane, you might as well try to cross the Himalayas in a rowboat."

In the case of the C-47, America's air leaders were adapting the commercial airliner, the DC-3, which made its debut in 1936. With timely foresight, the Army ordered the first C-47s in 1940. By the end of the war, 9,348 planes had been produced, carrying personnel and cargo. In combat areas, they were employed to tow troop-carrying gliders and drop paratroopers into enemy territory.

The plane was small compared to the bombers and the C-54 cargo plane that came along later in the war. The C-47 was sixty-five feet, five inches long, with a wingspan of ninety-five feet.

When loaded, it weighed thirty-three thousand pounds. Two engines with twelve hundred horsepower each gave the "Gooney Bird," the Air Force nickname for the C-47, a range of 1,513 miles, 313 miles longer than the C-46. The '47 was operated by a crew of six, with no armament. Air Force personnel considered the Gooney Bird a bargain at a cost of $138,000, some $95,000 below the price tag on a C-46—$233,000.

Major General William H. Tunner, who became one of the leaders of the Berlin Airlift three years after World War II ended, said of the Hump operation, "Every drop of fuel, every weapon and every round of ammunition, and 100 percent of such diverse supplies as carbon paper and C rations, every such item used by American forces in China, was flown in by airlift."

While the airlift continued for three years, a campaign on the ground lasted just as long, fought by a specially trained American infantry combat team known as Galahad Force and commanded by Brigadier General Frank Merrill, along with two Chinese divisions. As they fought, they came to be known as "Merrill's Marauders." Two other leaders of the ground war in the C-B-I were General Stilwell and Field Marshal Sir William Slim, commander of the British Fourteenth Army.

The combined air and land campaign in Burma lasted three years. The Burma Road was not reopened to Allied convoys until 1945, only a few months before the war ended. By then, 850 airmen had been killed while flying the Hump.

"The Hump" was a story of sustained bravery under extreme conditions. Within the overall story were tales of bravery, ingenuity, and achievements that remain a source of pride to the men who made it happen.

Captain John L. "Blackie" Porter was one of those men. A stunt pilot before the war, he organized "Blackie's Gang" with two C-47s to help rescue downed airmen. Neither kind of plane had weapons built into it, but the planes carried two .30-caliber machine guns on board. The copilot held one on his lap, and the other was kept in the cargo area of the plane. At other times they carried Thompson submachine guns and hand grenades.

In 1943, according to C. V. Glines, "virtually every rescue of crew members was due primarily to the efforts of Blackie's Gang."

One of those rescue missions included a war correspondent for CBS who became a noted television reporter after the war— Eric Sevareid. In one of Blackie's first rescue missions, he was sent to search for twenty crew members and passengers who had bailed out of a C-46 in the Naga hill country of northern Burma. The presence of Japanese soldiers would be only one of the dangers on the mission. Another was headhunters who lived in the area. Porter's crew found the missing Air Force personnel and civilians and arranged for airdrops of supplies. A surgeon, Lieutenant Colonel Don Flickinger, and two medics parachuted into the area and provided medical assistance. Then a ground party walked in and escorted the party, including Sevareid, to safety.

Blackie Porter staged other successful rescues, enough so that the Americans established a special search-and-rescue organization, headed by Captain Porter. Then, in one of the cruelties of war, he was lost in action in December 1943, while on another search mission.

The Chinese people were encouraged by their government to give whatever aid and support they could to American airmen who had been shot down. One leaflet distributed in an area occupied by the Japanese showed an American pilot in front of an American flag. The leaflet said:

> Happy New Year! This American pilot helped you to chase the Japanese out of Chinese sky. Help him. The ancient, tired god of gates is sleeping now. The terror of Japanese devil entered millions of Chinese families. The ancient god cannot stop them anymore. This strong young soldier, this American fighting pilot, with the help of the courageous Chinese army, they together will

protect the old and the young in your family. But he and his Chinese colleagues need your help when they are hurt, lost, or hungry. They need your comfort and friendship. Help them! They are fighting the war for you. Friends of the occupied territory, attention. Please do not let anyone see this leaflet. If the Japanese should see this, they will torture you.

★ 8 ★

"While I Was Their Commander, By God . . ."

Meanwhile, flying the Hump steadily increased in effectiveness, and the amount of supplies and equipment delivered into China grew. In December 1943, the tonnage airlifted over the Hump topped the goals set for the operation, prompting President Roosevelt to approve a Presidential Unit Citation, the first time a noncombat unit was awarded the Citation. FDR sent his personal thanks to every officer and enlisted man who was participating in the flights over the Hump. Eleven thousand campaign ribbons were sent to the C-B-I.

In early 1944, supplies and equipment to China reached ten thousand tons a month, a goal that had been set earlier by President Roosevelt. As operations in China increased, however, with a corresponding increase in the number of planes and men involved, so did the need for still more supplies and equipment. By the end of that year, the monthly figure for tonnage delivered had more than doubled.

General Tunner, a 1928 graduate of West Point, took command of the India-China Division of the still-new Air Transport Command (ATC) in August 1944, and made major changes in the management of the airlift. By then, Tunner was accustomed to presiding over a large operation. He had been commander of the Ferrying Division of the ATC for three years—a command of more than fifty thousand men, including eight thousand pilots. His crews had delivered ten thousand planes a month to bases in the United States and over a thousand every month to overseas destinations.

Tunner wasted no time in establishing a businesslike atmosphere in the Air Transport Command, sweeping his way through an organization that had gained a reputation for unkempt appearances and sloppy living quarters because the men placed greater emphasis on mere survival in their dangerous missions over the Hump. Otha Spencer remembered the difference in his book: "General Tunner ordered the filthy living conditions of the crews cleaned up and full-dress inspections daily. . . . On Saturday, all base personnel not in the air or on flight alert would have a formal parade. Men shaved, cut their hair, cleaned up their uniforms, marched erect . . . and complained. But morale soon improved."

Spencer said Tunner defended his emphasis on discipline by saying, "I had been sent to this command to direct American soldiers, and while I was their commander, by God, they were going to live like Americans and be proud they were Americans."

Tunner wanted crews who were flying at night to be able to get their sleep during the day, so he ordered "Quiet" signs erected in the living areas. Mobile PX trucks brought snacks and drinks to the flight line. Cafeterias were opened up and stayed open twenty-four hours a day so hungry Hump personnel could find something to eat at any hour of the day or night.

Crews were trained in jungle survival and how to use the emergency equipment on their planes. Search-and-rescue squadrons were reorganized to achieve greater effectiveness in their missions. ATC personnel could even continue their college educations. Special correspondence schools were established so crew members could take courses in professional subjects for college credits.

Vacations even came to life in the ATC. The men were encouraged to take time to enjoy the beauty of the surrounding country. General Tunner wrote, "India is a strange, exotic country, a land of great beauty . . . a land of extremes. As long as our men were there, I considered it a command function to make it possible for them to see some of the fascinating sights."

Otha Spencer said it seemed too good to be true, but it was, being encouraged by your commanding general to take a vacation whenever you could, right there where you were fighting a war. "It seemed like the last meal before the execution," Spencer said, "but we were encouraged, on days off, to hop rides on 'administrative flights' and take short tours of India and China."

C. V. Glines described other sweeping changes in life under General Tunner:

> Planes brought in for maintenance would pass through three to ten stations as if on a factory production line. At each station, a plane would go through different maintenance functions. A rigorous inspection completed the procedure. If approved, each aircraft would be test-flown before being sent back to the line.

In talking with his flight surgeon, Tunner learned that many of his pilots were flying up to 165 hours a month so they could log flying hours quickly, making them eligible for reassignment back to the United States. The flight surgeon said at least half of the flying personnel were suffering from operational fatigue and that several accidents had clearly been caused by fatigue.

Tunner, a stern disciplinarian, promptly extended the length of every pilot's tour in the CBI Theater to a full year and increased the number of hours required before a pilot could be rotated out of the theater to 750. Tunner admitted later, "It didn't make the pilots happy, but . . . it kept quite a few of them alive. . . ."

At the same time, Tunner moved to attack another enemy—mosquitoes. He began a malaria prevention program by employing stripped-down B-25s to spray the Chinese countryside. The men called the planes "Skeeter Beaters." With repellents and nets added to the fight against the mosquitoes, the incidence of malaria dropped.

Weather was a constant foe. At a reunion in Cincinnati in the year 2000, several Hump pilots remembered how it was as they spoke with Lew Moores of the *Cincinnati Enquirer.* James Brewer, a Hump pilot from Marietta, Georgia, who remained in the Air

Force and rose to the rank of colonel, said, "In spite of all the war stories, weather killed more of our people than anything. We didn't have the navigational aids that they have today. You wouldn't believe how primitive it was."

Another Hump pilot, Bill Dees of San Antonio, who flew the Hump on seventy-eight missions, identified one of the most severe weather problems: thunderstorms. Winds of more than a hundred miles an hour were not unusual. Pilot Jack Distler of Louisville, Kentucky, identified another challenge: leaky oil drums. The planes often carried fuel in fifty-five-gallon drums stored in the rear of the planes. Some of the drums leaked, and when they did, the pilots and crews resorted to a simple solution. While flying at altitudes of from sixteen to twenty-six thousand feet, Distler said, "You just opened a door and threw out the leaking ones. It took two men."

Brewer said many pilots were unable to adjust to the weather conditions. "Quite often," he said, "the weather was so terrible that you, God and the copilot were all flying the airplane at the same time, just trying to keep it upright. The ice and snow and the turbulence and heavy rains. . . ."

In addition to supplies and equipment, the planes carried troops, including Chinese soldiers. The planes also carried a wide range of other "passengers"—chickens, geese, ducks, pigs, even mules. The pilots told reporter Moores that the mules left "an odor that took a day to clear out."

The pilots and their crews, without any guns mounted on their planes, occasionally ran into something else on those dangerous flights—enemy airplanes. "You'd see them every once in a while," Distler said. "When that happened, you'd duck into a cloud."

Then he admitted, "I'll tell you, in all frankness: I never made a single trip where I wasn't scared stiff."

There was good and sufficient reason for Hump personnel to be "scared stiff." Storms over the Himalayas were a constant threat, one that took a heavy toll. The worst storm in the history of the Hump missions struck on the night of January 6, 1945. A cold front swept across the mountains from Siberia and combined with warm, moist air from the Bay of Bengal. The ATC lost seven planes that night, with thirty-one crewmen and passengers killed. The China National Aviation Corporation, whose pilots were rated above those of any other organization in their ability to fly in hazardous weather, suspended operations after losing three planes and nine crewmen. Other commands lost four more planes—a total of fourteen planes downed and forty-two crewmen and passengers lost in one night's storm. The men of the Hump began referring to that date as Black Friday.

The bigger Douglas C-54s, with four engines, able to carry three times as much cargo, began replacing the twin-engine C-46s and C-47s in the early days of General Tunner's command. In 1944, Tunner revised the route for the C-54s to give those pilots a more direct route to China. However, it also put the planes in a position where they were flying over 150 miles of Japanese-occupied territory and within range of Japanese fighter planes. Tunner asked for, and got, protection from U.S. fighter planes. After that, he said later, "enemy action was of little consequence."

After the loss of Blackie Porter, the search-and-rescue operation needed to be improved. Tunner said it was "a cowboy operation" and appointed Major Donald Pricer, a Hump pilot himself, as commander of the rescue unit. He gave the unit four B-25s, a C-47, and a liaison plane, an L-5. All the planes were painted yellow. The unit's operational capabilities and versatility were improved considerably when a helicopter was added.

Tunner continued to make moves to strengthen the tonnage being flown to China to meet the constantly increasing needs. To minimize personnel losses of his own, he required all newcomers to attend a jungle indoctrination camp, where they received training in survival from experienced guides. He authorized the publication of a newspaper that reported tonnage amounts airlifted over the Hump by each unit.

Second Lieutenant J. D. Broughel of the Army turned to poetry to describe what it was like to be a pilot who flew the Hump in July 1943:

Oh! History's page through every age
Tells of men who accomplish things,
But few there are who shine a brighter star
Than those of whom this bard sings.

I've flown up and down the airways
From Hartford to Cooch-Behar
And have flown on instruments hours on end
With a line on a single star.

Up where the oxygen's needed;
Down where it's gusty and rough,
When the radio compass is bouncin' around
And the going is really tough.

I've flown from Natal to Ascension
When the scum wasn't drained from the sumps,
But it's nothin' compared to the thrills ya get
In a ship flying "Over the Hump."

Half around the world from home and Nell
Living in bamboo huts
('bashas' they call 'em), the heat and bugs
And the damp almost drive you nuts.

To the boys in the 13th Squadron
It's like saying your ABCs,
Cross the Hump to the Lake and Mount Tali,
Then over to Yunnanyi.

We take off from down by Doom Doom,
At a place called Sookerating,
With twenty-five drums of gasoline
To go Over the Hump to Kunming.

First there's the Fort Hertz Valley
And before the Taung Pit, which is green,
We cross the Yellow Mali,
Then the third, the dark brown Salween.

We're getting to eighteen thousand,
And the engines are singing a song
As the fourth, a red river slips by below,
The Lantsang Kiang or Mekong.

Across the grim Himalayas
There's a million rock peaks,
And you're sweatin' at twenty thousand
If the engine as much as squeaks.

For there's no landin' up in the mountains,
And those Japs are at Sumpra Bum,
And those window-makers crowd on ya
Like tenement homes in a slum.

In the best of weather the hazards
'Twould take a year to tell,
But on instruments up in the "Soup" and ice
The going is really hell!

Rocky and evil and awful,
So you're scared if you have to jump:
Crossing the ocean is easy
Alongside of flying the "Hump"!

And what if you're downed in the mountains
With thousands of rocky defiles?
If the tigers and cobras don't get you
A day's work will net you three miles.

And what if you get to a river?
A raft gets you down to the Japs!
And you know that Home or for flying again
For the duration (at least) it is "Taps"!

Did you say that you had met Bushey?
Well, in case you didn't know,
He went down on his first trip over,
A week and a half ago.

Looking? Hell, no! They're not looking!
Combing those rocky shelves?
A hundred years wouldn't be enough time!
They'll have to "walk out" by themselves.

Over the PanShan we're still going great;
To the south lies the town of Yangpi,
And we'll hit the south end of Lake Tali,
And then on to Yunnanyi.

Now there's many a cumulonimbus
That's turned a hair gray in my head,
And too many times have I trembled
When I thought the right engine went dead.

Cross the veldt up in Tanganyika
Each foot brings a "rockier" bump,
But it's nothing compared to the ride you get
With the boys flying "Over the Hump"!

It's great to hold the controls
On that giant man-made bird—
Pratt and Whitneys singing the sweetest
Concerto you've ever heard—

For your heart must be in your flying,
And you swell with intrinsic pride.
(You see, I'm a navigator,
And I just go along for the ride!)

Most of the danger is over
And we feel pretty safe with our load
When we "spot" that old ribbon of freedom
That's known as the Burma Road.

"Oil for the lamps of China"
Was it the poet said?
Oil and gas for American boys!
They need it like butter needs bread!

We follow the road 'cross the mountains,
And our airspeed jumps as we wing
Through the valley that leads for the last hundred miles
To our destination—Kunming!

Yes! I've flown from Natal to Ascension
When the scum wasn't drained from the sump,
But it's nothing compared to the thrill you get
In a ship flying "Over the Hump"!

Oh! History's page through every age
Tells of men who accomplished things,
But few there are shine a brighter star
Than the boys with the Silver Wings!

On August 1, 1945, five days before the first atomic bomb was dropped on Hiroshima, Tunner's Air Transport Command flew 1,118 round trips carrying a total of 5,327 tons. A plane crossed the Hump every minute and twelve seconds, and a ton of supplies and equipment landed in China four times every minute—all without even one accident. Author Glines reported in *Air Force Magazine* that after the war, historians for the Air Force calculated that "some 650,000 tons of gasoline, munitions, other matériel and men had been flown over the Hump during the airlift. . . ."

After the shooting stopped with V-J Day on August 14, the mission continued until it was ended in November after three years. In that three-month interim, flying the Hump became difficult for a different reason. "The last few months of flying were uneasy," Otha Spencer said. "To die in combat is a tragedy, but to die after the war, trying to clean up the mess of battle and marking time until you can go home, is a story of even greater anguish." In the final days of the operation, bad weather wiped out eleven of twenty-two planes in one day, killing four pilots—all without a shot being fired.

The Air Force history reported that the airlift did more than help to win the war in the Pacific. "Here," the history pointed out, "the AAF [Army Air Forces] demonstrated conclusively that a vast quantity of cargo could be delivered by air, even under the most unfavorable circumstances, if only the men who controlled the airlift, the terminals and the needed matériel were willing to pay the price in money and in men."

It was a tactic that was to be employed extensively and tested severely again—less than three years later—in Berlin.

From his own experiences as a pilot flying the Hump, Otha Spencer drew lasting lessons for humanity. "If war is inevitable," he said, "as it seems to be; if men must fight, as they always have, then it was best that young men, and women, who were called on to fight the war and fly the missions of supply were taught a skill that would help mankind, and themselves, in future years of peace."

The pilots who flew the Hump learned more than that, Spencer added. "As young pilots who flew over the Himalayas, my fellow crewmen and I learned three lessons, beyond price, as rules of living, not dying:

One: It is honorable to fight and (if need be) to die for your country, as long as good men, right or wrong in their honest actions, feel that it is necessary to push back a tyrant who seeks to enslave free men.

Two: Anything can be done when men set their minds and hearts to it. Nothing is impossible.

Three: There are better ways to settle disputes than war.

PART 6

Ploesti

★ 9 ★

Black Sunday and Big Week

Someone once wrote, "Ploesti! No other name from World War II promotes thoughts of courage and sacrifice on the part of U.S. Army Air Forces bomber crews."

Yet the name *Ploesti* is not nearly as familiar to the American public as other historic bombing missions of the same war—Doolittle's Raid over Tokyo, Curt LeMay's relentless pounding of mainland Japan into near submission with his newly acquired B-29s in late 1944 and '45, and the decisive atomic mission by Paul Tibbets over Hiroshima that brought an end to America's war against Japan.

Ploesti is an industrial city in the foothills of the Alps in Romania, about fifty miles north of Bucharest, and was known, until World War II, as the home of the mythical literary character Count Dracula. With the start of the war, however, it became one of the key bombing targets of the Allies because of its abundance of oil refineries and other industry. Allied strategists estimated that its refineries held 35 percent of the oil required by Hitler's war-making juggernaut.

For that reason, Ploesti became the subject of detailed discussions during a secret meeting in Casablanca, Morocco, in January 1943 involving Roosevelt, Churchill, and other leaders of the Allied nations. For ten days beginning on January 24, the Allies discussed and decided on their future strategy for the conduct of the war in Europe. As a critical part of that strategy, Ploesti was singled out as a key target for heavy bombing raids—a strategy that was implemented with devastating effects to Hitler's machine, but heavy losses to the Allies as well.

After an earlier bombing attack against Ploesti on June 12, 1942, American B-24 bombers and other Allied planes returned on August 1, 1943—"Black Sunday"—in the first major attack under the new strategy of the Allied leaders. In his series "Valor" in *Air Force Magazine,* John Frisbee said the mission "stands as a monument not only to the skill and courage of Air Force crews but also to the ability of our combat leaders to pull together strands of a broken plan and salvage limited success from the apparent certainty of disaster."

Frisbee wrote such a comment because the Ploesti raid, which was controversial even while still on the drawing board, became a near disaster for the Allies and yet dealt a lasting blow to the ability of Adolf Hitler to wage war.

It was a first in several strategic respects: the first large-scale, low-level strike by heavy bombers against a well-defended target, and the longest strike of World War II until that time—1,350 miles each way. And it was one of the most heroic missions of the war, producing five Medal of Honor winners.

Ploesti was the site of fourteen oil refineries in and near the city. Some of the mission's planners felt that if the Allies could destroy those refineries, where large quantities of oil were stored in drums, it might ensure the defeat of Germany. With such convictions, the planners of the mission worked meticulously, and the airmen involved rehearsed the flight thoroughly, including two full-scale practice missions against simulated targets that were laid out in a remote area of the desert in Libya. Using empty fifty-five-gallon oil drums welded together end to end, they built simulated short smokestacks that were some fifty feet high.

Air Force Magazine's Frisbee said the plan of attack "was simple: surprise and precision." The stream of B-24 bombers would be led by Colonel Keith K. Compton of the 376th Group, followed by four other bomber groups. Specific buildings were assigned to parts of each of the five groups of planes. Together the groups would make up a task force of 178 B-24s under the command of

Brigadier General Uzal Ent, who was flying in Compton's plane. The plans called for the planes to fly at low levels, below German radar, leaving their Libyan base between 4 and 5 A.M. on August 1. When they approached Ploesti, the pilots were to drop their planes to five hundred feet and then begin a bomb run over the next thirteen miles on refineries in the city and at Brazi. Before releasing their bombs, the planes were to drop to treetop level, virtually skimming the ground. All of the refineries were to be hit simultaneously in one wave of bombers, hence the name for the mission—Tidal Wave.

The B-24 was just coming into its own, emerging from the shadows of the now famous B-25 "Billy Mitchell Bomber" and the B-17 "Flying Fortress." Named the Liberator by pilots of England's Royal Air Force (the RAF), who were the first to fly the plane in combat, the B-24 was considered the most advanced four-engine bomber in the world when mass production began in 1941. The plane had a wingspan of 110 feet and was 67 feet long, with a gross weight of sixty thousand pounds—ten thousand pounds more than the B-17. The Liberator was a high-altitude bomber, with pilots flying them as high as twenty-five thousand feet on their missions.

More than nineteen thousand B-24s were manufactured during the war, most of them by Consolidated Aircraft Company in San Diego. The others were built by General Motors and the Ford Motor Company after the production of new cars was halted following the 1942 models and America's factories were immediately retooled to turn out vehicles of war. The number of B-24s was much greater than two other famous bombers of that war. The converted factories turned out twelve thousand B-17s during the war and four thousand B-29s.

The crews selected for Operation Tidal Wave practiced low-level flying in those new B-24s on simulated targets near airfields in Benghazi in Libya, even buzzing the camp and its observation towers. In contrast to their training in preflight school, where hedge-hopping was strictly prohibited, they now found themselves being encouraged to do it and to practice it because of the unique characteristics of their coming mission. One of the pilots, Major Bob Sternfels, a veteran of fifty combat missions and coauthor of the book *Burning Hitler's Black Gold: The True Story of Ploesti*, with Frank Way, said, "Now we were ordered to fly the B-24 as close to the ground as you dared." They were told that they could fly as low as they wanted to—"but don't kill the camels."

Sternfels, a native of Detroit who was twenty-two years old, said that this kind of flying "made the exercise very dangerous. However, after days of low-level flying in formation, no one was injured during the simulated bomb runs. The young pilots learned quickly."

First Lieutenant Harold F. Korger, the bombardier on Colonel Compton's plane, remembered the remarks of General Lewis Brereton, commander of the 9th Air Force, in what Korger described as "a pep talk" just before the mission. He said General Brereton told the airmen they "should consider ourselves lucky to be on this mission." Korger added, "A strange silence seemed to descend upon the almost 1,800 crew members assembled for the final briefing; it is possible that at least 446 of the young Americans—average age slightly under twenty-one—would not have agreed if they knew that in less than twenty-four hours they would be dead."

The mission encountered severe problems that gravely threatened its success. Accounts differ as to the nature of the problems and the reasons for them. One version is that weather foiled the plan for the mission when thick cumulus clouds rose above the mountains en route to Ploesti, resulting in the first two groups of bombers being separated from the three behind them. The first two groups were flying twenty-nine minutes ahead of the other three on a mission that called for all of them to arrive over the target at the same time.

Because strict radio silence had been imposed, General Ent and Colonel Compton were unable to contact the trailing bomber groups and did not know whether those groups had turned back. On their own, they elected to follow the operations order for the mission even if they were going to carry it out alone. John Frisbee pointed out in his magazine article that a surprise attack on the refineries in Ploesti "by a single wave of some 140 bombers, that dominant key to success at an acceptable cost," was now out of the question.

Another major complication developed when Compton's plane made a wrong turn by turning too early, taking two groups to the west of Ploesti, an error that went unnoticed until the planes were on the outskirts of Bucharest. In an interview with Major Sternfels in later years, Compton, a future three-star general, said,

> It was several minutes before I confirmed that we had made the wrong turn. I never heard anything on the radio such as "mistake, mistake," as has been reported. This is simply because I was on the plane's intercom and not on the command channel. . . . It was when we recognized the outline of the city of Bucharest that I realized my error.

Colonel Compton told Sternfels,

> I turned to General Ent and told him we had turned too early and had missed the target. There was little choice as we could not get back on the planned bomb run heading. I asked him for permission to bomb any other target. Ent agreed, so I then went on the command channel and ordered all other aircraft to "bomb targets of opportunity."

Compton also told Sternfels that other accounts of the incident saying that General Ent radioed the command to hit other targets as they came into view "are incorrect. That was my command on the radio with the approval of General Ent. By that time, we had bypassed Ploesti so I then turned to a heading of zero degrees and began to search for my own target to hit."

In *Burning Hitler's Black Gold,* Sternfels disagreed emphatically that weather was the cause of the error. In a series of e-mail messages and correspondence in 2002, Sternfels, who flew fifty combat missions during the war, declared flatly, "Weather was *not* the factor that caused separation!" Major Sternfels has said today that Compton and Kane applied different degrees of power to their engines, with Kane using lower power settings than Compton. For that reason, Sternfels said, "We lost sight of Compton's group long before reaching the mountains with the clouds. This is *fact.*" Sternfels has said today that the weather theory "comes from other books whose authors were not born when I went on this mission."

Sternfels added that the error "was realized *immediately,* but what to do to correct it took time, and by then they [Compton's group] had almost reached Bucharest." Separated, the two groups continued toward their target, but the plot thickened: They were detected by German radar. "Enemy defenses," Frisbee wrote in *Air Force Magazine*, "much heavier than anticipated, were thoroughly aroused. More than 230 antiaircraft guns, supported by many barrage balloons and smoke pots, surrounded the refineries, with perhaps 400 fighters in the area."

The result was "a maelstrom of ground fire." The leader of the 93rd Bomb Group, Lieutenant Colonel Addison E. Baker, spotted several refineries to his left. With his pilot, Major John Jerstad—who had completed his combat tour but volunteered for the mission—he zeroed in on the refinery, but his B-24 was hit by enemy fire short of it and erupted into flames. Baker and Jerstad had the opportunity to make a belly landing on the open fields below or pull up to a higher altitude and bail out. This, Frisbee pointed out, "was a mission on which some thought the outcome of the war might hinge." Obviously aware of the importance of their mission and the opportunities it offered for the Allies, they led the bombers behind them straight on to the refinery. Then they crashed into the ground. Both of them were awarded the Medal of Honor posthumously.

Another pilot in the raid was twenty-one-year-old Second Lieutenant Lloyd Hughes, on his fifth combat mission. His B-24 was hit by ground fire and began leaking streams of gasoline from fuel tanks in the wing and the bomb bay.

Like Baker and Jerstad, Hughes declined the opportunity to save his own life by landing in the fields below. Instead, he continued flying through the smoke and flames from the bombers ahead of him, bombed his target, and came away from his run with his left wing engulfed in flames. He tried to save his crew by crash-landing his plane on a lakebed but failed when one wing hit a riverbank, causing the plane to explode. Hughes became the mission's third Medal of Honor winner.

As Colonel Leon Johnson, a 1936 graduate of the U.S. Military Academy at West Point, flew his plane into the final stages of his bomb run, he saw thick columns of black smoke ahead of him, plus flames and explosions caused by delayed-reaction bombs dropped by the pilots in Compton's group who had arrived over the target ahead of him. Below him were tall chimneys and cables from barrage balloons, plus more delayed-reaction bombs that would explode in a matter of minutes.

Colonel John R. "Killer" Kane, commander of one of the groups on the raid, led forty-one planes into the thick and threatening unknown, described by Frisbee as "a scene that resembled the background of a medieval painting of hell." In doing so, Kane lost fifteen B-24s because of anti-aircraft gunfire from the ground, as well as fighters in the target area. He lost three more bombers to German fighters over Bulgaria. His own plane was missing one engine and was demolished in a crash landing at an Allied airfield on Cyprus.

Johnson flew through flak, explosions, heavy smoke, and blistering heat, leading fifteen other bombers. Only nine of the sixteen planes survived. Johnson, who later became a four-star general, and Kane were awarded the Medal of Honor.

As Major Sternfels piloted his B-24, the *Sandman,* toward his target, he spotted a "flak train"—a string of routine-appearing railroad freight cars connected to a speeding locomotive, traveling in the same direction as Sternfels. Instead of an innocent

freight train, however, it was a carefully disguised weapons em-
placement on wheels. Behind their closed doors, the cars were
equipped with eighty-eight-millimeter cannon and ammunition
and were manned by gun crews who were ready to take their fast-
moving train to any part of Ploesti and its surrounding area that
was being threatened by an enemy air attack.

Just as Sternfels spotted the "freight cars," their sides began to
roll down and, as he noted in his book about the raid, "We were
literally looking down the shiny gun barrels." The *Sandman* was
flying only fifty feet above the ground at almost two hundred
miles an hour, on a direct course to bomb the Astra Romana refineries at Ploesti. The flak train's guns opened fire at Sternfels
and his crew from barely a few hundred feet away.

Sternfels also had to maneuver his plane around and even
through steel cables hanging from "barrage balloons," with explosives dangling at the end of the cables ready to burst into flames
on contact.

In the confusion, the thick black smoke, the intense enemy
fire from the ground, and the threat of the barrage balloons, Sternfels wrote in his book, published in 2002, "Ahead of us through
our now dirty rain and grime-streaked windscreen our assigned
target is just now coming into view. But it's already ablaze"—the
result of the delayed-reaction bombs dropped by the 93rd Bomb
Group's B-24s that went ahead of him in the confusion. "Huge
clouds of black smoke are swirling upwards hundreds of feet.
Tongues of flames are belching skyward higher than our rapidly
approaching aircraft. As we watch, new explosions are scattering
flames and debris in our path. Bombs are exploding right before
our eyes."

The copilot on the *Sandman,* First Lieutenant Barney Jackson, yelled, "Somebody's already hit our target!"

"It was obvious," Sternfels wrote, "that our target, a vital oil
refinery for the German war machine, had been struck just minutes before. And preceding aircraft had strewn bombs that would
likely still be detonating just as we fly through their path at only
50-feet altitude."

Bombardier Dave Polacheck told Major Sternfels for his book,

When we got over the target area, we got into the smoke.
You couldn't see a thing, huge black clouds covering
everything . . . at 20 feet over the target. I couldn't see
anything. But when it came to the bomb run . . . I
couldn't see well, but I was going to drop anyway. I
dropped all ours into the smoke.

The *Sandman* became a symbol of the Ploesti raid on Black
Sunday. A camera mounted in the bomb bay of *Chug-A-Lug,* piloted by Captain LeRoy Morgan, whose plane also sliced through
a cable from a barrage balloon, photographed the *Sandman* seconds after Sternfels completed the bomb run. In the picture, the
plane is sharply etched against a solid mass of black smoke filling
the entire right half of the photo, with factory smokestacks visible on the left.

It became the most famous picture of Black Sunday. It was
published in the August 30 issue of *Life* magazine, then one of
American's most popular publications.

At about the time the picture was taken, pilot Sternfels, making sure not to look at the B-24s that were "going down in
flames," told copilot Jackson, "Full throttles, Barney. Let's get the
hell outta here!"

More than 30 percent of the B-24 Liberators that reached the
targets in Ploesti were shot down by enemy fire or were forced to
land in Turkey, a neutral nation, because of damage to the planes.
Their crews were imprisoned.

A study by T. E. Davidson Jr. showed that 178 B-24s were
launched for the air attack, with 161 reaching their targets. Of
these, forty-four planes were lost, and 532 American men did not
come back. Seven airmen were interned in Turkey. One plane
crashed on takeoff.

After the Ploesti raid, the GI newspaper *Stars and Stripes* told
the story under a bold headline that said bluntly:

9TH AIR FORCE GIVES PLOESTI HELL

A "Combat Action Report" by Colonel Jacob Smart, the chief planner for the mission, dated June 15, 1944, began:

> The Ploesti mission of 1 August 1943 was one of the major exploits of the United States Army and Air Forces in World War II—an epic of American valor— the longest large-scale bombing mission that had been undertaken to that time—a masterpiece of detailed and careful planning, training and briefing. Measured in terms of injury to enemy war potential, even though it fell short of expectations of its planners, the mission was significant.

From the beginning, the Black Sunday raid on Ploesti was dogged by controversy, a debate that continues to this day. Colonel Johnson opposed the plan, conceived by Colonel Smart, because he thought it was too risky. General Ent was opposed on the same grounds.

Estimates of the success of the mission vary. The head of the Air Force during World War II, General Henry H. "Hap" Arnold, wrote later, "The damage done to the sprawling miles of Europe's Number One Refinery was great—60 percent of the total production capacity temporarily knocked out, but the cost was heavy." For General Arnold, the raid was also a personal success. He had lobbied for daylight raids, a practice avoided in the early part of the war because Allied planes were harder to see at night and thus safer from enemy anti-aircraft fire and interceptor planes of the Luftwaffe—the German word for "air weapon." But the targets were also hard to see at night. General Arnold contended that daylight bombing would significantly increase the raids' degree of success.

Alfred Goldberg, in his *History of the USAF* in 1957, said, "About 40 percent of the cracking and refining capacity of Ploesti had been destroyed, but the enemy, undisturbed by further attacks, succeeded within a few months in getting production back almost to its former level."

Others expressed similar views, pro and con, with varying statistics to back up their claims. Bob Sternfels was convinced that the raid "was necessary." On the subject of Compton's mistake, he said it

> was the error that caused the deaths of many airmen and this damaged the total concept of the Ploesti plan. First, two groups did not bomb their assigned targets. Second, the 93rd Group bombed the 98th's target, which caused the 98th to fly into a wall of fire. Worst of all, the ground fire from the German guns hit the 98th's bombers and accounted for a 42 percent loss of their planes. Third, Compton did not lose many planes. In fact, only one was lost over Ploesti. Fourth, the fact that Compton's bombs were dropped in a *safe* condition means he flew almost 3,000 miles, apparently never hit a refinery—all other groups that hit refineries had three to four times the loss rate—and dropped bombs that could not explode!

The debate continues to this day and presumably will never be resolved. But then came "Big Week."

By February 1944, Allied planners were designing a full-scale air attack to cripple Germany's ability to manufacture more airplanes for its Luftwaffe. Once again, Ploesti would be a key target, along with Hamburg, Germany's main seaport. The reasoning was that the attacks on the targets themselves, plus the losses sustained by the Luftwaffe in trying to defend against the attacks, could combine to deal a crippling blow to Hitler's Air Force, commanded by Reich Marshal Hermann Göring.

For Göring, this was his second war in the air after becoming an ace in World War I. After that war, he became one of Hitler's closest accomplices and founded the dreaded Gestapo to maintain a tight grip on Germany's leaders and its citizens when Hitler forced his way to command of the German government as a dictator in 1933. As one of Hitler's henchmen, Göring ran the German economy from that time until 1943, under his slogan, "Guns instead of butter." At the same time, he was commander in chief of the Luftwaffe. Surely it was one of the strangest combinations of official duties imaginable, an arrangement comparable to an American general serving as chief of staff of the Air Force and chairman of the Federal Reserve Board at the same time.

Big Week was launched on the night of February 19–20, despite foreboding weather conditions. The ceiling over England, where planes of the RAF would take off in what was going to be a combined U.S.-English operation, was only eight thousand feet, with severe icing in the clouds. Plans called for the British to bomb by night and the Americans by day, but the U.S. strike force would have to take off before dawn on the first day because of the shortness of daylight in that month. Despite the weather, General Carl Spaatz, commander of U.S. Strategic Forces in Europe, made the decision to launch the mission, sending in more than a thousand airplanes—all against aircraft plants in Germany—escorted by seventeen groups of fighter planes. At the height of Big Week, the RAF attack force included twenty-three hundred bombers flying over Germany at night, with thirty-eight hundred U.S. planes over Germany during the days.

The American Heritage Pictorial History of World War II reported that Göring's Luftwaffe lost 450 planes, a staggering number for any of the nations involved, but especially crippling for Germany, which was already experiencing shortages of supplies and equipment. "By that same summer," the *American Heritage* history said in its 1966 volume, "Göring's air fleet had been crippled. Eisenhower was able to reassure his D-Day troops in early June, 'If you see fighting aircraft over you, they will be ours.' "

Eisenhower's bold prediction turned out to be justified. After Germany surrendered a year and three months following Big Week, officers of the Luftwaffe said the raids clearly had a crippling effect on the German Air Force. According to *American Heritage*, one Luftwaffe officer said, "There is no doubt that the Americans harmed us most. The Russians were negligible as far as the home front was concerned, and we could have stood the British attacks on our cities. But the Americans' devastation of our airfields, factories and oil depots made it impossible for us to keep going."

The *American Heritage* account of Big Week and the rest of

the air war in Europe shed a different light on the reasons for its eventual success:

> Contrary to what might be expected, it was not a shortage of planes but a lack of pilots that finally stopped the Luftwaffe. In their all-out assault the last part of February, 1944—the so-called "Big Week"—the Allies pounded German air industry with some 6,100 bombers, while fighters flew more than 3,600 sorties. Plane production was badly disrupted, but the irreparable loss was the pilots killed when 450 German planes went down during the week; the Luftwaffe could not train new pilots that fast.

As in any war, there were heroes among the statistics. One was Second Lieutenant James Lewis, copilot of a B-24 that was hit by enemy fire on the first day of Big Week. At the "bombs away" point in the mission, one of the early bursts of enemy fire knocked out the right engine and damaged the fuselage of the plane, piloted by another second lieutenant, Frederick Rawson. As it limped along on one engine, the plane became a sitting duck for swarms of Luftwaffe fighter planes. One waist gunner, Sergeant Robert Shultz, was killed instantly.

Pilot Rawson sent copilot Lewis to the rear of the plane to give the order to bail out. As Lewis prepared to jump, he saw that Rawson, who was struggling to keep his plane under control until the crew could bail out, could not get out of his seat. Another problem was that there was no parachute available for his use.

As described by John Frisbee in his "Valor" series, "Lewis released Rawson from his seat, found the pilot's chute and buckled it on him. Satisfied that Rawson could make it out of the shot-up plane, Lewis entered the bomb bay to make sure all crew members had left or were able to parachute out." There he saw Sergeant Russell Wapensky, a tail gunner who had been wounded. Wapensky was standing, his clothing smoldering and his chute riddled by twenty-millimeter shells. There was not another parachute on board.

Lewis refused to leave the wounded gunner even though he

knew the plane was destined to crash. "He saw only one alternative," Frisbee wrote. "Lewis hoisted Wapensky onto his back and dove out the bomb bay. The shock of the chute opening broke Wapensky's grip from around Lieutenant Lewis's neck, and the tailgunner fell to his death."

The crew landed in a farm field. Another member, Second Lieutenant William Johnson, the navigator, was killed when his chute did not open. Two other members, Staff Sergeant Richard McCoy, the flight engineer, and the ball turret gunner, Sergeant Julian Winfree, survived the crash and were taken to a nearby hospital. Both had been wounded during the attack. They died there.

The others were taken to Frankfurt to be interrogated and remained prisoners of war until the war was over. By the time Big Week was over, as Frisbee wrote, "The achievement of Allied air superiority and eventual collapse of the Third Reich were in sight over a still-distant horizon."

PART 7

Hiroshima

Lieutenant Benjamin Foulois (left) and Orville Wright enjoy a moment at Fort Myer, Virginia, on July 30, 1909, the day the Army accepted Wright's "U.S. Army Aeroplane No. 1." (*Carroll V. Glines Collection.*)

Captain Foulois stands beside his military "aeroplane" in 1916, which he flew that year in the mission to track down Pancho Villa in Mexico. (*Carroll V. Glines Collection.*)

Benjamin Foulois, one of America's first three Army pilots, was a retired major general when he looked over his model of Army Aeroplane No. 1. (*Carroll V. Glines Collection.*)

In 1929, three future generals, then young officers, flew over southern California for six days in the plane with the question mark to test the feasibility of in-flight refueling. That plane is being refueled by RP#1 through a fire hose. The officers named their plane *Question Mark* because nobody knew how long they would be able to stay up. (*Via Robert F. Dorr.*)

Lieutenant General Elwood R. "Pete" Quesada, the first commanding general of the Tactical Air Command, was one of the officers aboard *Question Mark*.
(*Via Robert F. Dorr.*)

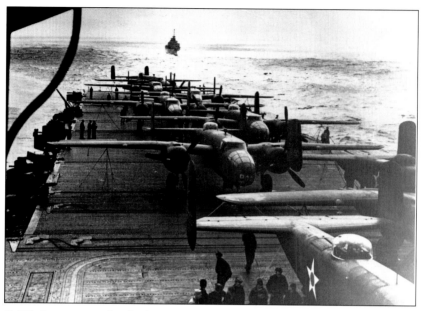

B-25s line up on the flight deck of the carrier USS *Hornet* on April 18, 1942, on their way to bomb Tokyo. (*Via Robert F. Dorr.*)

Only four months after the Japanese staged their surprise attack on Pearl Harbor, Lieutenant Colonel Jimmy Doolittle leads fifteen other B-25 pilots in a surprise attack of their own, over Tokyo. His was the first plane off the flight deck of the USS *Hornet* in the first carrier-based bombing mission in history. (*Via Robert F. Dorr.*)

President Franklin D. Roosevelt awards Jimmy Doolittle the Medal of Honor at the White House on May 19, 1942, for his leadership in planning and carrying out the stunning raid over Tokyo. With them in the White House are (from left) Lieutenant General H. H. "Hap" Arnold, commander of the Army Air Forces, Mrs. Doolittle, and General George C. Marshall, Army chief of staff. FDR also promoted Doolittle from lieutenant colonel to brigadier general, jumping him over the rank of full colonel. (*C. V. Glines Collection.*)

Eighty silver goblets honor the members of the Doolittle Raid over Tokyo. Those turned upside down represent the deceased. The last two survivors will open the bottle of brandy in the middle and drink a final toast. Between reunions, the goblets—a gift from the city of Tucson, Arizona—are on display at the Air Force Academy Museum in Colorado Springs, Colorado. (*Air Force Photo, C. V. Glines Collection.*)

Jimmy Doolittle rose from lieutenant colonel to the three-star rank of lieutenant general during World War II.
(*Via Robert F. Dorr.*)

"Doolittle's Raiders"—Lieutenant Colonel Jimmy Doolittle (second from left) and his crew: from left, Lieutenant Henry A. Potter, the navigator; Colonel Doolittle, the pilot; Staff Sergeant Fred A. Braemer, the bombardier; Lieutenant Richard E. Cole, the copilot; and Staff Sergeant Paul J. Leonard, the engineer-gunner.
(*Air Force Photo, C. V. Glines Collection.*)

Hitler's oil refineries in Ploesti, Romania, literally go up in smoke during the American raid of August 1, 1943. (*Bob Sternfels Collection.*)

First Lieutenant Bob Sternfels, in his B-24, misses the smokestacks on the left by only sixty-five feet while bombing the oil refineries in Ploesti. (*Bob Sternfels Collection.*)

B-24 Liberator bombers in mass production, and the final product.
(*Bob Sternfels Collection.*)

★ 10 ★

"Extremely Powerful Bombs of a New Type"

Almost a hundred thousand Japanese men, women, and children were killed in one bombing raid by the Americans, and another forty thousand were injured. One-quarter of the city—sixteen square miles—was destroyed. It was the most devastating mission of World War II, and it remains the most destructive air raid in history to this day. The fire department estimated that ninety-seven thousand people had been killed, 125,000 injured, and another 1.2 million left homeless.

It was not Hiroshima on August 6, 1945. Instead, it was Tokyo, five months earlier, on the night of March 9–10 of the same year. That was not the only difference in the two raids. The other, largely unknown to the American public and the rest of the world even to this day, is that the raid on Tokyo killed more people than the atomic bomb attack on Hiroshima.

The Tokyo raid of March 9–10 was one of the most notable in a long series of extremely heavy and destructive bombing missions intended to end the war and bring victory to the United States. If the Japanese were going to continue their stubborn resistance, sacrificing tens of thousands of lives in hopeless stands in the Pacific islands, then the Americans would simply pound them into defeat in their homeland, armed with the air power and the weaponry to continue this strategy for as long as it took. Night after night, American bombers continued their relentless air assaults, raining thousands of incendiary bombs on the modern and ancient buildings of Japan's major cities, spreading fires over what was left after the explosions.

A Japanese factory worker described the raid on Tokyo on the night of March 9–10. He found safety in a school compound during the raid. "The fires were incredible by now," he said:

> with flames leaping hundreds of feet into the air. There seemed to be a solid wall of fire rolling toward the building. . . . The great bombers were still coming over Tokyo in an endless stream. . . . Fire-winds filled with burning particles rushed up and down the streets. I watched people—adults and children—running for their lives, dashing madly about like rats. The flames raced after them like living things, striking them down. They died by the hundreds right in front of me. Wherever I turned my eyes, I saw people running away from the school grounds seeking air to breathe. They raced away from the school into a devil's cauldron of twisting, seething fire. The whole spectacle with its blinding lights and thundering noise reminded me of the paintings of Purgatory.

A Japanese newspaper reporter wrote, "The city was as bright as at sunrise. Clouds of smoke, soot, even sparks driven by the storm, flew over it. That night we thought the whole of Tokyo was reduced to ashes."

Three major developments in America's favor made these air assaults possible:

- The arrival of the B-29 bombers from America's factories after their conversion from automobiles and other peacetime products to wartime weapons and delivery systems.
- Victory over Japan in the Mariana Islands, providing ground for U.S. landing fields only 750 miles from the Japanese mainland, well within reach of the new long-range B-29s.
- An enormous increase in American air power, told convincingly in figures from the end of World War II showing the strength of the Army Air Corps:

193,000 pilots
50,000 navigators
45,000 bombardiers
297,000 aerial gunners

The story of Hiroshima, however, goes back considerably before the formation of this vast aerial armada, to a time even before the start of World War II.

On August 2, 1939, the month before Hitler invaded Poland to begin the Second World War, Albert Einstein, a world-famous physicist and a refugee from Germany, sent a letter to President Roosevelt alerting him to the growing possibility of producing what became the atomic bomb. He wrote to FDR from his home on Nassau Point at Peconic, Long Island. Einstein's full letter said:

F. D. Roosevelt
President of the United States
White House
Washington, D.C.

Sir:
    Some recent work by E. Fermi and L. Szilard, which has been communicated to me in manuscript, leads me to expect that the element uranium may be turned into a new and important source of energy in the immediate future. Certain aspects of the situation which has arisen seem to call for watchfulness and, if necessary, quick action on the part of the Administration. I believe, therefore, that it is my duty to bring to your attention the following facts and recommendations:
    In the course of the last four months it has been made probable—through the work of Joliot in France as well as Fermi and Szilard in America—that it may become possible to set up a nuclear chain reaction in a large mass of uranium, by which vast amounts of power and large quantities of new radium-like elements would be generated. Now it appears almost certain that this could be achieved in the immediate future.

This new phenomenon would also lead to the construction of bombs, and it is conceivable—though much less certain—that extremely powerful bombs of a new type thus may be constructed. A single bomb of this type, carried by boat and exploded in a port, might very well destroy the whole port together with some of the surrounding territory. However, such bombs might very well prove to be too heavy for transportation by air.

The United States has only very poor ores of uranium in moderate quantities. There is some good ore in Canada and the former Czechoslovakia, while the most important source of uranium is Belgian Congo.

In view of the situation you may think it desirable to have more permanent contact maintained between the Administration and the group of physicists working on chain reactions in America. One possible way of achieving this might be for you to entrust with this task a person who has your confidence and who could perhaps serve in an unofficial capacity.

His task might comprise the following:

(a) to approach Government Departments, keep them informed of the further development, and put forward recommendations for Government action, giving particular attention to the problem of securing a supply of uranium ore for the United States.

(b) to speed up the experimental work, which is at present being carried on within the limits of the budgets of University laboratories, by providing funds, if such funds be required, through his contacts with private persons who are willing to make contributions for this cause, and perhaps also by obtaining the co-operation of industrial laboratories which have the necessary equipment.

I understand that Germany has actually stopped the sale of uranium from the Czechoslovakian mines which she has taken over. That she should have taken such early action might perhaps be understood on the ground that the son of the German Under-Secretary of State, von Weizsacker, is attached to the Kaiser-

Wilhelm-Institut in Berlin where some of the American work on uranium is now being repeated.

Yours very truly,
Albert Einstein

On October 9, 1941, President Roosevelt, aware that Nazi Germany was also attempting to develop the kind of bomb that Einstein was talking about, authorized stepped-up research to determine the feasibility of building an atomic bomb. The final decision to produce the bomb on a priority basis was made on December 6, 1941, the day before the Japanese attack on Pearl Harbor. At the height of "Project Manhattan" in 1944, some 129,000 people were involved in developing the bomb, most of them without knowing it, at a cost of two billion dollars. The project represented a massive commitment of money and manpower that was beyond Germany's capability.

As American forces swept their way toward victory on both fronts—in Europe and in the Pacific—a former big-league baseball player was assigned to a spy mission to determine how close Germany was to the United States in the race to build an atomic bomb. Although some have questioned it, the story goes that Moe Berg, a journeyman catcher for fifteen years in the major leagues and also a lawyer and a Ph.D. after being educated at Princeton and the Sorbonne, was working for the Office of Strategic Services, the forerunner of today's Central Intelligence Agency.

On December 18, 1944, two days after the start of the Battle of the Bulge, Berg, then 42 years old, was sitting face to face with Hitler's most prominent atomic physicist, Dr. Werner Heisenberg. They were in Bisingen in Germany's Black Forest, the nerve center of the project like America's Project Manhattan complexes in Oak Ridge, Tennessee, and Los Alamos, New Mexico. Heisenberg was delivering a lecture. Berg was disguised as a Swiss graduate student. Elsewhere in the room, Berg spotted agents of Hitler's feared SS security force.

Berg's orders were to listen carefully. If he thought from Heisenberg's lecture that Germany was getting dangerously close to the United States in the development of an atomic bomb, or had even passed the U.S., Berg's orders were to take out the loaded Beretta revolver he had hidden in a shoulder holster under his suit coat and kill the German scientist. Then he was to take the cyanide pill in his pocket and swallow it, killing himself. Fortunately, Berg concluded from Heisenberg's comments that the United States still had a comfortable lead over Germany in the race to build an "A-bomb," so he did not have to resort to such dire actions.

On the other side of the world, America's fighting men were advancing toward victory step by step, capturing Japanese-held islands that were bringing those new U.S. superbombers, the B-29s, closer to the Japanese mainland and the empire's major cities—Tokyo, Kobe, Honshu, and Yokohama. On June 11, 1944, five days after the Allies landed in Europe on D-Day, a U.S. naval task force bombarded the Mariana Islands, only thirteen hundred hundred miles from Tokyo.

After another eight days, on June 19, the Japanese soldiers who had been defending Saipan, one of the islands in the Marianas chain, in frantic resistance ducked into limestone caves and began a suicidal last stand, aware of Saipan's strategic importance because of its proximity to their island nation. On July 18, Hideki Tojo, the Japanese premier, said the Japanese defense of Saipan had been a "great disaster" and resigned as premier. Three days later, U.S. forces landed on Guam, the largest island in the Marianas, and after only another three days, on July 24, they landed on Tinian, which was to play a key role in the dropping of the world's first atomic bomb. Tinian fell to the Americans on August 3, and the battle for Guam ended in an American victory a week later when organized resistance by the Japanese ended. The Americans, flying at the B-29's higher altitudes beyond the range of the anti-aircraft guns on the ground, were now close enough to Japan to bomb it from the captured islands.

The threat of U.S. bombing raids against Japan's major cities was worsening because of events in China as well. On February 7,

1944, President Roosevelt authorized the spending of five hundred million dollars to build five B-29 staging airfields near Chengtu in far northern China.

Otha Spencer made the argument in *Flying the Hump* that this construction project was "one of the most fantastic engineering feats of World War II, equal, as an engineering project, to the Great Wall of China. In a country where there were no graders, bulldozers, steamrollers or trucks, the huge base was built by hand."

CBS correspondent James Stewart reported from Chunking: "The roads for miles around were jammed with men, simple farmers in blue cotton trousers and jumps and straw sandals, each with two long poles over his shoulder and enough rice to last until he arrived at one of the sites." The men built their own tepee-like huts of straw and lived in them for months—430,000 of them. They worked from sunup to sundown seven days a week. Between the American victories in the Mariana Islands and the new staging areas in China, B-29s would be able to bomb Japan on a daily basis. The fate of the empire was sealed.

The first B-29 attack against Japan happened on November 24, 1944, when B-29s flew from their new base on Saipan and staged an air raid over Tokyo. The aerial assaults against Tokyo continued. On December 29, B-29s from Saipan bombed Japan's capital city again. After still more raids, ninety Superfortresses bombed Tokyo. B-29s, which the Japanese people called *B-san*—"Mr. B."—were flying from Guam, Saipan, and Tinian to the Japanese mainland at regular intervals and bombing its population centers, including Tokyo, Honshu, and Kyushu.

Thousands of Japanese were being killed in the raids, and their cities were being destroyed. In a lengthy feature article in *Air Force Magazine* in 1994, editor in chief John T. Correll described the desperation in Japan. The nation's military leaders pulled their troops back from their island battles in the Pacific, anticipating a final pitched battle against the Americans on the Japanese mainland. Manpower became scarce, and the Japanese cabinet extended the draft to more civilians, including men from age fifteen to sixty and women from seventeen to forty-five.

When the Air Force chief, General Arnold, visited Guam in June

1945, he said the B-29 campaign "would enable our infantrymen to walk ashore on Japan with their rifles slung." With this degree of military superiority by the United States, Arnold thought the use of the bomb in full combat conditions might not be necessary.

Bill Lawrence, who covered the White House for the *New York Times* during the administrations of six presidents after World War II, produced hard statistics displaying the air power of the Americans over the Japanese. In his 1971 autobiography, *Six Presidents, Too Many Wars,* Lawrence reported that from November 24, 1944, through the end of the war, B-29s flew 318 missions from the Marianas that dropped approximately 159,000 tons of bombs on Japanese targets. The targets included sixty-four industrial areas with a combined population of 21.2 million. Lawrence quoted Air Force statistics that showed the attacks burned out 157.98 square miles of Japanese urban industrial areas and left 8.4 million people dead or homeless.

The Japanese placed increased emphasis on the defense of their country, a marked contrast to the days less than four years earlier when Japan was on a sweeping offensive drive in the Pacific. By 1945, instead of attacking, Japan was defending. Correll wrote that new plans called for a defensive force of ten thousand airplanes, most of them the kamikaze suicide planes in which pilots would knowingly sacrifice their lives to strike an enemy target.

He added, "Suicide boats and human torpedoes would defend the beaches. . . . Civilians were being taught to strap explosives to their bodies and throw themselves under advancing tanks. Construction battalions had fortified the shorelines of Kyushu and Honshu with tunnels, bunkers and barbed wire."

Eventually there would be little left of the Japanese empire, with the disastrous raid on the night of March 9–10 demonstrating in alarming terms what the future held for the Japanese people.

On June 22, 1945, the same month that General Arnold made his optimistic prediction, Emperor Hirohito told his Supreme War Council bluntly, "We have heard enough of this determination of yours to fight to the last soldiers. We wish that you, leaders of Japan, will now strive to study the ways and means to conclude the war. In so doing, try not to be bound by the decisions you have made in the past."

Hirohito was making his remarks on the same day that one of the bloodiest battles of World War II, on Okinawa, ended in defeat for his nation. Japan lost more than a hundred thousand men. The United States lost seventy-five hundred in fighting on land and another five thousand Navy men, almost all of them in kamikaze attacks. John Correll pointed out in his magazine article, "Kamikaze attacks in that battle sank 28 U.S. ships and did severe damage to hundreds more. The Japanese force on Okinawa was only a fraction the size of the one waiting in the home islands."

Even with the extremely heavy casualties experienced by both sides in the Pacific, there were proposals on the part of some American officials to explode the atomic bomb in a demonstration rather than using it in an actual bombing. Correll pointed out that supporters for using it in an air raid countered that argument by saying a demonstration "would not be sufficient. Reasons included the possibility that the bomb might not work, that the Japanese might think the demonstration was faked, and that there was no way to make the demonstration convincing enough to end the war."

At a Big Three meeting at Potsdam in July attended by Truman, Churchill, and Stalin, U.S. leaders continued the discussion. Secretary of State Jimmy Byrnes, Secretary of War Henry Stimson, Admiral William Leahy, President Roosevelt's military aide, and General Arnold reached a consensus that the bomb should be dropped in an actual air raid, not as a demonstration. In Correll's article in *Air Force Magazine,* he reported, "Although Arnold supported the decision, he repeated his view that the use of the bomb was not a military necessity."

However, Truman's biographer, David McCullough, disagreed in his Pulitzer Prize–winning *Truman.* "Had the bomb been ready in March and deployed by Roosevelt," McCullough wrote, "had it shocked Japan into surrender then, it would have already saved nearly 50,000 American lives lost in the Pacific in the time since, not to say a vastly larger number of Japanese lives."

While the Potsdam conference continued, Truman sent an order to the Pentagon that the 509th Composite Group—headed by Colonel Paul Tibbets—should deliver the first "special bomb" as soon after August 3 as weather permitted, over one of the four cities on the list of targets.

Churchill agreed with the decision, and in later years was emphatic in continuing to support Truman. He said the decision by the president "saved Western civilization."

At the end of their conference, the Big Three issued a proclamation on July 26 warning Japan that it faced "utter devastation of the Japanese homeland" if it did not surrender unconditionally. "We shall brook no delay," the proclamation said tersely.

On the same day, an American warship, the cruiser USS *Indianapolis,* dropped its anchor just off the shore of Tinian and transferred a fifteen-foot wooden crate to a landing ship tank (LST), a naval craft built to land tanks and other heavy equipment. At the same time, two men climbed down a ladder from the *Indianapolis* and into a motor launch while carrying a heavy lead bucket. The crate contained the firing mechanism for the atomic bomb. Inside the bucket was a slug of uranium.

The two men, Major Robert R. Furman, an engineer, and Colonel James F. Nolan, a physician and radiology officer, had accompanied their top-secret cargo all the way from San Francisco on a ten-day journey. Both officers were attached to the Manhattan Project. During their entire trip, the two men took turns guarding the bucket. Meanwhile, a B-29 from Hamilton Field in California delivered a second slug of uranium to Tinian, at the same time that two other B-29s were delivering plutonium for a second atomic bomb.

Japan's response to the Potsdam Proclamation was almost predictable. Two days after it was issued, Baron Kantaro Suzuki, the new premier (who had succeeded Tojo), said the Potsdam Proclamation was a "thing of no great value."

Two days after that, on July 30, the *Indianapolis,* with a crew of 1,196 sailors and Marines, was sunk after delivering the material for the atomic bomb to Tinian. The ship had been headed for the island of Leyte. Survivors literally fought for their lives in shark-infested waters for five days until help arrived on August 4. Of the 900 men who survived the sinking, only 316 were still alive, two days before the atomic bomb, armed by their cargo, was dropped on Hiroshima.

One of the central figures in the progress of Project Manhattan, which was headed by a two-star Army general, Leslie Groves, was a twenty-nine-year-old lieutenant colonel, Paul W. Tibbets Jr., a product of America's heartland who spent his first years in Quincy, Illinois, and two cities in Iowa—Davenport and Des Moines. When he was nine years old, he moved with his family to Miami, Florida, after his father discovered that the people there didn't have to shovel snow in the winter or keep a furnace fired up.

Tibbets began his path to history by dropping candy bars from an airplane instead of bombs. His father was in the candy business, and twelve-year-old Paul experienced any boy's dream when he was chosen to scatter a cargo of a new product from the Curtiss Candy Company—Baby Ruth chocolate bars—from a Waco 9 plane over Miami's Hialeah racetrack in January 1927. The bars floated to the crowd below from miniature parachutes, something repeated for far more humanitarian reasons twenty-one years later in the Berlin Airlift.

In his 1998 autobiography, *Return of the* Enola Gay, Tibbets wrote "As I look back on both events, I'm obliged to report that the mission to Hialeah was more exciting than the one to Hiroshima. There is nothing to match the thrill of a twelve-year-old boy's first airplane ride."

Well before Hiroshima, Tibbets was selected for critical missions after earning his pilot's silver wings at Kelly Field in San Antonio in 1938. In one of the new B-17 Flying Fortress bombers, named *Butcher Shop,* he led the first daylight raid by an American bomber squadron over German-occupied France on August 17, 1942. "This was not only a first for me and my crew and for the eleven B-17s that were following us on this mission to Rouen," Tibbets said in his book. ". . . The mission, of which I was the leader, was a small beginning for us, but the beginning of the end for Hitler." By the end of the war in Europe less than three years later, planes of the American 8th Air Force had dropped 4.3 million bombs on Europe, delivered by 332,645 bombers.

The B-17 got a head start on World War II. It went from drawing board to flight testing in less than twelve months and was flown for the first time on July 28, 1935. The big bomber saw combat in Europe even before America entered the war. The plane was being flown by pilots of England's Royal Air Force in 1941 for high-altitude bombing missions. It was a war machine of the air, with eleven to thirteen machine guns and the capacity to carry twenty thousand pounds of bombs. It was easily recognized because it was the first Boeing airplane with a high tail for improved control and stability during high-altitude bombing. With a crew of ten, the plane had a top speed of 287 miles an hour and cruised at 150 mph, powered by four twelve-hundred-horsepower engines. It was suitable for long-range bombing because of its range of 3,750 miles and was able to bomb from almost seven miles up, beyond the range of ground fire.

During their return flight to their base in England, Tibbets said, "A feeling of elation took hold of us as we winged back across the Channel. All the tension was gone. We were no longer novices at this terrible game of war. We had braved the enemy in his own skies and were alive to tell about it."

After flying twenty-five combat missions in his B-17 over Europe, Tibbets was selected for two important assignments leading up to Operation Torch, the Allied invasion of North Africa, to stop Germany's Desert Fox, Field Marshal Erwin Rommel, in his attempt to capture that region for Hitler's Nazi machine. In October 1942, Tibbets flew General Mark Clark on Tibbets's plane, the *Red Gremlin,* to a secret rendezvous with French leaders in North Africa during the desert war there. He was also chosen as the pilot to fly General Eisenhower to Gibraltar for the start of Operation Torch. In November, Tibbets led the first bombing missions supporting the invasion.

While still flying missions over North Africa in March 1943, Tibbets was told to report to the office of the Allied air commander there, General Jimmy Doolittle, who told him, "I've just received a message from Hap Arnold"—General H. H. Arnold, commander of the Army Air Forces, the forerunner of today's U.S. Air Force. Doolittle continued, "He wants an experienced bombardment officer to come back to the States and help with the development of a big new bomber. I've recommended you for the job."

The "big new bomber" was the B-29.

Big may have been an understatement. The plane, being built by Boeing Aircraft, would be 99 feet long and 27 feet, 9 inches, high, with a wingspan of 141 feet, 3 inches. It was the largest airplane used by any country during the war and was used only in the war in the Pacific.

By comparison, the B-17 was 75 feet long with a wingspan of 103 feet. The B-29 would be able to carry a bomb load of twenty thousand pounds. With a full payload, it would weigh 141,000 pounds. With four engines providing twenty-two hundred horsepower, the B-29 would be able to fly 3,250 miles at a peak speed of 360 miles an hour.

Doolittle told Tibbets the request from Arnold was of the highest priority. Tibbets was to leave for Washington immediately. The general had his staff car waiting outside to take Tibbets back to his quarters to pick up his clothes. A C-47 was standing by to fly him to Liberia on the first leg of his trip back to the United States.

On his return to Washington, Tibbets learned that the program to build the plane, which had been on the drawing boards since 1940, was in a state of disarray. General Eugene Eubank, who commanded the first overwater flight of B-17s across the Pacific

Ocean in 1940, told him bluntly, "I don't know whether we'll ever have a B-29." Eubank had justification for his comment. The week before, Boeing's chief test pilot, Eddie Allen, and ten top technicians were killed in Seattle when a B-29 crashed during a test flight. An engine caught fire, and the flames spread to the fuel tanks in the wing.

Tibbets blamed the plane's early problems on the maximum effort to get it into the skies and on its powerful engines. "It was the largest airplane engine built up to that time," he has remembered, "and its difficulties stemmed from an effort to put them and the new airplane into operation before all the bugs had been worked out." As evidence of the push to get B-29s airborne, Tibbets received a transfer to Wichita, Kansas, where B-29s would soon be rolling off the production line at Boeing's new plant.

The Army had ordered 1,664 planes to replace the B-17. The B-29s, which flew higher, faster, and farther than the B-17s, were intended for the war in the Pacific. The commanding general of the Army Air Forces, General H. H. "Hap" Arnold, felt that their longer range made them more useful in knocking Japan out of the war. The B-17s, with a shorter range, were doing an effective job in Europe. Boeing was turning the B-29s out with maximum effort, producing them at plants in Wichita; Renton, Washington; Omaha, Nebraska; and Marietta, Georgia.

On August 31, 1944, Tibbets received another urgent phone call, this one from General Uzal Ent, commander of the 2nd Air Force. Ent told Tibbets to pack his bags immediately and take his B-29 to Colorado Springs, Colorado. "There was something cryptic in the way he spoke of my new job," Tibbets said. Ent told him only that the job would take him overseas. To Tibbets, that meant the Pacific, because of the B-29's value there with its long-range bombing capability.

What followed was a carte blanche assignment that was beyond the imagination of any member of the military. After a grilling by agents of the FBI to determine that he was not a security risk, Tibbets was briefed on the Manhattan Project. Then came the shocker: He was to be the man who would drop the atomic bomb on Japan. He was given blank-check authority to recruit and train the necessary personnel, organize them into a combat organization, determine what modifications to the new B-29 might be necessary, and see to it that their mission was carried out.

Tibbets was told by a superior officer, "You are on your own." He was told to use normal channels of communication "to the extent possible. If you are denied something you need, restate your need is for Silverplate and your request will be granted without question."

Armed with this virtually unlimited authority, Tibbets requisitioned fifteen new B-29s, specifying modifications that he wanted that would make the planes faster and enable the pilots, including Tibbets, to fly above the range of Japan's anti-aircraft guns. At the same time, he recruited a B-29 bombardment squadron from Wendover Field in Utah, close to the Nevada border, and reorganized it into the 509th Composite Group. On December 17, 1944, the day that the Battle of the Bulge began in Europe, formal orders were issued activating the 509th. It was the forty-first anniversary of the world's first flight in a powered aircraft, by the Wright brothers at Kitty Hawk, North Carolina. Three months later, in March 1945, Tibbets established the 1st Ordnance Squadron to carry out the technical phases of his top-secret operation.

"We would be organized," Tibbets said, "for the purpose of dropping a bomb that hadn't been built on a target that hadn't been chosen."

The 509th eventually consisted of eighteen hundred men. "The organization," Tibbets wrote in his book, "was to be completely self-contained with its squadron, troop transport aircraft, military police and a medical unit with specialists in the field of radiology." Recognizing the unheard-of nature of his operation, Tibbets said clearly, "There had been nothing like it in this or any other war. Some were to call it 'Tibbets's Individual Air Force' because I was given the authority to requisition anything needed to carry out my assignment. . . . My job, in brief, was to wage atomic war."

* * *

In the planning that led to the bombing of Hiroshima, Tibbets encountered questions that had no known answers. One of them was just how much damage this all-powerful bomb might do, not only to the target city, which had not yet been determined, but also to other parts of Japan and even to other parts of the world. "There were formulas which indicated that, if it were 100 percent efficient, the resulting explosion might crack the earth's crust," Tibbets wrote.

Planners assumed that such a high degree of efficiency probably could not be achieved, but there were other questions as well, especially concerning radiation and fallout from the atomic cloud. In addition, there was the safety of the plane's crew. Tibbets said those planning the mission, including General Ent and himself, agreed quickly in a meeting that conventional bombing procedures would not work. To avoid destroying themselves, the crew "would have to put as much distance as possible between itself and the point of the blast."

At that point in the discussion, Tibbets asked, "What do you consider a safe distance?"

A Naval Academy graduate in the group, Captain William "Deak" Parsons, offered an answer. He was an associate director of the Los Alamos bomb laboratory in charge of atomic bomb ballistics. "We're not sure," he said, "but our best calculations indicate that an airplane should be able to withstand the shock waves at a distance of eight miles."

Tibbets then raised another question: "How much will the bomb weigh?"

Parsons said the bomb, which had not yet been built, was expected to weigh nine to ten thousand pounds, about the same as the bomb load carried by B-29s on a typical mission.

A plane with such a load and enough fuel to make it back to its base could reach an altitude of thirty thousand feet over the target, slightly less than six miles above the ground. Tibbets knew that meant another job for him: "Find a way to increase the distance between blast and bomber to eight miles."

He solved the problem by factoring in a "slant-line" tactic in which the plane would fly slightly more than five miles in the opposite direction after releasing the bomb. With its six-mile altitude, the combination would give the B-29 a slant-line distance of eight miles from the point of the bomb's detonation. "My strategy, then," Tibbets wrote in 1998, "was to make a tight turn that, when completed, would have our plane flying almost directly away from the aiming point. Calculations convinced me that the most effective maneuver would be a sharp turn of 155 degrees. This would put considerable strain on the airplane and would require a degree of precision flying unfamiliar to bomber pilots. Nevertheless, it seemed our best bet for survival."

On May 9, 1945, the day after V-E Day—"Victory in Europe," when the Germans accepted the Allies' terms calling for "unconditional surrender"—Colonel Tibbets selected his B-29 at the Martin Omaha plant in Nebraska. It was delivered nine days later.

The selection of the target for the first atomic bomb continued to be a matter of discussion as 1945 unfolded. At a meeting in the newly completed Pentagon building just across the Potomac River from Washington in Northern Virginia, a "Committee of Operations Analysis," headed by General Groves and composed of Colonel Tibbets and others, compiled a list of target cities— Kyoto, Hiroshima, Yokohama and Niigata. Orders went out to the Army Air Forces not to firebomb these cities. Kyoto was later stricken from the list by Secretary of War Stimson because it had been the ancient capital of Japan and therefore held particular historical and religious significance for the people of Japan. Hiroshima, the seventh largest city in Japan and an industrial and military shipping center on Honshu, became the first target. Nagasaki, another important military target, was added to the list in place of Kyoto.

The list of targets might have been considerably longer if Germany had not surrendered as planning for dropping the bomb continued. Tibbets says today that while the war on Europe was still going on, "All our early planning assumed that we would make almost simultaneous bomb drops on Germany and Japan." That planning was quickly revised with the surrender of Germany, because completion of the bomb was still three months away. Tibbets adds, "It is my belief that Berlin would have shared the fate of Hiroshima if the war in Europe had still been in progress in August, 1945."

With the war in Europe over, the target committee agreed to drop the bomb during the first week in August.

★ 11 ★

What Truman Wrote
in His Diary

While Project Manhattan was racing toward the day when the United States would possess the world's first atomic bomb, named Little Boy, parallel planning was under way for a corresponding operation—the invasion of Japan. To be more accurate, the planning actually called for *two* invasions involving two million American military personnel. Operation Olympic would be launched on or about November 1, 1945, on the southern part of the Japanese island of Kyushu, with almost eight hundred thousand American soldiers and Marines storming ashore. A second invasion, Operation Coronet, would take place around March 1, 1946, on the main Japanese island of Honshu, near Tokyo.

The chiefs of the U.S. military services estimated that a total of five million troops, most of them American, would be involved in the two invasions. Casualty estimates varied then and still do today. Military planners assumed that the invasion of Kyushu would cause between thirty-one and fifty thousand U.S. losses in the first month, and that the total American casualties from the two invasions would exceed half a million. Losses to the Japanese people were assumed to amount to far greater figures.

Tibbets, then a twenty-nine-year-old lieutenant colonel, wasn't sure the invasions would ever happen. As one of only a handful of officers who knew about the atomic bomb project, he realized something that was almost unimaginable: His organization of only eighteen hundred men and eighteen bombers would be doing the work of two million soldiers. "We were confident," he wrote, "that we would end the war and save hundreds of thousands of lives, both American and Japanese."

On June 18, 1945, two months and six days after Vice President Harry Truman became president on the death of Franklin Roosevelt, he gave preliminary approval to the invasion plans as presented by General George Marshall, the Army chief of staff. On July 17, Truman wrote in his diary of the possibility that Russia might enter the war against Japan, then added, "Believe Japs will fold up before Russia comes in. I am sure they will when Manhattan appears over their homeland."

With the arrival of the plutonium and the firing mechanism, everything was ready for the mission that was to shake the world, both literally and figuratively. The only element remaining to be reckoned with now was the weather, a factor of even greater concern because the bomb would be dropped by sight rather than by radar. Tibbets departed from conventional strategy on this point and abandoned the usual practice of preparing weather forecasts developed from long range. Instead, he elected to send three weather planes ahead of his plane to report on conditions over Hiroshima and two alternate targets.

Seven planes would be involved in the mission. Two would accompany the Tibbets plane, one with scientific instruments to measure the intensity of the bomb's blast and another to take photos and produce a pictorial record of the event. Another plane would be on standby and would land at Iwo Jima in case Tibbets's plane developed mechanical problems.

General Thomas Handy, acting chief of staff of the Army, sent a memorandum to General Carl "Tooey" Spaatz on July 25 telling him that the 509th Composite Group commanded by Colonel Tibbets "will deliver its first special bomb as soon as weather will permit visual bombing after about 3 August 1945 on one of the targets: Hiroshima, Kokura, Niigata and Nagasaki. . . . Additional bombs will be delivered on the above targets as soon as made ready by the project staff. Further instructions will be issued concerning targets other than those listed above."

General Handy stressed the need for the tightest security. "Dissemination of any and all information concerning the use of the weapons against Japan," his memo said, "is reserved to the Secretary of War and the President of the United States. No communiqué on the subject or release of information will be issued by Commanders in the field without specific prior authority."

Handy concluded his memo by directing General Spaatz to deliver the information to the highest American military authorities in the Pacific. "The foregoing directive is issued to you by direction and with the approval of the Secretary of War and of the Chief of Staff, USA. It is desired that you personally deliver one copy of this directive to General MacArthur and one copy to Admiral Nimitz for their information."

Four days later, in the wake of the Potsdam conference, General Spaatz arrived on Saipan and took command of the Strategic Forces in the Pacific. He carried an order from Washington, issued by General Groves, that authorized the dropping of "the first special bomb" on one of the four target cities some time after August 3. At a meeting of Spaatz, General Curtis LeMay, the commander of the XXI Bomber Command in the Pacific, and Tibbets, the young lieutenant colonel, assured the two generals that all was in a state of readiness. The bomb had been assembled. Only one more thing needed to be done—inserting the two small slugs of uranium—and that would not occur until Tibbets and his crew were in the air. In the meantime, the slugs were being kept under guard twenty-four hours a day in the ordnance area on Tinian.

From the start of the planning, Tibbets had favored making Hiroshima the target of the atomic attack. He knew Hiroshima was an important industrial and military center. He and his fellow planners also believed that there were no prisoner-of-war camps in Hiroshima, unlike some of the other target cities. After the war, they learned that this information was wrong. Then it was revealed that twenty-three American airmen who had been shot down in the area around Hiroshima were imprisoned in a castle in Hiroshima.

Following up on the order from General Groves, Colonel Tibbets drafted a detailed directive for LeMay's signature ordering Special Bombing Mission Number 13 to be carried out and identifying Hiroshima as the target. In the event of poor visibility caused by clouds, the secondary target was to be Kokura. Nagasaki was listed as the third choice.

"My old bombardier from our days in Europe, Tom Ferebee, and I studied a large aerial photo of Hiroshima and its surrounding areas and selected a T-shaped bridge near the heart of the city as our 'aiming point,' " Tibbets remembered.

> Although there were many bridges in the city crossing the branches of the Ota River, this one stood out because of a ramp in the center that gave it the "T" shape that would be easier to spot than other landmarks. The people of Hiroshima called it the Aioi bridge. Now we were ready for what we decided to call *Operation Centerboard*. We made one other decision: We would drop the atomic bomb on Hiroshima on the morning of August 6.

Before that, on August 2, the Americans staged another air raid of immense proportions. On that date, 855 B-29s blasted six Japanese cities from the face of the earth in one massive aerial attack, using so-called "conventional" bombs. Volume II of *The American Heritage Pictorial History of World War II* stated, "It was thus entirely plain before the first nuclear bomb was dropped that the so-called conventional plane using the so-called conventional explosive was, all by itself, a weapon of staggering destructive capacity." Then, with an eye toward what happened four days later, *American Heritage* added, "The bomber, so long considered the ultimate in strategic might, had reached its moment of total and awful triumph."

※　※　※

After making the final decisions on Operation Centerboard with Tom Ferebee, Tibbets made a decision of his own. Fully aware that his airplane would be engraved forever in the history books, he knew he needed a name for it, the one he had picked out personally on the production line at the Glenn L. Martin factory in Omaha, Nebraska. "Considering the historical importance of the event," he wrote in his autobiography, "it seemed hardly fitting to announce that the world's first atomic bomb had been dropped from an unnamed B-29 bearing the number 82."

Remembering his mother's strong support for him, especially when he decided to enter an aviation career instead of pursuing the one in medicine that his parents had hoped for, he wanted to honor her by naming his plane for her. He said he considered her name "pleasing to the ear." Besides, he reasoned, it was rare. He had never heard of anyone with that name. He decided "it would be a fine name for my plane: *Enola Gay.*"

On the same day that he named his plane, Colonel Tibbets received confirmation of the plans to stage the air raid on August 6, the next day. Takeoff time was set for 2:45 A.M., 0245 in Army-Navy time. A coded message was flashed to Washington alerting General Groves and General Marshall.

At the final briefing before the mission, Captain Deak Parsons dropped a bomb of his own. He voiced his concern over the intention to take off with a live atomic bomb in the bomb bay. "If we crack up and the plane catches fire," he said, "there is danger of an atomic explosion that could wipe out half of this island."

Having raised a critical question, he also had an answer. He suggested that he be permitted to assemble the bomb in its completed state in the first stages of their flight. He proposed to do this by inserting one of the uranium slugs and the explosive charge into the bomb casing after takeoff. In that way, he reasoned, if the plane crashed, the only losses would be the B-29 and its crew, including Parsons himself—and Tibbets.

General Thomas F. Farrell, the ranking officer of the Manhattan Project on Tinian at the time, asked, "Are you sure you can do it?"

Parsons gave him a direct answer: "No, but I've got all day to learn."

As Tibbets watched the bomb being loaded onto the *Enola Gay*, he reflected on its significance, especially in comparison to the bombing missions that pilots on both sides of the war were flying up until that day. He thought it "seemed incredible that a single bomb should have the explosive force of 20,000 tons of TNT . . . 40 million pounds—surely the scientists were exaggerating. This would be equal to 200,000 of the 200-pound bombs which I carried over Europe and Africa three years before."

He also wondered why they were calling this monster killer with a blunt nose and four tail fins Little Boy. "It was not little by any standard," he has noted today. "It was a monster compared to any bomb I had ever dropped." Little Boy was twenty-eight inches in diameter and twelve feet long. It weighed more than nine thousand pounds. Whatever the fate of the historic mission might be, Little Boy was destined to be the only bomb of its kind ever produced. If a second atomic bomb were to be used later, it would be shaped more like a pumpkin—hence it was nicknamed Fat Man.

As the loading process continued, some of the other men on Tinian stopped by and wrote messages on sides of the bomb. One was addressed to Emperor Hirohito and was signed FROM THE BOYS OF THE INDIANAPOLIS.

After playing a few hands of blackjack because they couldn't sleep, Tibbets and some of his fellow officers assembled for their final briefing at eleven o'clock—2300 hours—on the night of August 5. William Laurence, the science reporter for the *New York Times,* who had arrived on Tinian only the day before, took notes on what Colonel Tibbets told his crew:

> Tonight is the night we have all been waiting for. Our long months of training are to be put to the test. We will soon know if we have been successful or failed. Upon our efforts tonight it is possible that history will be

made. We are going on a mission to drop a bomb different from any you have ever seen or heard about. The
bomb contains a destructive force of 20,000 tons of
TNT.

As the men sat in the briefing, they still had never been told
that they would be dropping an *atomic* bomb—the world's first—
on Japan. "The word 'atom' had never been spoken in our nearly
one year of training," Tibbets wrote. "Nor was it in this briefing."

Tibbets reviewed the operational plans for the mission. Then
he reminded all personnel to have their goggles ready for use as
soon as the bomb was released, to protect their eyes from a brilliant flash, one that would be brighter than the sun. As the briefing ended, the group was led in prayer by Chaplain William B.
Downey, the pastor of the Hope Lutheran Church in Minneapolis
before he entered the service.

After the briefing and the prayer, the airmen walked to the
mess hall—Dogpatch Inn—for a preflight breakfast prepared by
their mess sergeant, Elliott Easterly. Since this was no ordinary
mission, the meal was not ordinary either. Easterly had decorated
the walls with paper pumpkins and handed out mimeographed
menus decorated with his own drawings and comical comments.
The menu consisted of real eggs instead of the powdered kind
usually served to military personnel in a combat zone, plus sau-
sage, rolled oats and apple butter, with coffee or milk.

Even though the round trip would take thirteen hours, Tibbets
ate lightly. He drank several cups of black coffee, sitting around
the table and making conversation with his fellow history mak-
ers.

As the crew of the *Enola Gay* arrived at the mess hall, those of
the three weather planes—the *Straight Flush, Jabbitt III,* and
Full House—now were leaving, to report for takeoff an hour ahead
of Tibbets and his crew. Each of the three planes was to fly to one
of the target cities and radio back what the weather conditions
were.

After the men of the *Enola Gay* finished their meals, the flight
surgeon, Don Young, came to the Tibbets table and slipped him a

small cardboard pillbox, saying, "I hope you don't have to use these."

Tibbets answered, "Don't worry. The odds are in our favor."

Tibbets admits that the subject was a grim one despite their brave front. The pillbox contained twelve cyanide capsules, one for each member of the crew of the *Enola Gay*. Tibbets didn't have to be told what they were for. If the men were shot down and captured, they were to take the pills and kill themselves.

When Tibbets arrived at the flight line, he was surprised to see his *Enola Gay* sitting in floodlights like something in a Hollywood premier. Movie cameras had been set up, and still photographers were ready with their own equipment. The event was about to be recorded for posterity.

The three weather planes took off at 1:37 A.M. Slightly more than an hour later, at two forty-five, Tibbets roared down the runway at Tinian in the *Enola Gay,* carrying seven thousand gallons of gasoline and their nine-thousand-pound bomb. On board and flying their way into the history books were Tibbets and eleven other airmen:

The copilot, Captain Robert A. Lewis of Ridgefield Park, New Jersey.

The bombardier, Major Thomas W. Ferebee of Mocksville, North Carolina.

The navigator, Captain Theodore J. Van Kirk of Northumberland, Pennsylvania.

The radar countermeasures officer, Lieutenant Jacob Beser of Baltimore, Maryland.

The weaponeer and ordnance officer, Captain William S. Parsons of the Navy, from Santa Fe, New Mexico.

The assistant weaponeer, Second Lieutenant Morris Jeppson of Carson City, Nevada.

The radar operator, Sergeant Joe Stiborik of Taylor, Texas.

The tail gunner, Staff Sergeant George R. Caron of Lynbrook, New York.

The assistant flight engineer, Sergeant Robert H. Shumard of Detroit, Michigan.

The radio operator, Richard H. Nelson of Los Angeles, California.
The flight engineer, Technical Sergeant Wyatt E. Duzenberry of Lansing, Michigan.

Tibbets pointed out that every section of the United States was represented in the crew—the East and West Coasts, the Midwest, the North, and the South. All twelve of the men were wearing coveralls that bomber crews usually wore. With two exceptions, the men also wore the long-peaked flight caps that were a standard part of the in-flight dress of bomber crews. The two exceptions were Van Kirk, who wore an overseas cap, and Caron, who wore a Brooklyn Dodger cap in honor of his favorite baseball team.

As they sped down the runway under the power of their four twenty-two-hundred-horsepower engines, they passed four grim reminders of the dangers of flight—B-29s that had crashed the night before. There were no survivors.

At the end of the runway, Tibbets radioed the tower and the tower responded, in this brief exchange:

> Dimples Eight-Two to North Tinian tower. Ready for takeoff on Runway Able.
> Dimples Eight-Two. Dimples Eight-Two. Cleared for takeoff.

The B-29, with its new name, headed down almost two miles of runway, then lifted off as Special Bombing Mission 13. As they lifted off the ground and into the Pacific air, Dutch Van Kirk wrote his first entry into the plane's log. In the space marked for "Time Takeoff," he wrote "0245," precisely the time specified in the operations plan for the mission. The night was pleasant enough, almost ironically so, with puffy clouds and a crescent moon.

Eight minutes after takeoff, Parsons and Jeppson lowered themselves into the plane's bomb bay to insert the slug of uranium and the explosive charge into the core of Little Boy. As Jepson held a flashlight, Parsons inserted the charge. Parsons was working in cramped quarters and cutting his fingers occasionally on the bomb's tooled steel. Parsons finished the job in only twenty-five minutes. Little Boy was now a monster, ready to become the first atomic bomb dropped in the history of warfare. On a tablet, copilot Bob Lewis wrote, "The bomb is now alive. It is a funny feeling knowing it is right in back of you. Knock wood."

As Tibbets puffed on his favorite Kaywoodie brier pipe, the *Enola Gay* flew over Iwo Jima, the scene of another of the war's bloodiest battles only six months before. From February 19 to March 16, Marines fought the Japanese in a fierce battle that claimed four thousand American lives and wounded another sixteen thousand Marines. The ferocious engagement ended in an American victory that gave Tibbets and his fellow airmen land for an air base only 750 miles from Yokohama.

Now the *Enola Gay* was only three hours from its target—and Tibbets and his crew still did not know what that target was: Hiroshima, Kokura, or Nagasaki. They waited for word from the three weather planes ahead of them—*Straight Flush,* piloted by Major Claude Eatherly, which was headed for Hiroshima, near the southern tip of Honshu, Japan's main island; *Jabbitt III,* being flown by Major John Wilson, who was headed for the secondary target, Kokura; and *Full House,* the plane piloted by Major Ralph Taylor, who was going to check the weather over Nagasaki.

If the first-priority target, Hiroshima, was under a cloud cover, Tibbets and his men were to turn westward to Kokura or Nagasaki on the coast of Kyushu, the smaller island to the southwest. The question of clouds was crucial because the men on the *Enola Gay* were still under orders to drop their bomb on a visual run instead of relying on radar.

Still not knowing which city would be his target, Tibbets climbed his B-29 up to the bombing altitude of 30,700 feet. At 8:30 A.M., the word came in code from one of the weather planes, Eatherly's *Straight Flush,* high over Hiroshima. Eatherly's radio operator, Sergeant Pasquale Baldasaro, tapped out the message in code—a cryptic combination of letters and figures: "Y-3, Q-3, B-2, C-1."

Tibbets translated the message: The cloud cover was less than three-tenths at all altitudes. *C-1* meant to bomb the primary target—Hiroshima. For Tibbets and his crew, the word on Hiroshima was what they wanted. They had trained mostly to hit that target instead of the others, studying maps and aerial photos of the approach path and the city. "We knew every feature of the terrain over which we would be flying," Tibbets remembered. "And now the Japanese landscape was unfolding below us just as the pictures had promised."

As they came closer to their target, Tibbets got on the plane's intercom and reminded the members of his crew to put on their polarized goggles and keep them on their foreheads until the bomb was released. At that time, they were to slip their glasses over their eyes to protect them from the blinding glare of the blast caused by Little Boy. The reason: The bomb was expected to produce the intensity of ten suns.

They were only ten miles from their target when Major Ferebee, the bombardier, pointed dead ahead and said, "Okay, I've got the bridge." Captain Van Kirk, the navigator, glanced at an aerial photograph, looked over his shoulder at the ground below, and said, "No question about it."

Tibbets noticed that the T-shaped bridge "was easy to spot. Even though there were many other bridges in this sprawling city, there was no other bridge that even slightly resembled it."

Copilot Lewis entered a few more comments into his flight log: "As we are approaching our primary, Ferebee, Van Kirk and Stiborik are coming into their own, while the Colonel and I are standing by and giving the boys what they want."

Ninety seconds from bomb release, Tibbets put the plane on autopilot and turned its controls over to Lewis, saying, "It's all yours." Then he took his hands off the controls and slid back in his seat, trying to relax but not having much success. He fixed his gaze on the center of the city as it glowed in the day's early sunlight. While he looked, Tibbets knew that much of what was below him was about to be destroyed.

Another question on the mind of Tibbets—and the other eleven crew members—was how many of the people below would be killed. He learned later that Eatherly's weather plane had set off air-raid sirens in Hiroshima forty-five minutes before the arrival of the *Enola Gay* in the same skies. When the Japanese noticed that Eatherly's *Straight Flush* didn't do anything and then left, they ignored the sirens when they sounded again forty-five minutes later with the arrival of the *Enola Gay*. It remains another of the countless questions about Hiroshima: How many more lives would have been saved if more people in Hiroshima had heeded the warnings of the air-raid sirens and taken cover before Tibbets and his crew dropped their bomb?

The Japanese did not fire their anti-aircraft guns at the *Enola Gay*, probably because they knew that the new American planes, the B-29s, were beyond the range of their guns on the ground. No fighter planes intercepted either American plane that morning because the Japanese had begun to think that most American flights over their cities were only reconnaissance missions.

Tom Ferebee pressed his left eye against the viewfinder of his bombsight and said, "We're on target." Sixty seconds before the scheduled release of the bomb, Ferebee flicked a switch that set off a high-pitched radio tone, which sounded in the earphones of the men on the plane as well as the crews of the two other planes and the three weather planes, which were already more than two hundred miles away on their return flight to Tinian.

One minute later, the radio tone stopped. The pneumatic bomb-bay doors opened automatically and out tumbled Little Boy, seventeen seconds later than the scheduled release time. In a flash, more than half of Hiroshima vanished from the force of the atomic bomb. Estimates of the number of buildings destroyed run as high as 80 percent, in an area of more than four square miles—60 percent of the city's size. It was 8:15 A.M., Hiroshima time.

The *Enola Gay* immediately became nine thousand pounds lighter, causing problems for Tibbets because the plane's nose pointed sharply into the air, complicating the most important part of the mission—to put as much distance as possible between the plane and the bomb as it exploded on the ground. Tibbets turned his plane 155 degrees to the right and banked it 60 degrees. Bob Caron said later that he had a wild ride in his tail gunner's section and felt as if he were the last man in a game of crack-the-whip.

At the same moment that the *Enola Gay* released its bomb, pilot Chuck Sweeney's plane also opened its bomb-bay doors and dropped out three instrument packages to measure the effects of the bomb's blast in shock waves, radioactivity, and other categories. The instruments sent back the results by radio. As they glided toward the earth, they were suspended from parachutes, causing erroneous reports that the bomb had been dropped by parachute.

Tibbets remembered:

> From the pilot's seat of my airplane, I saw the city shimmering six miles below in the bright sunlight of an August morning. Suddenly there was a blinding flash beside which the sun grew dim. In a millionth of a second, the shimmering city became an ugly smudge.
>
> For eleven months I had worked day and night to plan the delivery of that bright and devastating flash. Now that I could say "Mission accomplished," I was stunned.

Tibbets felt a physical reaction to the bomb's explosion. "At the moment of the blast," he said in his book, "there was a tingling sensation in my mouth and the very definite taste of lead upon my tongue. This, I was told later by scientists, was the result of electrolysis—an interaction between the fillings in my teeth and the radioactive forces that were loosed by the bomb."

Tibbets continued to head his plane away from the blast and the shock wave, which was due to arrive almost a minute later. As he did, he got on the plane's intercom again and said, for the record, "Fellows, you have just dropped the first atomic bomb in history." He estimated that he and his crew were nine miles from the point of the explosion when the shock wave reached their plane. As they waited and flew, another question was about to be answered: Would the plane be able to withstand the blow?

Caron was the only man on the plane with a direct view of the awesome blast below. He saw the shock wave as it approached the plane at the speed of sound, almost eleven hundred feet a second. Before Caron could shout a warning to the others, the wave hit the plane with a violent force. Tibbets said, "Our B-29 trembled under the impact, and I gripped the controls tightly to keep us in level flight. From my experience of flying through enemy flak over targets in Europe and Africa, I found the effect to be much like that produced by an anti-aircraft shell exploding near the plane."

That's what Deak Parsons thought had happened. He yelled, "It's flak!" Then he realized the jolt was what they had been told to expect. Bob Lewis told reporters the next day that the impact from the shock wave felt as if a giant had hit the plane with a telephone pole. After that first blow, a second arrived, what scientists call an echo effect.

The now familiar mushroom cloud caused by the blast had already risen to forty-five thousand feet, three miles above the *Enola Gay,* when the rest of the crew spotted it. It was still "boiling upward," Tibbets remembered, "like something terribly alive. It was a frightening sight, and even though we were several miles away, it gave the appearance of something that was about to engulf us."

Tibbets said the sight on the ground was even scarier. Fires were "springing up everywhere amid a turbulent mass of smoke that had the appearance of bubbling hot tar." The city, so clearly visible on that summer morning only minutes before, was now obscured under a blanket of smoke and fire.

At that point, Lewis wrote the final entry into his log: *"My God!"*

For the record, Tibbets has disputed the Hollywood version, contained in the movie *Above and Beyond,* starring Robert Taylor and Eleanor Parker. In the movie, the comment is attributed to Tibbets, and improved upon, in Hollywood's opinion, to read, "My God, what have we done?" Tibbets said, "These words were put in my mouth by the authors of the movie script for *Above and Beyond."*

In *Return of the* Enola Gay, Tibbets wrote,

I'm sure those dramatic words were not spoken, but they probably reflect the thoughts of all 12 men aboard the *Enola Gay*. . . . Whatever exclamation may have passed our lips at this historic moment, I cannot accurately remember. We were all appalled and what we said was certain to have reflected our emotions and our disbelief. It is unfortunate that there is no way to reconstruct, with complete accuracy, the excitement that seized all of us aboard the *Enola Gay*.

In fact, there was a way. Tibbets, with an eye on the historical value of the moment, had told Jake Beser to record everything said aboard the plane during the bomb run on a wire recorder, plus everything said after the bomb drop. Beser did, and turned the spool of wire over to an information officer on their return to Tinian. Tibbets said, "It has never been heard of since."

Captain Parsons radioed a report back to Tinian in code: "82 V 670. Able, Line 1, Line 2, Line 6, Line 9." Meanwhile, Tibbets sent a radio transmission of his own back to their headquarters, using words and phrases that had been agreed on earlier. When translated, the message informed headquarters that his plane had bombed the primary target visually with good results and without interference by Japanese fighter planes or anti-aircraft fire.

As their plane headed back to Tinian, Tibbets told Bob Lewis in the copilot's seat, "I think this is the end of the war."

The radio transmission from Tibbets was decoded and relayed to General Groves in the Pentagon and then on to President Truman, who was having lunch with a group of enlisted men aboard the cruiser USS *Augusta* on his way home from the Potsdam conference. When he got the word, Truman exulted, "This is the greatest thing in history."

Meanwhile, the mushroom cloud was still visible over Hiroshima an hour and a half after the explosion, as Tibbets and his men flew home. They were almost four hundred miles from ground zero when Bob Caron, with the best view from his tail gunner's roost, finally reported that he could not see the cloud.

A Japanese journalist later described the devastation, chaos, and tragedy that quickly followed:

> Suddenly a glaring whitish-pink light appeared in the sky, accompanied by an unnatural tremor that was followed almost immediately by a wave of suffocating heat and a wind that swept away everything in its path.
>
> Within a few seconds, the thousands of people in the streets and the gardens in the center of the town were scorched by a wave of searing heat. Many were killed instantly, others lay writhing on the ground, screaming in agony from the intolerable pain of their burns. Everything standing upright in the way of the blast—walls, houses, factories and other buildings—was annihilated, and the debris spun around in a whirlwind and was carried up into the air. . . .
>
> Beyond the zone of utter death in which nothing remained alive, houses collapsed in a whirl of beams, bricks and girders. Up to about three miles from the center of the explosion, lightly built houses were flattened as though they had been built of cardboard. Those who were inside were either killed or wounded. Those who managed to extricate themselves by some miracle found themselves surrounded by a ring of fire. And the few who succeeded in making their way to safety generally died 20 or 30 days later from the delayed effects of the deadly gamma rays. . . .

The journalist said a violent wind arose, spreading the fires "with terrible rapidity because most Japanese houses are built only of timber and straw."

When the word flashed around the world, President Truman addressed the nation on radio, in the last year before television sets became available to the public. He spoke in somber tones into the radio microphones and the newsreel cameras:

> Sixteen hours ago, an American airplane dropped one bomb on Hiroshima, an important Japanese army base.

That bomb had more power than 20,000 tons of TNT. . . . It is an atomic bomb, harnessing the basic power of the universe. . . . What has been done is the greatest achievement of organized science in history. . . . If they do not accept our terms, they can expect a rain of ruin from the air the like of which has never been seen on this earth.

The headline at the top of the *Washington Post* stretched all the way across page one and ran three lines deep:

SINGLE ATOMIC BOMB ROCKS JAPANESE ARMY BASE WITH MIGHTIER FORCE THAN 20,000 TONS OF TNT TO OPEN NEW ERA OF POWER FOR BENEFIT OF MAN

In contrast, the Japanese government announced on the radio that evening that "a few B-29s hit Hiroshima city at 8:20 A.M. August 6 and fled after dropping incendiaries and bombs. The extent of the damage is now under survey." By the next morning, the Japanese people were still being told that the damage to Hiroshima was caused by incendiary bombs. By midafternoon, the people were being told something closer to the truth. "It seems," their radios proclaimed, "that the enemy used a new-type bomb."

However, the word was getting to the Japanese people one way or the other. The U.S. Office of War Information printed several million leaflets, plus a newspaper, in Japanese, showing one of Sergeant Caron's pictures of the atomic cloud as it rose over Hiroshima. The leaflets were dropped on cities all over Japan, carrying this message:

To the Japanese people:

America asks that you take immediate heed of what we say on this leaflet.

We are in possession of the most destructive explosive ever devised by man. A single one of our newly-developed atomic bombs is actually the equivalent in explosive power to what 2,000 of our giant B-29s can carry on a single mission. This awful fact is one for you to ponder and we solemnly assure you that it is grimly accurate.

We have just begun to use this weapon against your homeland. If you still have any doubt, make inquiry as to what happened to Hiroshima when just one atomic bomb fell on that city.

Before using this bomb to destroy every resource of the military by which they are prolonging this useless war, we ask that you now petition the Emperor to end the war. Our President has outlined for you the thirteen consequences of an honorable surrender. We urge that you accept these consequences and begin the work of building a new, better and peace-loving Japan.

You should take these steps now to cease military resistance. Otherwise, we shall resolutely employ this bomb and all our other superior weapons to promptly and forcefully end the war.

Evacuate your cities now!

The Soviet Union, with an eye toward grabbing more land for itself after the war, jumped into what was left of World War II two days later, on August 8. The next day, a second atomic bomb was dropped on Nagasaki, the seaport on the west coast of Kyushu, by Frederick Bock's B-29, *Bocks Car*. One of Japan's industrial giants, Mitsubishi, operated a steel and arms plant at Nagasaki, plus a shipyard, an electrical equipment production plant, steel factories, and an arms plant. The bomb struck the Mitsubishi Steel and Arms Works at 11:20 A.M. and killed forty thousand people. In Tokyo, the military and political leaders of Japan were left with one staggering question: Just how many more of these bombs do the Americans have?

President Truman took to the airwaves again on the day of the bombing of Nagasaki. He said sternly that the United States used the atomic bomb

against those who attacked us without warning at Pearl Harbor, against those who have starved and beaten and executed American prisoners of war, against those who have abandoned all pretense of obeying international laws of warfare. We have used it to shorten the agony of war, in order to save the lives of thousands and thousands of young Americans. We shall continue to use it until we completely destroy Japan's power to make war. Only a Japanese surrender will stop us.

On the same day, the Japanese cabinet met at two-thirty in the afternoon and continued to debate the question of surrender until two o'clock the next morning. Japan's war minister, General Korechika Anami, one of the members of a stubborn faction that continued to oppose surrender, told the rest of the cabinet, "We cannot pretend to claim that victory is certain, but it is far too early to say the war is lost. That we will inflict severe losses on the enemy when he invades Japan is certain, and it is by no means impossible that we may be able to reverse the situation in our favor, pulling victory out of defeat."

Emperor Hirohito, however, overruled Anami. In words that ended history's worst war, Hirohito said that "the time has come to bear the unbearable." Then he said, "I give my sanction to the proposal to accept the Allied Proclamation on the basis outlined by the Foreign Minister."

At noon on August 14—V-J Day—Emperor Hirohito told his cabinet, "A peaceful end to the war is preferable to seeing Japan annihilated." At eleven-thirty that night, he recorded a message to be broadcast to the Japanese people the next day. Five and a half hours later, at 5 A.M. on August 15, General Anami committed suicide. Hirohito's message was broadcast to his subjects at noon on August 15, the first time he had ever talked to them. He told them,

> Despite the best that has been done by everyone—the gallant fighting of the military and naval forces, the diligence and assiduity of our sergeants of the state, and the devoted service of our one hundred million people, the war situation has developed not necessarily to Japan's advantage, while the general trends of the world have all turned against her interest.

Hirohito continued:

> Moreover, the enemy has begun to employ a new and most cruel bomb, the power of which to do damage is, indeed, incalculable, taking the toll of many innocent lives. Should we continue to fight, not only would it result in an ultimate collapse and obliteration of the Japanese nation, but also it would lead to the total extinction of human civilization.
>
> Such being the case, how are we to save the millions of our subjects, or to atone ourselves before the hallowed spirits of our imperial ancestors? This is the reason why we have ordered the acceptance of the provisions of the Joint Declaration of the Powers.

On September 2, 1945, leaders of the United States and Japan, with General Douglas MacArthur presiding, signed the surrender treaty on the decks of the battleship *Missouri*. Twenty-seven days after the first atomic bomb was dropped, World War II was over.

★ 12 ★

The Aftermath, Then and Now

Shortly after he dropped the atomic bomb on Hiroshima, Paul Tibbets was called to the White House by President Truman. With his commanding knowledge of history and other military controversies, Truman anticipated the furor that would follow in the months ahead, not to mention the controversy that has lingered over years, decades, and into another century. Truman told Tibbets, "Don't you ever lose any sleep over the fact that you planned and carried out that mission. It was my decision. You had no choice."

In his book, Tibbets wrote fifty-three years later, "His advice was appreciated but unnecessary. This was exactly my view from the start. But it was good to know that we had a president with the guts to take the heat. I have often thought of the well-known sign on his desk: *The Buck Stops Here.*"

Tibbets also wrote candidly:

> Let it be understood that I feel a sense of shame for the whole human race, which through all history has accepted the shedding of human blood as a means of settling disputes between nations. And I feel a special sense of indignation at those who condemn the use of a nuclear explosive while having no lament for the fire-bombing attacks in the same war on the city of Tokyo, where thousands of civilians were literally burned to death in a single night, and on Dresden, a great German city that was all but leveled in a dreadful mass attack.

President Truman described his feelings about being the one who had to make the decision on whether to use the atomic bomb. In his personal papers, edited by his daughter Margaret and published in 1989 under the title *Where the Buck Stops: The Personal and Private Writings of Harry S. Truman*, the president wrote, "Some people have the mistaken impression that I made it on my own and in haste and almost on impulse, but it was nothing like that at all." He said he would never forget when he learned about the overpowering bomb "if I live to be a hundred." He was told about the bomb only a few hours after President Roosevelt died on April 12, 1945, "no more than half an hour after I was sworn in as president at 7:09 P.M."

Secretary of War Henry Stimson took the new president aside and informed him secretly of the project to build a "super bomb" and told him it was "almost ready." On April 26, Stimson and General Groves came to the White House for a meeting that was "so secret that Groves came into the White House by the back door." Stimson gave Truman a memo saying, "Within four months we shall in all probability have completed the most terrible weapon ever known in human history, one bomb which could destroy a whole city."

Stimson said he wasn't sure whether the United States "could or should" use the bomb because he was afraid it "could end up destroying the whole world." Truman said, "I felt the same fear as he and Groves continued to talk about it, and when I read Groves's 24-page report." By June 18, when Truman met with the Joint Chiefs of Staff, "we still hadn't decided whether or not to use the atomic bomb. . . ." Instead, they discussed plans to invade Japan. Truman said, ". . . the statistics that the generals gave me were as frightening as the news of the big bomb. The Chiefs of Staff estimated that the Japanese still have 5,000 attack planes, 17 garrisons on the island of Kyushu alone, and a total of more than two million men on all of the islands of Japan."

General Marshall told Truman that the Japanese would "unquestionably fight even more fiercely than ever on their own homeland," leading to the probability that the United States would "lose a quarter of a million men and possibly as many as a half-million in taking the two islands." Truman declared in his papers, "I could not bear this thought, and it led to the decision to use the atomic bomb."

On July 29, the Americans voiced the latest in a series of appeals to the Japanese to surrender, and it was, in Truman's words, "rejected immediately." He wrote in his papers, "Then I gave the final order, saying I had no qualms 'if millions of lives could be saved.' I meant both American and Japanese lives." Truman said that "a number of major Japanese military men and diplomats later confirmed publicly that there would have been no quick surrender without it. For this reason, I made what I believed to be the only possible decision."

Truman later said in a letter to his sister, Mary, "It was a terrible decision. But I made it. And I made it to save 250,000 boys from the United States, and I'd make it again under similar circumstances."

In a speech ten years later, Truman elaborated:

> It was a question of saving hundreds of thousands of American lives. . . . You don't feel normal when you have to plan hundreds of thousands of . . . deaths of American boys who are alive and joking and having fun while you're doing your planning. You break your heart and your head trying to figure out a way to save one life. . . . The casualty estimates called for 750,000 American casualties—250,000 killed, 500,000 maimed for life. . . . I couldn't worry about what history would say about my personal morality. I made the only decision I ever knew how to make. I did what I thought was right.

In his personal papers years later, Truman added for emphasis, "I still think that."

Tibbets said he and his crew members answered questions "for at least 20 years" from reporters who wanted to know the state of their health. "It has been implied," he wrote, "that some of us have died mysteriously and that others have fallen victim to disease or insanity." On the contrary, Tibbets is a healthy eighty-seven years old at this writing, living in Columbus, Ohio, after retiring from the Air Force as a brigadier general and then pursuing a successful business career as president of Executive Jet Aviation, Inc., a position from which he retired in 1986.

The Hiroshima controversy erupted with the arrival of the postwar period and simmered over the years of the Cold War and into today's age, with the global concern over terrorism and the possible use of nuclear weapons by "rogue states." It reached a peak in 1994, with the announcement of plans by the Smithsonian Institution in Washington to build a display, *The Last Act: The Atomic Bomb and the End of World War II*, in connection with the fiftieth anniversary of the *Enola Gay*'s historic mission. The controversy was caused by heated objections from various quarters over the wording proposed for the display and because of what some considered a lopsided collection of photographs.

One of those leading the fight against the display as proposed was John T. Correll of *Air Force Magazine*. Correll, along with millions of others, took heated offense to one particular paragraph that said, "For most Americans, this war was fundamentally different than the one waged against Germany and Italy—it was a war of vengeance. For most Japanese, it was a war to defend their unique culture against Western imperialism."

Correll counted forty-nine photos of Japanese casualties in the first draft of a Smithsonian report proposing the exhibit in connection with the anniversary of General Tibbets's flight compared to only three of American casualties. Correll also counted four pages of information on Japanese atrocities, compared to seventy-nine pages describing Japanese military casualties and civilians injured in conventional bombing raids as well as from the two atomic bombs.

In a letter to the editor, Correll said in the *Washington Post* that the 295-page script "gives less than one page to Japanese military actions before 1945." In contrast, he said, "The emphasis on Japanese death and suffering is so pronounced—84 text pages and 97 photos—that visitors to the exhibit might well perceive Japan as the victim, rather than as the aggressor, in the Pacific war."

Correll concluded,

> The *Enola Gay*'s task was a grim one, hardly suitable for glamorization. On the 50th anniversary of its occurrence, however, it should be remembered in historical context and balance, and the story should be told with fairness and accuracy. The exhibit planned by the National Air and Space Museum does not meet that standard. It is a partisan interpretation of what happened and historical revisionism at its worst.

General Tibbets was among those upset over the plans for the exhibit, calling them "a package of insults." In his autobiography, Tibbets offered other arguments in behalf of his mission over Hiroshima in 1945 and against the designers of the planned 1995 exhibit. He wrote that the American people in 1945 "were almost unanimously thankful that such a miracle weapon had been developed." He added later, "President Roosevelt and Prime Minister Churchill were in complete agreement on the bomb, and both of these men are regarded as enlightened humanitarians."

Tibbets offered additional evidence on the subject of saving lives through use of the bomb. "The people of Hiroshima and Nagasaki would not have been spared," he noted, "because, had these cities not been reserved for A-bombings, they certainly would have been destroyed by conventional explosives or incendiaries." He reminded his readers that the Potsdam declaration, which called for unconditional surrender by the Japanese and warned them of the consequences they would suffer if they insisted on continuing the war, "was firmly rejected by the Japanese."

The Committee for the Restoration and Display of the *Enola Gay* gathered more than ten thousand signatures of protest, and the Air Force Association (AFA) said the exhibit as proposed was "a slap in the face to all Americans who fought in World War II." The AFA said the display as proposed "treats Japan and the U.S. as if their participation in the war were morally equivalent."

Columnist Hugh Sidey wrote in *Time* magazine that the veterans "are well aware of the grim nature of the subject. They are not asking for a whitewash." Correll added, "Nobody is looking for glorification. Just be fair. Tell both sides."

Tony Snow wrote in *USA Today* that the display "raises a racism charge." To support his claim, Snow quoted another portion of the text: "Some have argued that the atomic bomb would never have been dropped on the Germans, because it was much easier for Americans to bomb Asians than 'white people.'"

Syndicated columnist Charles Krauthammer wrote that the exhibit

> promises to be an embarrassing amalgam of revisionist hand-wringing and guilt. What to do? General Paul Tibbets, the man who commanded the *Enola Gay,* has the right idea: Hang the plane in the museum without commentary or slanted context. Display it like Lindbergh's plane, with silent reverence and a few lines explaining what it did and when.
>
> Or forget the whole enterprise and let the Japanese commemorate the catastrophe they brought on themselves.

The American Legion demanded that the exhibit be canceled. In January 1995, with the Hiroshima anniversary less than seven months away, the Legion's national commander, William M. Detweiler, wrote to President Clinton, saying that officials of the Smithsonian's Air and Space Museum included "highly debatable information which calls into question the morality and motives of President Truman's decision to end World War II quickly and decisively by using the atomic bomb." He urged the president to cancel the exhibit.

The *Washington Post* published an editorial on January 20 saying, "The fuselage of the *Enola Gay* is an emotion-soaked artifact and a piece of historical heritage that the American people deserve to get a look at. They also deserve a historical presentation worthy of the subject and of the standards the Smithsonian unaccountably let slip in this chaotic case."

More than eighty members of the House of Representatives, Democrats and Republicans, demanded the dismissal of the Air and Space Museum's director, Martin Harwit, for his "continuing defiance and disregard for needed improvements in the exhibit." The letter was signed by Congressman Dick Armey of Texas, the House majority leader, and Congressman Tom DeLay, also of Texas, the House Republican whip.

The display was revised extensively during the winter in attempts to overcome these objections, but the furor continued. Columnist George Will said those in charge of the exhibit "obviously hate this country." TV commentator Cokie Roberts said, "to rewrite history makes no sense." David Brinkley, the veteran TV journalist, said, "What I don't understand is why a very strong element in the academic community seems to hate its own country and never passes up a chance to be critical of it." Speaker of the House Newt Gingrich said the "revisionism" could be permitted if it were limited to the "faculty lounge." But he said the American people should not be subjected to "historically inaccurate, anti-American and distorted history."

The *Washington Post* spoke out again, blaming the entire controversy on what it called the "narrow-minded representatives of a special interest and revisionist point of view" who were attempting "to use their inside track to appropriate and hollow out a historical event that large numbers of Americans alive at that time and engaged in the war had witnessed and understood in a very different—and authentic—way."

When the critics were still not satisfied, the exhibit was canceled and the director of the Air and Space Museum, Martin Harwit, resigned. Eventually, another exhibit was produced. It opened in 1995, fifty summers after General Tibbets led the raid over Hiroshima in the *Enola Gay*. The exhibit that finally survived and opened its door to the public was a scaled-down version of the original. It included part of the plane and the casing for the Little Boy bomb dropped by Tibbets and his crew. The exhibit was open to the public for three years, until 1998.

✻　✻　✻

Tibbets has pointed out that the atomic bomb almost certainly would have also been unleashed on Germany if the war in Europe had not ended three months before Hiroshima. He wrote that Japan might have been the target of a third atomic bomb. "If indeed a third had been necessary," he said, "there was serious discussion of making Tokyo the next target. Although much of that city had been burned out by incendiaries, it was still the seat of government and the center of the empire's military planning."

At a press conference back on Guam, with Tibbets sitting between General LeMay and General Spaatz, reporters asked the young pilot a range of questions:

> *How did you feel about dropping the first atomic bomb in history?*
> There was a sense of shock to all of us on the plane.
>
> *Was the sight more awesome than you expected?*
> Yes.
>
> *Do you think this will end the war?*
> Yes, unless the Japanese have taken leave of their senses.
>
> *How was Hiroshima chosen as the target?*
> Because it was an important center of military operations which we had spared from conventional bombing.

On the same day, a story from Washington reported on savings in dollars and cents produced by the bomb. It said the atomic bomb project had cost two billion dollars but would pay for itself if it shortened the war by only nine days, based on the war's cost to the United States of seven billion dollars a month.

Despite all the furor that was kicked up half a century later, the strongest and maybe the most persuasive argument in defense of President Truman's decision to drop the atomic bomb came not from General Tibbets or General Curt LeMay, or President Truman, or any other ranking official in the U.S. government in 1945. The most convincing statement on the controversy came not from an American but from an Englishman—Winston Churchill, the wartime leader of Great Britain who rallied the British people and steadfastly blocked Hitler's Nazi juggernaut from overrunning Europe from its invasion of Poland in 1939 until the United States declared war on Germany the day after the attack on Pearl Harbor.

In an address before the House of Commons on August 16, 1945, two days after the Japanese surrendered, Churchill declared:

> There are voices which assert that the bomb should never have been used at all. I cannot associate myself with such ideas. Six years of total war have convinced most people that, had the Germans or the Japanese discovered this new weapon, they would have used it upon us to our complete destruction with utmost alacrity. I am surprised that very worthy people, but people who in most cases had no intention of proceeding to the Japanese front themselves, should adopt the position that, rather than throw this bomb, we should have sacrificed a million American and a quarter million British lives in the desperate battles and massacres of an invasion of Japan. Future generations will judge these dire decisions, and I believe if they find themselves dwelling in a happier world from which war has been banished, and where freedom reigns, they will not condemn those who struggled for their benefit amid the horrors and the miseries of this gruesome and ferocious epoch.

PART 8

The Berlin Airlift

★ 13 ★

When Millions Looked Skyward

The Berlin Airlift is not the story of one dramatic, dangerous flight. It is the story of 277,569 of them.

Less than three years after the end of World War II, the world teetered again on the brink of war. This time the setting was not some aggressor nation but the conquered and divided city of Berlin, carved into four parts by the Allies at the end of that war, to be occupied by the United States, Great Britain, France, and the Soviet Union. At a meeting on March 19, 1948, Soviet premier Joseph Stalin and Wilhelm Pieck, the leader of the German Communist Party, discussed the possibility of trying to force the Allies out of West Berlin. Pieck warned that the coming elections, scheduled for Berlin in October, could be a disaster—unless the Allies could be pressured to leave the city beforehand.

Stalin responded, "Let's make a joint effort. Perhaps we can kick them out."

On the morning of June 26, 1948, the world woke up to shocking news. The banner line across the top of page one in the *New York Times* told the story:

BERLIN SIEGE ON AS SOVIET BLOCKS FOOD

The article below the headline reported the stunning overnight development:

About 2,250,000 Germans in the Western sectors of Berlin came face to face with the grim specter of starvation today as the siege of those sectors began in earnest.

In the hottest crisis yet of the young Cold War, one fraught with the dreaded possibility of World War III, the Soviet Union—"the Russians"—had sealed off the residents of West Berlin. The people of the sector had been surrounded by the hostile territory not only of East Berlin but of East Germany itself, since the postwar map drawn up by the Allies in 1945 awarded the land around Berlin to the Russians. The two-million-plus Germans in West Berlin were always more than a hundred miles from the friendly territory of West Germany, and now Stalin and his henchmen in the Kremlin had flashed the signal to let all of them starve to death if necessary.

The Soviet officials were already furious with the Allies over the establishment of a separate West Germany. The "Berlin Crisis" itself was triggered when the Allies then introduced a new currency into the western zone to prevent the "Reds" from flooding it with more money, which they had done before. The Russians, who were lusting for the rest of the territory in Berlin for themselves, were also upset with the results of the first free election of a mayor in Berlin since 1933, the year of Adolf Hitler's rise to power. They vetoed the voting results, saying the mayor-elect, Ernst Reuter, was "anti-Soviet."

They made repeated threats to drive the Allies out of Berlin. That kind of tough talk prompted the American commandant, Colonel Frank Howley, to issue a stern warning: "Any joker who thinks the United States, Britain and France are going to be dealt out of Berlin has another guess coming."

For Howley and every other American official, the timing could hardly have been much worse. Responding to the demands of the American people as soon as World War II ended, the U.S. military system had been reduced both in size and budget. As of February 1948, only twenty-nine months after the Japanese surrendered as the final act to end the war, the nation's military strength was down to 552,000 Army personnel, 476,000 in the Navy—including 79,000 Marines—and 346,000 in the Air Force, compared to a total of 15.1 million who served during the war.

The Russians, however, began backing up their threats. They started applying pressure to West Berlin's lifelines with a ten-day blockade in April. On June 20 they blocked all rail lines into the city. Three days later, they cut off electrical power to three-quarters of the western zone. Then on June 24, while Americans listened to the delegates in the Republican convention in Philadelphia nominate Thomas Dewey for president, or watched it on the new luxury called "television," the Russians made their blockade alarmingly complete. They hoped to force all Allied troops out of the other three sectors of the city and impose Communist rule on the Berliners. Suddenly, the city became the world's flash point.

On the same day, President Truman signed a bill reinstating the military draft and calling for the drafting of up to a quarter of a million young men between the ages of nineteen and twenty-five. The rapidly worsening situation in Germany, especially in Berlin, was cited as one of the critical reasons for the action.

The U.S. military governor of West Germany, General Lucius D. Clay, warned that the Russians would not be able to force the Allies out of Berlin "by any action short of war." Great Britain's wartime leader, Winston Churchill, said the issues caused by the Berlin crisis were "as grave as those we now know were at stake in Munich ten years ago."

Churchill, the co-leader with Franklin Roosevelt of the Allied victory in Europe, added, "There can be no doubt—the Communist government of Russia has made up its mind to drive us and France and all the other Allies out and turn the Russian zone in Germany into one of its satellite estates under the rule of totalitarian terrorism." He urged firm resistance as "not only the best but the only" way of preventing another world war, warning against "yielding to dictators—whether Nazi or Communist."

Overnight, Soviet troops slammed shut all highway and water access to West Berlin in their boldest and scariest move since the end of World War II only three years before. The *Times* article from Berlin, by Drew Middleton, said the Soviet military administration took the action as part of the Soviet's "calculated policy of starving the people of the Western sectors into the acceptance of the Communist demand for the withdrawal of the Western powers."

Now the residents of West Berlin were marooned, deprived not only of their daily shipments of food but also medicine, fuel, clothing, and all other items necessary to sustain human life. There was another complication: The agreement reached by Roosevelt, Churchill, and Stalin at Yalta in February 1945, three months before the end of the war, provided no ground routes for the Allies in and out of West Berlin over the Russian-occupied land of East Germany.

An Associated Press dispatch dated June 25 said, "The blockade left the air the only way to get food in to the 2,000,000 inhabitants of the American, British and French sectors. Allied experts said that would prove unworkable in the long run." For the short run, however, the Allies could buy time. Certain supplies had been stockpiled by officials in April because of the growing tensions. As of June 30, reserve amounts stored in the Allied sector included a twenty-five-day supply of flour, sugar that could last eighty-one days, nineteen days of meat, fifty-six days of fat, an eighteen-day supply of potatoes, fifty-four days of cereal, nineteen days of milk, and enough coffee for eighteen days.

The next day, fifty American C-47 cargo planes, the twin-engine military version of the DC-3 then used by most airlines, flew in powdered and canned milk for the babies of West Berlin, "who can get no fresh milk now that the Russians have stopped the flow from dairies in their zone," the AP reported. The wire service described the flights as "makeshift measures," while the British commander called on the Russians to "lift their food blockade at once or take the blame for starving 2,000,000 Germans."

The AP story added,

> Officials said the American Air Force beginning Monday would double its flights to Berlin to 100 a day to bring in food and as many other "essential items" as

possible. These will carry about 200 tons a day. But American experts declared it would be impossible to bring in all the 2,000 to 2,500 tons of food daily needed by Western Berlin's population

Still, those men, women, and children living in the Allied zones of West Berlin began looking to the sky at the American and British planes as their pilots flew their precious cargo into the city. For those millions, the skies were now their only avenue of hope.

President Truman faced another of the crucial decisions that marked his presidency. "The situation was extremely dangerous," David McCullough wrote in his book *Truman*. "Clearly Stalin was attempting to force the Western Allies to withdraw from the city. Except by air, the Allied sectors were entirely cut off. Nothing could come in or out. Two and a half million people faced starvation. As it was, stocks of food would last no more than a month. Coal supplies would be gone in six weeks."

The Army chief of staff, General Omar Bradley, who had helped to mastermind the Allied victory in Europe, wrote later, "We were nose to nose with massive Soviet military power."

His advisers offered options to Truman. One was for the Allies to force their way into Berlin behind an armored convoy. Another was for the United States to retaliate by slapping on its own blockade, closing all U.S. ports and the Panama Canal to Russian ships.

Truman rejected all such ideas. At a meeting in the Oval Office, Secretary of Defense James Forrestal, Undersecretary of State Robert Lovett, and Army Secretary Kenneth Royall began debating whether American forces should stay in Berlin. Truman cut off the discussion with his typical firmness and bluntness: "We stay in Berlin. Period."

McCullough writes, "On Monday, June 28, Truman ordered a full-scale airlift." In deciding on such a plan Truman consulted "none of the White House staff or any of his political advisers" despite "all the political heat and turmoil of the moment," McCullough wrote.

With the presidential election barely four months away, McCullough said, "There was no talk of how the President's handling of the crisis would make him look, or what political advantage was to be gained. And neither did Truman try to bolster the spirits of those around him by claiming the airlift would work. He simply emphasized his intention to stay in Berlin and left no doubt that he meant exactly what he said." Thus, the Berlin Airlift was born.

Despite his public firmness, Truman showed strain in private. In a letter back home to Missouri to wife Bess and daughter Margaret in the first months of the airlift that summer, he wrote, "It is hot and humid and lonely. Why in hell does anybody want to be a head of state? Damned if I know."

The airlift was the suggestion of Lieutenant General Albert Wedemeyer, who mentioned it over dinner with General Clay while the crisis was building. Wedemeyer knew what he was talking about. He was the commander of U.S. ground forces in China during World War II, where American pilots "flew the Hump"— the Himalayan Mountains between China and Burma—to keep his troops supplied during their fight against the Japanese Army.

The Air Force began flying supplies into West Berlin in a massive, in-your-face act of defiance, an around-the-clock operation that lasted more than a year, always balanced delicately against the menacing presence of the Russians and their bellowing threats from East Berlin and Moscow.

Overnight, some of the same American and British pilots who had rained thousands of tons of bombs on Berlin and its people only three years before were delivering food and other supplies to the same people. And that was not the airlift's only irony.

At the peak of the operation, planes were landing every forty-five seconds, many of them from Wiesbaden Air Base, an American field used by the German Luftwaffe, where forty of Hitler's bombers had once taken off every three hours. For that reason, American fliers had made Wiesbaden a prime target in the closing months of the war. When they had captured the field, they had counted seventy-six bomb craters on the runway—the same strip they were now using to head toward Berlin with their life-saving supplies.

On the first day of the airlift, thirty-two C-47s carried eighty tons of supplies from Wiesbaden to West Berlin. By late July, the operation included fifty-four C-54 "Skymasters" and 135 C-47s. The British were doing their part with ninety transport planes from their Royal Air Force. Eventually a fleet of between two and three hundred four-engine C-54s, whose twenty-thousand-pound capacity was triple the C-47's, formed the backbone of the joint U.S.-British operation. The British made a major additional con-tribution—their RAF planes evacuated fifteen thousand children to foster homes in West Germany.

The planes of the airlift became angels of aluminum, deliver-ing coal from the Ruhr Valley, milk and other dairy products from Denmark, wheat from the United States for bread, coffee from Brazil, and sugar from Cuba. The airlift was sustaining the peo-ple, and a *sea*lift was sustaining the airlift. Twelve million gallons of fuel were delivered by sea each month to "keep 'em flying"— the Air Force slogan of the 1940s.

Halfway around the world, a twenty-five-year-old Air Force pilot from Iowa, Captain Ken Herman, was test-flying new YC-97 Boeing Stratocruisers in California when he suddenly received orders to proceed to Rhein-Main Air Base in Frankfurt in the ear-liest days of the airlift.

"My orders were to go there for two weeks to pinch-hit for a pilot whose wife was threatening to divorce him," Herman has said today. "There were a lot of divorces being threatened as a re-sult of pilots being ordered over there, and some of those mar-riages collapsed under the pressures caused by the airlift. It was a military crisis that produced marital crises. Many wives felt they had sacrificed enough during World War II, and that they shouldn't have to go through this only three years later. They had a point."

The orders to Captain Herman in California were part of an alert flashed to Air Force bases around the world from Wash-ington:

PREPARE TO RELEASE ALL AVAILABLE C-54 SKY-MASTERS TO THE UNITED STATES AIR FORCE'S COMMAND IN EUROPE

For Captain Herman, with World War II experience flying C-54s in Alaska, the airlift began even before he found out where he was going to live. He flew two round-trip missions on the day of his arrival before being told where his living quarters were.

The military has a way of changing your orders under a catchall expression—*due to the exigencies of the service.* That's exactly what happened to Captain Herman. "Right after I got over there," he said, "my orders were extended to ninety days. Then they were extended to 180 days. Eventually, everyone who was ordered over there was required to serve 180 days."

For Herman, his new home was the 11th Troop Carrier Squadron. His living quarters were at Fassberg, where you could play poker by getting into any one of several twenty-four-hours-a-day, seven-days-a week games. Looking back, he rates his quarters as "much worse than what our pilots and crews told us they had in England during World War II." The European winter brought another adjustment—life without hot water for showers. That winter complicated the already stringent flying conditions with what some called Europe's harshest weather of the twentieth century.

In the first months of the airlift, the men in Herman's barracks were forced to endure something else—cuckoo clocks. These were and are a popular German export, and one pilot, a young captain named Willard Bergeron, was so fascinated by the timepieces that he began a collection. "The only problem," Herman remembered, "was that he kept them running. He had more than thirty of those things, and they weren't in precise synchronization with each other. When they started chiming the hour, it would drive you nuts. Twelve o'clock was a real experience."

Worse than that, the clocks were depriving the airlift pilots and copilots of their sleep. One pilot who'd had enough threatened to blow them to bits with his shotgun if Bergeron didn't unhook them. When he refused, the man with the shotgun waited until Bergeron was flying, then went into his room and blew the biggest clock he could find to smithereens.

Bergeron came back, surveyed the disaster area, and didn't say a word. "He took them all down right away," Herman said, "and put them into boxes. We never heard another cuckoo again—and we could get some sleep."

Herman, now a retired colonel living in Arizona, was tapped along with his entire squadron of planes, pilots, mechanics, and maintenance and administrative personnel. Their mission: to fly C-54s into the American air base at Tempelhof and other Allied bases in West Berlin as the world held its breath. He flew 190 of those missions of mercy in what the Allies called "Operation Vittles," always worried about two things: the weather and the Russian Yak fighter planes that stalked their every flight, hoping that one of the Allied planes would accidentally stray off course and into Russian airspace, providing the Yak pilots with an excuse to shoot it down.

And there was a third danger—the Russian-occupied territory next to the north corridor into Berlin. When the Allies began flying the airlift, the Soviets innocently built a bombing range, dropping their bombs on practice runs as Herman and others passed by at three-minute intervals twenty-four hours a day.

The Russians had a worry of their own—they didn't have the atomic bomb, and the Americans did. In the first days of the airlift, Truman dispatched two squadrons of B-29 bombers to England, knowing that everybody in the world remembered B-29s were the planes that dropped the atomic bombs on Hiroshima and Nagasaki.

"Our intelligence in London spread the word that we had a squadron of B-29s based in England and loaded with atomic bombs, ready to take off for Russia on a moment's notice," Herman said. "They let it be known that if one of those fighter planes hassling us ever really started something, or if one of those bombs from their new bombing range landed somewhere on Tempelhof accidentally on purpose, our B-29s would flatten Moscow in a day."

The Americans never worried about getting involved in a nuclear bombing of Moscow over something that might flare up during the airlift. "The Russians didn't know it," Colonel Herman said, "but the English refused to let us keep atomic weapons on British soil. Something else they didn't know: The B-29s sent to England had never been modified to carry atomic bombs."

He said in 1997, "There never was a squadron of B-29s loaded with atomic bombs. Those Russian Yak fighters never forced any fights with us in the three narrow air corridors that we followed into Berlin—via Hamburg, Frankfurt, and Hanover—and they kept their bombs exploding on their territory and not ours. That talk our intelligence people were spreading about those B-29s worked. The Russians fell for it."

The danger of war was grave. After leaving the presidency, Truman wrote, "There was always the risk that Russian reaction might lead to war. We had to face the possibility that Russia might deliberately choose to make Berlin the pretext for war. . . ."

History shows that in the same month the airlift ended—September, 1949—President Truman announced that the Russians had exploded their first atomic bomb.

★ 14 ★

"The Easter Parade"

In each corridor, Berlin Airlift pilots flew in accordance with an extremely rigid system of traffic control, which required them to follow an exact route at predetermined speed and altitude. They had to squeeze their planes into the corridors as if they were using an aerial shoehorn at altitudes as low as fifteen hundred feet. The corridor was twenty miles wide. Planes flew in "blocks" forty to fifty planes deep. There was virtually no margin for error. Any misjudgment or inattentiveness could lead to their deaths, and a worsening of the already tense international situation.

Earl Moore, whose comfortable flying duty in Shanghai was interrupted by a swift transfer to Germany, remembered the need for pilots to fly in strict compliance with the route assigned to them. "You had to stick to that," he said. "You'd better, because someone might chop your tail off."

Another pilot, Lewis Huston, remembered the tight squeeze coming into Tempelhof. "We had to land at the minimum safe airspeed," he said. The runway, which was turf, was short, and "if you weren't careful, you could run off the end of it. We came in so low to make sure we didn't overshoot the runway that we barely cleared the rooftops of apartment buildings around the base."

A second runway was built, of perforated steel. "This one was a little longer," Huston said. "Not much, but a little. To land on that run, you had to fly *between* the apartment buildings. You came in so low on the final approach that you could look *up* and see the people in those apartments."

In the midst of all this, the airlift pilots had to endure the intentional harassment by the Soviets—jamming the Allies' radio channels and buzzing the airlift planes with their Yak fighters. The operation reached its peak on Easter Sunday in April 1949, when 1,383 flights in twenty-four hours delivered 12,941 tons, prompting the men of the airlift to call it "the Easter Parade."

The Allies used loading fields at Fassberg, Celle, Rhein-Main, Wiesbaden, and other locations in West Germany, including a seaplane base, and unloaded their cargo in West Berlin at Tempelhof, the U.S. base, the British field at Gatow, and the French base at Tegel. They even landed seaplanes on Berlin's lakes.

The cargo wasn't always food. Captain Herman always carried twenty thousand pounds of coal for heating, cooking, and generating electricity. But it didn't make any difference what they had on board. "We were gung-ho pilots," Colonel Herman said. "We enjoyed our role in helping to stick it to the Russians."

Another Air Force test pilot, Russ Steber, flew 415 airlift missions, was captured by the Russians, and has given credit for his survival to his dog, a boxer he bought as a puppy and named Vittles. The dog accompanied his master on 131 flights into Berlin from their base at Erdin in Germany.

Steber remembered the danger in the flights—"there was nothing but noise, sea fog, and cold weather"—and the Russian fighter pilots "buzzing" the American planes. But at least he wasn't alone. Vittles was there.

"Vittles started flying with me, and he became the Berlin Airlift mascot," Steber said. The airlift's commander, General Curtis LeMay of Hiroshima immortality, who later became the Air Force's chief of staff, had a parachute made to fit Vittles.

"Sometimes if I had to take off and he wasn't around, he'd hop another plane," Steber remembered. "Or if he didn't find me, he'd bum a ride back. Everybody flew with him."

Steber was one of the pilots who crashed, but he was lucky— he lived to tell about it. "My plane was sabotaged, and my crew had to bail out. It's a good thing the dog wasn't with me that time, or we probably both would have gotten killed."

The Russians interrogated him for three days but released him when he didn't give them any useful information. At the end of his airlift tour, he was awarded four Air Medals for his missions.

Colonel Herman had his share of close calls. Fog was a threat every day and night, and on several nights he had to "divert" and land at an alternate site, never sure he had enough fuel left to make it. Once he crashed into the runway when his nose gear caved in.

On another flight, he was roaring down the runway at Fassberg preparing to lift his C-54 into the air and head for Berlin when his number four engine, the outboard engine on the right side, quit barely five minutes into the mission. He made the split-second decision to attempt an immediate landing. While the control tower operators held the next C-54 on the ground and kept the runway clear, Herman landed his plane safely on only three engines—and preserved his shipment of 20,000 pounds of coal.

As the summer wore on, General Clay was concerned. Despite the enormity of the operation, the Berlin Airlift was not meeting his goals. In a secret cable to Washington, Clay wired, "We are not quite holding our own." But someone who could more than hold his own was on his way.

Major General William H. Tunner, the Air Force's greatest expert on transportation by air, arrived at Wiesbaden in a C-54 on July 28. Tunner, forty-two years old, had already made his name as one of the geniuses behind the success story of flying the Hump in the China Burma India Theater during World War II.

Roger G. Miller, an Air Force historian in Washington and the author of *To Save a City: The Berlin Airlift, 1948–1949*, described General Tunner in his book as "a brilliant, dedicated, meticulous leader whose steel-blue eyes and index-card mind missed nothing." Miller also said Tunner was a workaholic. "He labored long hours," Miller wrote, "at an intense pace and drove his staff relentlessly."

Miller wasn't Tunner's only admirer. He quoted General LeMay as saying Tunner was "the transportation expert to end transportation experts." LeMay wrote later that assigning Tunner to the Berlin Airlift was "rather like appointing John Ringling to get the circus on the road."

Miller cited Tunner's credentials: helping to establish the U.S. Army Air Forces Ferrying Command at the start of World War II, not to mention his role in the C-B-I Theater. "His imagination, determination and organizational skills," Miller wrote in *To Save a City,* had made flying the Hump into China a legend in the history of the Air Force.

Tunner, like his top boss, President Truman, considered the crisis in Berlin to be "the first conflict between the free and the slave world," convincing himself that "We can't afford to lose it."

Tunner offered this commentary, which was an insight not only into the composition of an airlift but also a revealing look at his own personality:

> The actual operation of a successful airlift is about as glamorous as drops of water on stone. There's no frenzy, no flap, just the inexorable process of getting the job done. In a successful airlift, you don't see planes parked all over the place; they're either in the air, on loading or unloading ramps, or being worked on. You don't see personnel milling around; flying crews are either flying, or resting up so that they can fly again tomorrow. Ground crews are either working on their assigned planes or resting up so they can work on them again tomorrow. Everyone else is also on the job, going about his work quietly and efficiently.

General Tunner was a firm believer in something that was admittedly unexciting but was also, in his view, an essential ingredient in a successful airlift. In Miller's words, "Under Tunner, the monotony of repetition replaced the romance of flying. The more humdrum things were, the better." He quoted General Tunner as saying, "The real excitement from running a successful airlift comes from seeing a dozen lines climbing steadily on a dozen charts—tonnage delivered, utilization of aircraft and so on—and the lines representing accidents and injuries go sharply down. There's where the glamour lives in air transport."

Tunner wanted efficiency—*maximum* efficiency—all day, every day. Only then, he was convinced, could the Berlin Airlift become a victory for the Allies and for the United States in particular. Tunner himself wrote in later years, "This steady rhythm, constant as the jungle drums, became the trade-mark of the Berlin Airlift. I don't have much of a natural sense of rhythm, incidentally. I'm certainly no threat to Fred Astaire, and a drumstick to me is something that grows on a chicken. But when it comes to airlifts, I want rhythm."

Tunner didn't leave the airlift's chances of success to chance; nor did he confine his leadership to rallying speeches. Employing many of the same management techniques he used in the C-B-I Theater, he set goals for each of the bases involved. Those statistics he talked about, covering tonnage delivered, the maximum use of aircraft, accident rates, and other revealing numbers, were published in the airlift's own newspaper, *Task Force Times,* and displayed on Howgozit Boards for all of the sixty thousand airlift personnel to see.

One incident illustrated the Tunner technique perfectly. After U.S. planes delivered massive amounts of supplies on 1949 in the Easter Parade, General Tunner visited the base at Celle, which was delivering 12 percent more cargo than its quota required, then traveled to Fassberg, where the commander proudly informed him that his base was delivering 10 percent over his quota. "That's fine," Tunner commended him, "but of course it's not up to what they're doing over at Celle. They're really on the ball over there."

In his book, Roger Miller reported, "By the time Tunner left Fassberg, its commander had charged down to the flight line to urge his people to redouble their efforts."

In his long and distinguished military career, General Tunner, like some other commanders, picked up a collection of nicknames, including Tonnage Tunner. Congressman L. Mendel Rivers of South Carolina called him Mr. Airlift. Miller, however, reported that "thanks to his ruthless drive for absolute precision on the Berlin Airlift, the nickname that stuck was 'Willie the Whip.'"

* * *

The Berlin Airlift was a prolonged story of compassion, heroism, and even death. In the worst accident, two C-47s collided in midair in thick fog near Frankfurt. All four crew members—the two pilots and their copilots—were killed.

One of the greatest heroes was First Lieutenant Royce Stephens, whose C-54 developed a fire in one engine shortly after takeoff. The other four crew members bailed out, but Stephens stayed with his plane. It crashed into an open field, still carrying its load of coal for the people of Berlin. Lieutenant Stephens was killed in the crash.

The strain tolled on everyone associated with the airlift, even in stories that had happy endings. An experience involving Bill Michaels was a case in point. With twelve hours between shifts, Stephens, an airlift pilot, went to visit his fiancée in Celle and found her distraught and crying, explaining she had a dream the night before that Bill was killed on one of his missions to Berlin.

Michaels was inclined to shrug it off, especially after she told him his aircraft number in the dream was 236. The number of his plane was 233, but that aircraft had been shipped back to the States for its thousand-hour inspection. While his plane was back in this country, Michaels, with more than 150 airlift missions already to his credit, was taken off flying status and assigned to maintenance work while another crew and another C-54 filled in.

The replacement plane burst into flames on one of its flights. The pilot and co-pilot were killed. The plane's number: 236.

Another pilot, Lieutenant Gail Halvorsen, was a hero of a different sort. He became known as the Berlin Candy Bomber because he always stashed his own private supply of candy aboard his plane and "parachuted" his gifts to the children of West Berlin. It started early in the airlift, when he strolled out to the runway at Tempelhof between flights to watch his colleagues make their landings and found himself in a conversation with kids who were watching, too, from the other side of the barbed-wire fence that lined the runway.

The kids, thirty of them, were more worried about freedom than getting enough to eat. Halvorsen, a Mormon from Garland, Utah, was struck by their priorities. They told him, "We don't get *enough* to eat. Just give us a little. Someday we'll have enough. But if we lose our freedom, we may never get it back."

Halvorsen promised to drop some candy to them from his plane the next day. He persuaded his copilot and flight engineer to join him in donating their week's ration of candy and gum, tied the treats into handkerchiefs to form miniature parachutes, and dropped them from his plane. He began doing it every day.

The word got out, in a big way, when one of his "parachutes" almost hit a German newspaper reporter on the head. He asked questions, then wrote an article about Halvorsen's humanitarian operation—and the story went around the world in a flash.

His colonel summoned him and told him that what he was doing was suddenly getting worldwide publicity. "The general called and congratulated me," the colonel said, "and I didn't know anything about it. It made me seem stupid. Why didn't you tell me about it?"

"Because I didn't think you would approve, sir."

"You're right," the colonel admitted. Then, in a comment that anyone who ever put on a uniform can relate to, the colonel said, "But the general thinks it's a great idea. Keep it going—but keep me informed."

Suddenly, hundreds of pounds of candy, in handkerchiefs, began pouring into Halvorsen's base from America. In one batch, the American Confectioners Association sent more than three tons. Military volunteers helped distribute them to the aircrews flying into Berlin through the three corridors. The candy was dropped in the new makeshift parachutes to schools, playgrounds, and other spots all around West Berlin. Another pilot, Captain Eugene Williams, thought about the kids who couldn't run after the parachutes. He delivered a special load of candy to a hundred children who were patients at a hospital in the American sector of Berlin.

The deluge continued. Eventually Halvorsen's success story grew to such dimensions that he was assigned a full-time secretary to handle his mail, something that just doesn't happen for first lieutenants who aren't even working in an office but are flying airplanes instead. You don't need a secretary to fly an airplane in an airlift, unless you were Gail Halvorsen in 1948. Some of his mail was addressed to him as *Der Schokoladen-flieger*—"The Chocolate Flier."

Many of the German kids who were gleefully picking up the parachutes were tasting chocolate for the first time. It had never been available in Germany in their lives.

Meanwhile, the folks back home were keeping the men of the airlift supplied with what they wanted most—news. Having just gone through a war that ended only three years earlier, they were removed from their country again, so they yearned to hear what was going on back in the States.

They learned from their mail, Armed Forces Radio, and the daily newspaper for American military personnel, *Stars and Stripes,* that Truman's battles weren't only with the Soviet Union. He was feuding with the Republican Eightieth Congress, calling it "the worst in history." Enough of the American people agreed to give him his historic upset victory over Dewey in November.

The song hits from back home made their way to the barracks in Germany—Dinah Shore's "Buttons and Bows," "Now Is the Hour" by Bing Crosby, and a novelty tune in December, "All I Want for Christmas Is My Two Front Teeth."

While the men of the airlift were away, cortisone and vitamin B_{12} were discovered. Joe Louis retired, and Babe Ruth died. Truman integrated the armed forces. Seven Japanese war leaders were hanged in Tokyo just after shouting *"Banzai!"*—a battle cry meaning, "May you live ten thousand years."

The folks were writing in their letters about new products suddenly appearing on the market in those first postwar years—Honda motorcycles, radial tires, a game called Scrabble, Dial soap, and a new chain of ice cream stores named Baskin-Robbins. And Hollywood's biggest stars were still advertising Chesterfield cigarettes—Cary Grant, Gregory Peck, and Ethel Barrymore.

The men in Berlin gathered around radios in their few spare moments, especially to enjoy that now legendary blockbuster Sunday-night lineup of Jack Benny, Fred Allen, *Stop the Music*, Sam Spade, and others.

Their families back home were gathering around something else besides just their radios—television screens seven and ten inches in size, black and white, turning out the lights in the living room—nobody had a "family room" in those years—to watch two of the first "TV" stars, Milton Berle and Ed Sullivan, who made their debuts in 1948. Berle, on the *Texaco Star Theater,* became the top-rated star in television before the airlift ended, beating out Sullivan's *Toast of the Town* and Arthur Godfrey, *The Lone Ranger, Ted Mack's Original Amateur Hour, The Goldbergs,* and *Kukla, Fran and Ollie.*

The folks back home remembered the men of the airlift at Christmas. Bob Hope left the States and brought his show to Berlin with his wife, Delores, Irving Berlin, Jinx Falkenberg, and the Radio City Music Hall Rockettes; but General Tunner learned that the troupe would be appearing only in downtown Wiesbaden and downtown Berlin. No show would be performed at an airlift base—until Tunner hit the roof. Through Air Force channels, he demanded that either Hope would put on a Christmas show for the men of the airlift, or the airlift would not be mentioned in any of the publicity. Tunner knew that such a restriction would have aroused the curiosity of the American reporters, who would then start asking why Hope wasn't entertaining the very troops he was there for—the airlift personnel.

Within twenty-four hours, Air Force headquarters in Europe managed to make arrangements for airlift personnel to receive priority treatment at Hope's two shows—and three other shows were scheduled for airlift bases.

✢　✢　✢

The German people expressed their gratitude toward the American pilots, and not just at Christmastime. They were well aware that these airmen had been the enemy only a short time ago but were now saving their lives and the lives of their children and grandchildren. At Christmas 1948, one German merchant offered Christmas cards showing a tree, accompanied by a verse that described the feelings of the Berliners in four simple lines:

> *A tree grows in Berlin*
> *Struggling for life.*
> *Nurtured by Airlift*
> *Defiant of strife.*

The folks back home remembered the men of the airlift, too. The *New York Times* published an editorial that Christmas saying, "We were proud of our Air Force during the war. We're prouder of it today."

★ 15 ★

"Blockade Free!"

There were thirteen plane crashes in which Americans were killed in the Berlin Airlift, along with several other nonfatal accidents. Thirty U.S. airmen and one American civilian lost their lives, in addition to those from other nations. But the operation continued to develop into an international success story, so much that with success came problems of another kind.

More C-54 cargo planes arrived in August, along with their crews and ground support personnel. The increase in takeoffs and landings became a challenge on both ends of the airlift, with runways feeling the strain of the heavier planes and the constantly rising number of flights. The more severe part of the problem was in Berlin: The runways at Tempelhof and Gatow had simply never been intended to handle the heavy burden of air traffic, with the planes landing every few minutes, twenty-four hours a day, with far heavier loads than ever.

Over the summer, General LeMay ordered new runways built, and construction began on a new strip at Tempelhof on July 8, 1948, with American enlisted men operating the heavy equipment such as graders and bulldozers and German civilians doing everything else by hand. Groups of German workers, women as well as men, wielded shovels, picks, crowbars, and other tools in a masterful demonstration of split-second timing that rivaled the air operations themselves. The minute a plane landed, the German civilians hurried onto the runway and immediately began to fill holes and build up the landing surface.

An earsplitting whistle would alert them that another plane was approaching, at which point they would rush off the runway until it passed their work point. Then they would hurry out and jump into action again. They finished repairing the south runway at Tempelhof on September 12, then moved on to repeat their performance on Tempelhof's other runway and on the runways at the other airlift bases.

The Air Force became a separate and equal branch of the U.S. armed forces in 1947. On September 18, 1948, it celebrated its first birthday with "Air Force Day," a tailor-made opportunity for the motivational General Tunner. He wanted to set a one-day record in tonnage delivered, and he made it by having his planes plus the British deliver almost seven thousand tons of coal, five and a half thousand tons of it aboard U.S. planes, from noon on the seventeenth to noon on the eighteenth.

Speed in unloading the cargo was one of the main factors for the record. In Berlin, C-54s were unloaded in as little time as seven and a half minutes, C-47s in three and a half. In one twelve-minute period, German ground crews unloaded more than nineteen tons of coal. Army Secretary Royall wrote to Stuart Symington, the first secretary of the Air Force, that he was "sure that the record of 5,500 tons of coal carried by your planes on Air Force Day, with all its implications, did not escape the attention of our Russian friends."

Then came another serious problem, which the Russians called "General Winter." Bad weather set in during November, and leaders on both sides of the airlift believed the operation might be brought to a stop by the weather, which, as noted, turned into one of the most severe European winters of the twentieth century. Colonel Howley, the American commandant in Berlin, wrote later, "General Winter, the unconquerable Russian general, positively frowned on us, and we could almost hear the Russians guffawing through the Iron Curtain."

General Clay arrived at Tempelhof in early November and later recorded his reaction to the weather and the skill of the Air Force personnel running the landing field's GCA—the ground-controlled approach system operated by radar.

> Thanks to the effectiveness of GCA and its well-trained operations, we landed without accident but with our brakes hot. When the tower directed us to the taxiway, we found the visibility so poor that we dared not move farther down the runway. We were unable to follow the jeep that was sent to guide us and finally reached the unloading ramp guided by an airman under each wing signaling with flashlights.

November was the worst month of the winter for the airlift, especially the fog. Colonel Howley was quoted in one of the histories of the airlift:

> The worst enemy of air operations is not cold but fog, and we had plenty of that, too—thick, impenetrable fog. November and December were bad months. During November, 15 of the 30 days were almost impossible for flying, and December wasn't much better. . . . Fog-bound November and December were the acid test of the Airlift. If we could put these two normally bad flying months behind us without serious disaster to the people we were feeding, and could get well into January, we should know that we had the blockade licked.

They did, but not without cutting it uncomfortably close. The estimates were that forty-five hundred tons of supplies were needed every day to keep West Berliners alive. In November, the planes of the airlift recorded their smallest tonnage delivered since July, an average of 3,786 tons a day. Concern was growing that the mission might not survive the winter. Fortunately, things improved in December. The weather was less severe than November's, and tonnage increased correspondingly, up to an average of 4,562 tons a day.

Coal remained the essential ingredient in the airlift because it was related to sustaining so many elements in the lives of the Germans, such as heat, light, and power. The people were limited to four hours of electricity a day, and they never knew when they would get those four hours. Meals for the whole day were cooked whenever those four hours began, even if it was midnight. One woman married to a dentist pedaled a bicycle to generate electricity for her husband's drill. Streetcar service was reduced by 40 percent, and subway service was cut in half.

Despite the hardships caused by the Russian blockade and the harsh winter of 1948–49, Berliners remained strongly united in their support of the airlift. Even with unemployment rising to 10 percent, Roger Miller wrote, "The population of the Western sectors of the city exhibited a resilient, hard-bought toughness that rejected surrender to the Soviet Union and ensured the success of the Airlift."

Determination to continue the airlift and its success was strong on both sides of the Atlantic. On December 7, James Forrestal, America's first secretary of defense under the new reorganization act signed by President Truman the year before—the same act that had established the Air Force as a separate branch of the armed forces—ordered the Department of the Army to draw up plans for the long-range operation of the airlift. He told the Army to prepare for the possibility that the Russians would maintain their blockade of Berlin for as long as three years.

An Army intelligence report dated January 13, 1949, said, "Faith in the Airlift and in the Western Powers . . . to remain in the city has increased since the beginning of the winter." The report concluded, "Unless the situation becomes definitely worse, the population of the West sectors of Berlin may be relied upon to support the policy of the Western Powers through this winter."

On February 18, despite a return of severe winter weather, the airlift delivered its millionth ton of cargo to Berlin. Secretary of State Dean Acheson wrote to General Clay that the airlift had "sustained the physical existence and elemental human rights of more than two million Berliners." He added, "Our government offers its grateful commendation, in particular to the personnel of the Air Forces. . . ."

As the airlift continued, its productivity actually increased. On Easter Sunday 1949, with two hundred C-54s and 154 British planes under his command, General Tunner reprised another motivational technique from his CBI experiences. "Things were going too well," he wrote later. "It was necessary, I thought, to do something to shake up the command." Like an athletic coach, he resorted to competition to achieve his goal. With his staff, he developed specific goals for the weekend of April 15–16, taking care to keep the information secret so the Russians could not make propaganda hay if the Allies fell short of the goals. The forecast was for good flying weather.

With no advance notice, sergeants from the operations office at each airlift base posted the quotas for the next twenty-four hours at noon on Saturday, April 15. Shortly after, General Tunner flew into Tempelhof and then continued on to each American and British airlift base, stimulating his personnel to achieve maximum amounts of tonnage shipped over that weekend. He succeeded. The Allies airlifted 12,941 tons of supplies into the western zone of Berlin in those twenty-four hours, most of it coal. With the operation almost a year old, the men of the Berlin Airlift were still setting records.

"Kremlinogists" detected signs as early as February 1949 that the Russian resolve to continue their blockade might be starting to crack, and by March 21 the Soviet delegate to the United Nations, Jacob Malik, was indicating clearly that the Russians were willing to discuss an end to their blockade. Working through the United Nations at meetings held in New York, the two sides reached an agreement on May 4. Russia lifted its blockade on May 12.

A dramatic announcement from the first secretary-general of the four-year-old United Nations, Trygve Lie, to his UN colleagues said:

> We, the representatives of France, the United Kingdom and the United States of America on the Security Coun-

cil, have the honor to request that you bring to the attention of the members of the Security Council the fact that our Governments have concluded an agreement with the Union of Soviet Socialist Republics providing for the lifting of the restrictions which have been imposed on communications, transportation and trade with Berlin.

The whole world breathed easier for the first time in more than a year. The confrontation was over, and the tension disappeared—at least most of it and at least for the time being. The most serious face-to-face showdown up to that time between the two "superpowers" of the world in the Cold War was over, and the United States, with her allies, won. When the Soviets finally caved in, a city's entire population had been saved from starvation.

At one minute after midnight on Thursday, May 12, 1949, two jeeps and a convoy of seventy-five cars, buses, and trucks roared out of Berlin toward the western zone under a bright moon, complying with an order from the Russian high command three days earlier, announced by General V. I. Chuiko, the Soviet commander in Germany.

At the same moment that the vehicles motored out of Berlin, a flotilla of cars moved out of Helmstedt in the British zone, headed for West Berlin to reconnect the sectors and the people in them. They arrived an hour and forty minutes later. By dawn, traffic was flowing freely along the Autobahn.

At the stroke of midnight, the lights came on again in West Berlin, literally. Berliners, after fifteen months of being limited to those four hours of electricity a day, never knowing when they would start, could finally return to their previous life of getting electricity the same way people in most of the rest of the world did—by flipping a switch.

When the Russians finally lifted the blockade, the atmosphere was compared by some to the fanfare for a Hollywood movie premiere. The people, one news report said, "whooped it up in the flag-decked city." Two giant celebrations were attended by 250,000 Berliners.

Middleton of the *Times* said, "With the end of the blockade approaching, Berlin's mood varied from that of a front line just before battle to that of a circus day in a small town." Schools and businesses were closed. An Associated Press photo showed excited schoolchildren waving their lunch boxes over their heads on the news that there would be no school and holding a sign saying, BLOCKADE FREE!

Another photo showed a freight train leaving for Berlin with gondolas of coal, the first transported into the city by train since Captain Herman and his fellow airmen began flying it in at the start of the airlift. The train was one of seventeen traveling into West Berlin that day. On the side of the railroad cars was a hand-lettered message: BERLIN, WE GREET YOU.

Secretary of State Dean Acheson praised the airlift pilots and crew members for a "superb performance" but added, "While we are delighted that their efforts have brought an end to the blockade, we must not regard that act alone as having solved the German problem."

Acheson warned world leaders that lifting the blockade "has contributed toward our being in a position where, perhaps over a long period of time, we can move toward a solution. The lifting of the blockade puts us again in the situation in which we were before the blockade was imposed. It was an arbitrary, and, in our view, an illegal measure."

The Western Allies were keeping their powder dry, figuratively if not literally. The airlift went on. Orders were to continue the operation for at least another month, building a stockpile of supplies—just in case. On the first day after the end of the blockade, the planes landed in Berlin at their usual rate.

As the C-54s continued flying, an American military presence in another of the world's trouble spots ended. On June 29, the last U.S. forces were withdrawn from South Korea. One year later almost to the day, North Korean troops, using Russian weapons and on signals from Stalin in the Kremlin, stormed across the thirty-eighth parallel that divides North from South and started the Korean War.

The Berlin Airlift finally ended on September 30, 1949, a year and three months after it began. When it was over, one C-54 crew posted a sign next to its plane: BLOCKADE ENDS—AIRLIFT WINS. The box score showed the results of this massive lifesaving mission on behalf of America's former enemies:

462 days
277,264 flights
2,300,000 tons of supplies
60,000 flying and administrative personnel

One official described the airlift by saying, "It was born in peace, lived in peace and died in a peaceful world—it kept the peace in Europe."

The men of the Berlin Airlift did more than save two and a half million lives, which was heroism enough. Their achievement was historic for other reasons as well:

- The Berlin crisis was the first confrontation of the Cold War, and thus the first great victory by the Allies, led by the United States.
- It was the first time an airlift was used as an instrument of policy. The Truman administration adopted the position that it would stop the spread of Communism in Europe. The Berlin Airlift was instrumental in implementing that policy.
- It was the first major operation of the new United States Air Force, established by President Truman the year before.
- The airlift established techniques for airlift operations that are still employed today. Airlift practices based on the Berlin experience were part of U.S. military operations in the Korean and Vietnam Wars as well as other U.S. military engagements in Panama, Hungary, the Persian Gulf, and even stateside

crises such as the nuclear scare at Three Mile Island in Pennsylvania in 1979.

So grateful were the people of Berlin, then and now, that they established their own organization, Luftbruckedanke—"Airlift Thanks"—immediately after the airlift ended. Over the years, it has provided college scholarships for the children of the men killed during the operation, financial assistance to their widows, and funds to airlift veterans experiencing financial difficulties.

The organization's help continues to this day. So does the genuine international friendship forged out of that harrowing time. On a trip to Berlin in 1994, paid for by Luftbruckedanke, Ken Herman was thanked literally hundreds of times by Berliners for his role in the airlift. "Everywhere I went, people couldn't thank me enough, even that many years later," he said.

One man told Herman, "My son was five months old when you began the airlift. You saved his life." As he spoke, he cried. When Herman tells the story, he also cries.

The story is more than just a moving account of two men who were caught up in those times. It is also a one-on-one illustration of the gravity of that worldwide crisis and the individual heroism of the men of the brand new U.S. Air Force, in the frightening ordeal that gripped the world for more than a year, half a century ago.

PART 9

Korea

★ 16 ★

The Biggest Bombing Raid
of the War

When armed troops from the army of North Korea charged across the thirty-eighth parallel into South Korea in the rain at five o'clock on the morning of June 25, 1950, to start the Korean War, the military confrontation was a mismatch. North Korea had 150,000 troops under arms plus 150 Soviet-made tanks, heavy artillery, and at least fifty Russian Yak fighter planes. In stark contrast, South Korea's fighting force, even in the face of a series of threats extending over the entire previous year, still numbered fewer than one hundred thousand men, none with combat experience, and no combat airplanes. The South Korean Army's ability to defend itself and its nation included almost no artillery and enough ammunition to last only a few days.

President Harry Truman, weekending at his home in Independence, Missouri, immediately ordered American air and sea forces to support the South Korean Army. Three days later, he authorized the use of ground forces. At the same time, Truman signed Public Law 599, extending the military draft until July 9, 1951, and authorizing the call-up of reserves and National Guard units for as long as twenty-one months of active duty. Only five years after the end of World War II, the United States was back in a major war.

American military strength was almost as much of a concern as South Korea's. General Omar Bradley, chairman of the Joint Chiefs of Staff, wrote later that the reduction in American military forces following the end of World War II had slashed the Army to a "shockingly deplorable state." He warned that the Army at that point "could not fight its way out of a paper bag." Another Army general, Lieutenant General Hobart R. Gay, commander of the 1st Cavalry Division in Korea, called the Army's lack of combat readiness an "utter disgrace."

Clay Blair agreed. He was an author and military correspondent who wrote in his 1987 book *The Forgotten War,* "For various reasons, it [the Army] was not prepared mentally, physically or otherwise for war. On the whole, its leadership at the Army, corps, division, regiment and battalion levels was average, inexperienced, often incompetent, and not physically capable of coping with the rigorous climate of Korea."

Reporter Bill Lawrence of the *New York Times* wrote in his autobiography, *Six Presidents, Too Many Wars,* "The battle in Korea was one for which the United States was ill prepared. The five peacetime years of drastic cutbacks in military expenditures at home, plus some cockeyed ideas of economy-minded Secretaries of Defense, had given us an army so under-equipped and so badly organized that the troops lacked the power to fight well."

The Air Force, only two years old, underwent a rapid buildup with the start of the war. With only one basic training center, at Lackland Air Force Base in San Antonio, Texas, the air arm of America's military establishment suddenly found itself swamped with volunteers, young men eighteen or nineteen years old or in their early twenties.

They flocked into the Air Force in the summer and fall months of 1950. The Air Force was quickly forced to open two more basic training centers, reopening a former Navy base at Geneva, New York—renamed Sampson Air Force Base—and opening Parks Air Force Base outside San Francisco. Proof of the need for the two additional bases: On the night of January 16, 1951, with the Korean War still only six months old, Lackland, with facilities to handle a peak load of twenty-nine thousand basic trainees, had sixty-nine thousand young men in training, sleeping in tents on every spare piece of ground on the base, shivering under as many as seven blankets in a freak cold wave.

As the men kept coming into the Air Force, so did new aerial might. World War II propeller-driven P-51 fighter planes were being replaced by America's first jet fighter, the F-80, and soon the F-86, which performed yeoman service in Korea, followed by the F-84 all-weather fighter. B-29 bombers, which had provided America with such strong air power in the last years of World War II, were taking over the bombing load in Korea, after replacing their B-25 and B-26 cousins from earlier in the war before.

After sweeping shifts in the course of the war up and down the Korean peninsula in its first six months, the war settled into a stalemate during most of 1951 and 1952. By mid-1952, America's military leaders decided to launch an intensive bombing campaign intended to score important victories in both military and psychological warfare.

Their main target: Pyongyang, the capital of North Korea.

General Mark Clark, who had become the commander of the UN forces when President Truman had fired General Douglas MacArthur the year before, authorized the air strikes on July 3, 1952, naming specific military targets in and around Pyongyang but cautioning Air Force officials in the war to "avoid needless civilian casualties."

General Jacob E. Smart, once chief planner of World War II's Ploesti Raid and now deputy commander of the U.S. Far East Air Force (FEAF), wanted to go beyond any military objectives and use the raids to psychological advantage as well. He told his staff, "Whenever possible, attacks will be scheduled against targets of military significance so situated that their destruction will have a deleterious effect upon the morale of the civilian population actively engaged in the logistic support of the enemy forces."

As a part of this parallel effort, warning pamphlets were printed, to be dropped over Pyongyang by American planes several days in advance of the bombing raids, in a tactic reminiscent of the leaflets dropped over Hiroshima in 1945 before Paul Tibbets released the first atomic bomb. On the recommendation of the psychological warfare experts in the U.S. Far East Air Force who were responding to General Smart's orders, these pamphlets warned the North Korean civilians to avoid going onto military posts of any kind and even showed the main supply routes that would be bombed. The planes later dropped other leaflets with a second warning that all military installations along supply routes would also be the targets of the American bombers. After the bombing raids, the planes would drop a third edition of leaflets, reminding civilians that they had been warned by the American planes to stay away from military targets.

General O.P. Weyland set the date for the start of Operation Pressure Pump—July 11, 1952. Virtually every air unit in the Far East was going to participate in a harsh, all-day attack against thirty targets in Pyongyang. The risk for the American airmen was great: Pyongyang, because of its military and political prominence as the nation's capital, was defended by Russian-built fighter planes, forty-eight anti-aircraft batteries, and more than a hundred automatic weapons. With that much power available to fire flak at attacking planes, Pyongyang was considered one of the worst "flak traps" in Korea. In addition to Pyongyang, seventy-eight towns and villages were identified as key targets.

When July 11 dawned, the biggest air attack of the Korean War until that date was launched, with more than five hundred planes pouring fourteen hundred tons of bombs on the city during 1,063 sorties. The planes struck command posts, supply depots, factories, enemy barracks, railway facilities, and gun positions.

At least three of the thirty targets were destroyed, and all except two were damaged heavily. A direct hit on an air-raid shelter reportedly killed between four and five hundred Communist officials. Radio Pyongyang, the government's official voice and its propaganda outlet to the people of North Korea, was knocked off the air for two days. Then it announced that the "brutal" attacks had destroyed fifteen hundred buildings and had inflicted seven thousand casualties. The raids also knocked out most of North Korea's electric power for two weeks and crippled the nation's power to generate electricity for the remainder of the war.

But the worst was yet to come.

Another air operation, the "All United Nations Air Effort" against Pyongyang, was begun on August 29 in an effort to shock Russian and North Korean officials who were meeting in Moscow. What was destined to become the biggest bombing raid of the war, surpassing the raids of Operation Pressure Pump only the month before, included targets that sounded like a map of the capital city. In his 1983 book *The United States Air Force in Korea, 1950–1953*, Robert Frank Futrell wrote, "The list of targets marked for attack read like a guide to public offices in Pyongyang and included such points of interest as the Ministry of Rail Transportation, the Munitions Bureau, Radio Pyongyang, plus many factories, warehouses and troop billets."

Planes of the U.S. 5th Air Force began the assault at 0930 hours, with other waves of aerial assault following at 1330 hours and 1730 hours. The Navy joined in the operation with planes from the aircraft carriers *Boxer* and *Essex*. The overall United Nations effort totaled 1,403 sorties. Aerial photographs later showed moderate-to-severe damage to thirty-one targets.

The Associated Press reported from Seoul, "Black smoke poured from the factories, supply dumps and troop billets (barracks) at the outskirts of Pyongyang, which was forewarned of the raids by radio and leaflets." One pilot said the capital city "was blowing up all over."

Reports from the Air Force said some 420 planes poured four thousand gallons of flaming gasoline and 597 tons of high explosives on more than forty targets in raids over Pyongyang that began at dawn and did not stop until dusk. Pilots and crew members sprayed fifty-two thousand rounds of machine-gun fire on the area.

This time the targets were rings of 48 anti-aircraft guns surrounding the city, more than 100 automatic weapons, stockpiles of supplies, barracks, industries, and airfields. The U.S. Air Force pilots were joined by Navy and Marine Corps pilots as well as airmen flying the warplanes of South Africa, South Korea, and Australia.

The Air Force said the morning raid consisted of 420 fighter-bombers whose pilots and crew members shot up their targets below and dropped a hundred tons of bombs on two airfields, a power plant, factories, anti-aircraft batteries, and forty other vital military targets. Those on the raid reported that four large explosions ripped the area after the bombs were dropped.

In the afternoon, 245 planes went back for more. Air Force officials said the first two waves of fighter bombers destroyed forty-two buildings and damaged thirty-two others. In addition, they knocked out twenty gun emplacements, damaged a bridge, scored two direct hits on a factory, and bombed craters into two airstrips.

After describing the damage inflicted by the heaviest air raid of the Korean War, the Associated Press report added, "In accordance with U.N. policy of holding down civilian casualties by forewarning North Korean cities, Radio Seoul warned of the raid in advance and leaflets were dropped on Pyongyang, urging non-combatants to leave."

The U.S. Air Force's superiority in the skies continued to be demonstrated in bombing raids over the next nine months, reaching another awesome and damaging peak on May 13, 1953. That was when twenty American F-84 Thunderjet fighter-bombers of the Air Force's 58th Fighter-Bomber Wing blasted the Toksan Dam in North Korea and destroyed that region's irrigation system, a body blow to any Asian nation that depended heavily on its annual rice crop as an essential means of feeding its people—and its army. It was one of the most prominent raids of the war, employing the Air Force's tactic of "interdiction"—cutting off the enemy's transportation and supply routes.

The Toksan Dam was a stone-and-earth structure that held back the waters of the Toksan Reservoir. It stood twenty air miles north of Pyongyang and was 2,500 feet long and 270 feet thick at its base. The waters of the Potang River backed up in the reservoir for three miles and formed a lake a mile wide. Water flowed from the dam in a controlled release through irrigation canals that wound their way down each side of the valley to supply thousands of acres of rice paddies.

A major railroad entered the valley just below the dam and ran the length of the river valley to Pyongyang, parallel to a main highway. Both the railroad and the highway wound their ways past countless craters from American bombs during the three years of the war.

The missions to destroy North Korea's all-important irrigation system followed on the heels of successful raids to repulse the enemy's ground forces in heavy fighting in two mountaintop locations whose names had become familiar to the Americans back home—Old Baldy and Bunker Hill. A feature article in the 58th Fighter-Bomber Wing's own newspaper, the *Thunderjet Express,* quoted Major Douglas Montgomery as saying, "We've blown at least 50 feet off the top of the hill," which stood approximately nine hundred feet high before the bombardments by U.S. planes.

"From the beginning of dawn to the last glow of evening light," the *Thunderjet Express* said, "a steady stream of fighter bombers churned the top of the once wooded hill with an average of 200,000 pounds of bombs each day."

One pilot said, "We've been operating like a fleet of dump trucks. We haul up a load of bombs, dump it on the target, come back for another load and go right back and dump that one."

The newspaper described the job of the fighter-bomber pilots in graphic terms:

> The fighter-bomber pilot's job is one of the most grueling and dangerous of the air war. Bombing from altitudes of 2,000 feet on close support strikes at front-line targets, he is nakedly exposed to all the automatic weapons and rifle fire that the Red troops can throw at him. Many pilots come back with their Thunderjets full of holes, to the distress of their crew chiefs. Some pilots do not come home at all.

The article pointed out one group of unsung heroes in any raid, the men who keep the planes capable of flying their missions in the first place. "For maintenance crews and armament men," the wing's newspaper said, "whose job it is to present the pilot with a plane ready to fly and fight, this all-out air offensive has called for maximum endurance." One pilot told the newspaper, "My crew chief has deeper circles under his eyes than I have."

One member of the armament crew confirmed the demands on his time: "We've been working 16 and 17 hours a day instead of the 10 to 12 we normally work." As soon as he and his coworkers finished loading their bombs, he said, "the pilot is ready to take off again."

For the men of the 58th Fighter-Bomber Wing, the raid on the Toksan Dam was going to be another in a long line of raids, with every day bringing the same preparations, the same dangers, the objective to cripple the enemy's ability to fight, and the same day-in, day-out follow-up duties.

A feature article in the *Thunderjet Express* described the daily routine that contributed to the success of the bombing raids. The article, published in the issue of April 23, 1953, twenty days before the Toksan Dam raid, said, "Day and night, bomb-laden jets of the 58th roar out from the base to slash enemy transportation lines and strike supply and troop areas, rolling stock and frontline positions. Though the missions are often routine, each brings a new thrill of excitement to the men participating."

The article credited the daily routine as one of the major factors in the successful raids of the 58th:

> While each day's operation is reflected in the results of the mission, the complete—but silent—story lies in the daily routine involving everyone in the wing. The pre-dawn breakfasts for pilots, maintenance in the night when the cold seems to seep into working fingers, the all-night evaluation of intelligence reports, the careful inspection of flying clothes and combat equipment . . . all are part of the same sequence, day in and day out, supporting the combat air effort. Pilots themselves, be-

fore and after each mission, follow the same rigid routine of preparation and follow-up, checking and reporting upon the countless details which guide the control of each mission.

One of the admirers of the pilots was Ted Fusaro, a twenty-one-year-old staff sergeant from New Britain, Connecticut, who joined the Air Force a month after the war started. He was assigned to the 58th's Maintenance and Supply Group as its supply sergeant but served as the acting personnel officer during his tour from June 1952 to July 1953.

Fusaro, who now lives in retirement in Cocoa Beach, Florida, remembers that the Toksan Dam raid came after another of the harsh Korean winters. "I will always remember," he said in 2002, "trying to get a shower in during the winter. We had to leave our tent in full winter clothing, field jacket, boots, and hood and go through snow and cold for well over a hundred yards to where the shower was. We had to limit the hot water to about two minutes and then dress again and trudge back. But nothing compared to what the ground troops had to experience."

When the spring weather arrived, so did the monsoon season. During those months, he said, "I was in more mud than I had ever seen, and then the monsoon was over and it was just dust all over."

On May 13, the U.S. bombers came over the Toksan Dam at an altitude of three hundred feet and dropped high-explosive bombs into the dam's walls of packed earth. Flash floods from the bombs cascaded their way for twenty-seven miles through the valley below, wiping out huge chunks of a main transportation and communications route leading to the front lines of the war. Four other dams were attacked in the same series of raids. They were upstream from the army's supply routes and provided seventy-five percent of the water supply necessary to sustain North Korea's rice crop.

The U.S. pilots of the 58th were unable to assess their level of success because of the darkness at the end of their raid, but additional pilots staging a follow-up raid the next morning saw the results of the attack. When they looked down from their planes, they saw that their compatriots who had flown before them had scored a direct hit on the dam that caused one of its sections to collapse overnight, creating a hole 430 feet wide. The waters behind the dam had exploded through the opening and overpowered everything in their path as they unleashed a force of nature that overwhelmed everything in their path, emptying the reservoir in the process.

Aerial photos taken the next day showed that more than six thousand feet of the railroad bed had been washed out, plus a truck bypass route and three railroad bridges. Some twenty-seven miles of the river valley were flooded by the untamed waters. A statistical report on the damage showed:

- More than six miles of rail line destroyed.
- Five railroad bridges destroyed or damaged.
- Two miles of highway destroyed.
- Five highway bridges destroyed or damaged.
- Sunan airfield flooded and washed away.
- Floods in sections of the town of Sunan.
- Eight occupied anti-aircraft positions flooded.
- Sections of the railroad and highway systems seriously weakened.
- Heavy damage to thousands of acres of rice paddies.
- Irrigation canals washed out or clogged with silt.
- Flood conditions downstream from the dam as far as Pyongyang, causing extensive damage to North Korea's capital.

A second raid followed against the Chasan Dam, plus other attacks against two other irrigation dams named Kywonga and Kusong.

The success of the raids by the pilots of the 58th Fighter-Bomber Wing won high praise from General Otto Weyland, commanding general of America's Far East Air Force. On May 20, he sent an enthusiastic message to Colonel Victor Warford, commanding officer of the 58th:

Personal For Warford: Heartiest congratulations to you and your dam busters on the outstanding results attained on Toksan and Chasan Dams which washed out supply routes at Pyongyang. These strikes constitute two of the most crippling blows yet in the interdiction program. It will be a long time before trains or trucks roll over those two main supply routes to Pyongyang. Keep up the good work.

Signed—Weyland

Warford relayed Weyland's message to "all units" of his command and added his own congratulations:

It is extremely gratifying to receive messages of this nature which reflect the fine job being performed by all personnel of the "58th." Congratulations to one and all. Let's keep up the good work.

Victor E. Warford
Colonel, USAF
Commanding

Colonels and generals weren't the only ones who were impressed. The GIs of the 58th were, too. Staff Sergeant Fusaro has said today, "I truly admired the young pilots of the 58th, and looking back, it is hard to believe that they were only in their twenties."

A review of newspapers from that period shows that America's papers seem to have missed this critical development in the war at the time it happened, but military historians today consider the raids among the most significant developments of the war, certainly in terms of the air battle.

The military leaders of North Korea, however, needed no one to point out this significance to them. On the contrary, those leaders and political officials immediately took to the radio airwaves and their newspapers to do some firing of their own—with harsh propaganda blasts against the American airmen and their commanders. In a nation known for its strong government propaganda, the verbal attacks against the United Nations forces in general and the American Air Force in particular were considered some of the harshest language in the entire three years of the Korean War.

Pyongyang's radio stations and newspapers fired back at the United Nations forces, condemning America's "imperialist aggressors attempting to destroy the rice crop by denying the farmers the life water necessary to grow rice." In what appeared to be a deliberate attempt to manipulate world opinion, they referred to each of the five dams by seven or eight different names—two or three Korean names, the name in Japanese, even fictitious names—all intended to create the impression that dozens of dams had been attacked.

The propaganda attacks seemed to be convincing proof that the raids had struck at North Korea's jugular vein—its ability to feed its army and its general population. Asian nations, including North Korea, live in fear of what they call "rice famine"—a poor crop of their essential food commodity. In this case, the raids seemed to have accomplished what only nature could do in the past—cut off the supply of water for rice.

Reports today show that the bombing raids on the dams caused widespread flooding that washed out roads, railroad beds, and thousands of acres of rice fields. After the most pressing repairs were completed, the enemy was still faced with a serious complication. The North Koreans were compelled to maintain lower water levels in the dams to prevent additional floods that could be caused by future attacks. The lower water levels in the dams, however, reduced the amount of water available to feed what rice crops were left.

Now North Korea was faced with the urgency of obtaining rice from alternate sources—a serious enough problem that was compounded by existing conditions in 1953. Intelligence reports indicated that there was a serious rice famine in South China, a major source of the food for the entire region of Communist Asia. Even if rice were found elsewhere, it would have to be transported to North Korea via a transportation system overloaded by the demands of war and approaching a complete breakdown because of the American bombs that were striking North Korea day and night. One estimate was that if 10 percent of imported rice reached its destination—the same percentage of other goods getting through—it would not be enough to feed the North Korean Army.

The massive raids over North Korea on August 29, 1952, and May 13, 1953, plus those that American pilots flew almost on a day-in, day-out basis over most of the war, had an overwhelming impact on the enemy invaders. Units of the U.S. Far East Air Force flew 720,980 sorties during the war and dropped 476,000 tons of bombs. FEAF authorities estimated after the war that their raids killed almost 150,000 North Korean and Chinese troops and destroyed more than 975 enemy planes, eight hundred bridges, eleven hundred tanks, eight hundred railroad locomotives, nine thousand railroad cars, seventy thousand motor vehicles, and eighty thousand buildings. By the war's end, almost all of North Korea's modern buildings had been destroyed.

When the bombings of the irrigation dams began in 1953, North Korea's representatives had been emphatically and repeatedly rejecting Allied terms for a truce for two years. They were especially opposed to the voluntary return of prisoners of war and the establishment of a demilitarized zone (DMZ) between the two Koreas. Only a few days before the bombing raid against the Toksan Dam, the enemy had once again declared these provisions "absolutely unacceptable."

History shows that the Korean War ended barely two months later, when the Communist government of the North called for a resumption of the on-again, off-again talks at Panmunjom. Representatives of the warring nations signed a truce agreement there on July 27, 1953, a truce that remains in effect to this day.

Robert Futrell pointed out in his book that the strong outcry to reduce the strength of America's armed forces after World War II "had not been a cause for peace but had tempted the Communists to exploit war as an instrument of national policy." Secretary of Defense George Marshall, the five-star general and former chairman of the Joint Chiefs of Staff and secretary of state, agreed. "The final recognition of this fact," he said, "made it possible to start the rebuilding of the armed forces to the minimum strength required for the security of the United States. . . ."

When the Korean War began, the Air Force strength stood at 426,314 officers and enlisted men. Shortly after the start of the war, it added one hundred thousand Air Force Reservists. With the international situation worsening rapidly in Korea and in Europe, the Joint Chiefs of Staff authorized the Air Force to expand to 1,210,000 men in November 1950, only five months after the start of the war in Korea.

America's air power in the form of its planes as well as its personnel also expanded as the hot war in Korea and the Cold War elsewhere both continued. As early as 1951, the first full year of the Korean War, B-47 Stratojets were replacing the B-29 and B-50 bombers. By the time 1954 ended, all of the B-29s had left the Air Force's service. In 1955, the giant B-52 Stratofortress jet bombers began to replace the former Air Force heavyweight, the B-36.

"The Korean War," Robert Futrell wrote, "was one more tragic example of the failure of the existing patterns of international organizations to maintain harmonious relationships in a world where predatory nations were eager to plunder their weaker neighbors."

However, Futrell conceded that a certain amount of good came out of the war in Korea, including the show of force from the UN units that were supporting South Korea, which "must have given pause to the aggressor nations."

The American people, when the North Korean forces boldly invaded South Korea in 1950, "could now clearly see that world peace would come through strength and not through weakness," Futrell wrote. Then he quoted Thomas Jefferson's famous statement, "The price of peace is eternal vigilance," adding several words of his own—"vigilance to detect and halt aggression wherever it appears."

As one of those who helped to stop the Korean aggression, Ted Fusaro says today,

A B-24 bomber returns to an air base in the Libyan desert after the air attack on Ploesti's oil refineries on August 1, 1943. (*Via Robert F. Dorr.*)

First Lieutenant Bob Sternfels, later promoted to major, receives the Distinguished Flying Cross from General Jimmy Doolittle after the raid on Ploesti. (*Bob Sternfels Collection.*)

Twenty-nine-year-old Lieutenant Colonel Paul Tibbets stands next to the B-29 bomber, named for his mother, that dropped the atomic bomb on Hiroshima. (*Paul Tibbets Collection.*)

The crew of the *Enola Gay* before taking off for Hiroshima. Standing, left to right: Lieutenant Colonel John Porter, ground maintenance officer; Captain Theodore J. Van Kirk, navigator; Major Thomas Ferebee, bombardier; Colonel Paul W. Tibbets, pilot and commanding officer of the 509th Group; Captain Robert A. Lewis, copilot; and Lieutenant Jacob Beser, radar countermeasure officer. Kneeling: Sergeant Joseph Stiborik, radar operator; Staff Sergeant George R. Caron, tail gunner; Private First Class Richard H. Nelson, radio operator and the youngest crew member at age eighteen; Sergeant Robert H. Shumard, assistant engineer; and Technical Sergeant Wyatt Duzenbury, flight engineer. Not pictured: the ordnance officers, Navy captain William S. Parsons and Army Air Corps lieutenant Morris R. Jeppson.
(*Paul Tibbets Collection.*)

Colonel Paul Tibbets at the controls of his B-29 bomber, the *Enola Gay*.
(*Paul Tibbets Collection.*)

Smoke from history's first atomic bomb billows twenty thousand feet above Hiroshima and spreads ten thousand feet across the target at the base of the rising column. (*Via Robert F. Dorr.*)

Colonel Tibbets and his crew aboard the *Enola Gay* return to their base on Tinian after dropping the atomic bomb on Hiroshima on August 6, 1945. (*Via Robert F. Dorr.*)

Seven C-47s line up to be stocked with supplies for the two and a half million people cut off from the outside world during the Soviet Union's blockade of the Allied sectors of Berlin. President Truman ordered the Berlin Airlift in June 1948. It continued until the Soviets lifted their blockade a year later. (*National Archives Photo.*)

C-54s are loaded under floodlights and spotlights during the around-the-clock Berlin Airlift. (*National Archives Photo.*)

F-84s take off on another bombing mission during the Korean War. (*Via Robert F. Dorr.*)

A B-52 jet bomber is being loaded with bombs at Andersen Air Force Base on Guam during Operation Linebacker II in Vietnam at Christmas 1972. (*Via Robert F. Dorr.*)

A B-52 drops nineteen bombs in this photo, plus many more, over North Vietnam in December 1972, during Operation Linebacker II. The operation forced the North Vietnamese back to the conference table the following month and led to the end of the war. (*Via Robert F. Dorr.*)

The B-52 Stratofortress, one of the bombers used in Operation Desert Storm during the Gulf War against Iraq in January 1991. (*Via Robert F. Dorr.*)

The B-2 bomber saw heavy duty in Gulf War II. (*Via Robert F. Dorr.*)

I do not believe that the Korean War has had its rightful place in American history. I further believe that the effort to locate and return the thousands of POWs and MIAs has been terribly neglected. I get the feeling sometimes that the Korean "police action" is treated like an insignificant incident between World War II and Vietnam. You might say that I am somewhat resentful about that and felt real good when I heard Vice President Cheney speak to a group of Korean War vets recently and give appropriate tribute to their service.

As for the Air Force itself, Robert Futrell said, "From its growth and experience during the Korean hostilities, the fledgling United States Air Force emerged as a power better able to maintain peace through preparedness."

That power, and its ability to maintain peace, was to be tested again only one decade later, in another faraway place with a strange-sounding name—Vietnam.

PART 10

Vietnam

★ 17 ★

"Maximum Destruction"

The Air Force was a presence in the affairs of Vietnam as early as 1950, when the Pentagon dispatched "advisers" to help the French forces there maintain and operate American planes in the war against the Vietminh, the Communist-led revolutionary organization formed in 1941 to win independence for Vietnam.

The United States kept a wary eye on South Vietnam, concerned that the growing unrest there was being caused by Communist aggression from China and North Vietnam. President Eisenhower and his secretary of state, John Foster Dulles, dispatched "military advisers" and units of the Green Berets to South Vietnam. One of the rising stars in the Senate, John Kennedy of Massachusetts, supported the policy and agreed with what Eisenhower and Dulles called "the domino theory," that other countries would begin to collapse like dominoes into the Soviet orbit if South Vietnam were allowed to fall.

Kennedy restated his belief when he became president. "We have a very simple policy in Vietnam," he said. "We want the war to be won, the Communists to be contained, and the Americans to go home."

An incident that reportedly occurred in the Gulf of Tonkin on August 4, 1964, less than a year after Kennedy's assassination, ignited a sharp escalation in America's military involvement. Two American destroyers reportedly were hassled by North Vietnamese torpedo boats. On August 7, Congress overwhelmingly approved a resolution authoring President Johnson to "take all necessary measures to repel any armed attack against the forces of the United States and to prevent further aggression."

Johnson, the former Senate Majority Leader from Texas who was a master legislative strategist, knew the resolution gave him blank-check authority to take whatever action he considered justified. Further, the authority was open-ended, with no closing date. Johnson said the resolution "was like Grandma's nightshirt—it covered everything."

Seven months later, the Air Force launched Operation Rolling Thunder, the longest air campaign in American military history. With frequent interruptions, it lasted from March 2, 1965, to October 31, 1968. Pilots from the Air Force, Navy, and Marines flew one million sorties and dropped half a million tons of bombs on North Vietnam.

One of the operation's success stories was the raid on the Paul Doumer Bridge in Hanoi, the most important bridge in North Vietnam. It was named for the late president of France, assassinated four decades earlier. The bridge was named in his honor partly because of his leadership as governor-general of French Indochina in building railroads that would link northern Vietnam with southern Vietnam and also with China.

Nicknamed the "Doomer" Bridge by pilots anxious to blast it out of existence, the bridge had been off limits since the start of the Vietnam War because its southern end stretched into downtown Hanoi, which itself was restricted because of its special status as the country's capital. But the restriction against bombing the bridge was lifted suddenly at 10 A.M. on August 11, 1967. That was when orders were received directing that a bombing raid against the bridge be launched immediately—not next week or tomorrow but that same day.

The bridge was a railroad and highway span more than a mile long but only thirty-eight feet wide. It consisted of nineteen rail spans and a highway that ran along both sides of the track. Some twenty-six trains crossed it every day, plus countless trucks carrying more than six thousand tons of supplies to the North Vietnamese Army fighting in South Vietnam and Laos. It was the only rail link from the port of Haiphong to Hanoi. Four of five major rail lines came together to cross the bridge from the north in Hanoi.

Because it was the main link in Hanoi's logistics, it was heavily protected, surrounded by three hundred anti-aircraft guns, thirty surface-to-air missile sites armed with four to six missiles each, and MIG fighter planes on standby at several bases near Hanoi.

The mission commander for the strike was Colonel Robert M. White, a P-51 fighter pilot in Europe during World War II and a fighter pilot in the Korean War. He had flown the experimental X-15 plane to a record altitude of 59.6 miles and a speed of 4,093 miles an hour. He was the holder of the Harmon and Collier Trophies for outstanding achievements in aviation and NASA's Distinguished Service Medal.

White, who rose to the rank of major general, said the members of the 355th Tactical Fighter Wing immediately displayed a level of intensity "higher than I had seen since joining the Wing." He said preparations that normally took an hour were completed in twenty minutes. The support staff and the planners seemed to be setting speed records of their own for getting ready to fly a mission, White told John Frisbee of *Air Force Magazine*. He said, "You'd have to be there to understand" how eager all the personnel of the wing were to get a shot at that bridge at long last.

Takeoff was 1418 hours (2:18 in the afternoon). Shortly before four o'clock, Colonel White rolled into his bomb run from thirteen thousand feet, five thousand feet above the point where he was to release his bombs. He and those pilots behind him were flying smack into the teeth of a heavy barrage of flak and several missiles from the ground.

The strike force reached its target and released its bombs at two minutes before four. The skill and accuracy of the pilots and crew members produced direct hits on the bridge. One span immediately caved in and collapsed into the river. A few minutes later, as the attack continued, two spans from the highway portion of the bridge also fell away. To top off the success of their mission, all crews made it home safely.

The bridge was closed for two months, with three of its nineteen spans knocked out, and two additional strikes kept it closed the rest of the year.

Despite its duration of more than three and a half years, Rolling Thunder fell short of its goals. Even though the raids caused six hundred million dollars' damage and killed perhaps fifty-two thousand North Vietnamese civilians, they did not stop the Communists from launching a vigorous counteraction, the Tet Offensive, early in 1968, and did not force the North Vietnamese to the negotiating table. In addition to failing to meet its overall objectives, Rolling Thunder also imposed a heavy burden on the United States: a price tag of two billion and the loss of 919 planes. President Lyndon Johnson ordered a halt to the bombing on October 31, 1968.

Bombing over North Vietnam was resumed in the spring of 1972, when President Richard Nixon, completing his first term in office and preparing for a second, ordered the start of "Linebacker I"—a direct response to an invasion of South Vietnam by the North Vietnamese early that spring in what came to be called the "Easter Offensive." Nixon also authorized the mining of Haiphong and other harbors in North Vietnam.

It was another attempt to get the North Vietnamese to the negotiating table. Commanders were given wider authority to achieve the objectives of their operation than those who had been in charge of Rolling Thunder. They had full control over tactics to be employed and the selection of targets under White House guidelines. Unlike Rolling Thunder, the men in Linebacker I were able to use laser-guided bombs in large quantities and were free to attack targets that had been off limits early in Rolling Thunder.

Two of the heroes of Linebacker I were pilots, not of bombers or fighters but of helicopters; and not because they bombed something but because of a rescue.

Captain Roger Locher was forced to bail out when his chopper was struck by shells from two MIG-19s. The shots knocked out the helicopter's hydraulic system, making the craft uncontrollable. Then a fire erupted in the rear of the fuselage, forcing the crew to bail out.

Locher landed uninjured in trees near a MIG base, north of the Red River, 350 miles into enemy territory. His parachute and survival pack were stuck in the tree where he landed, above his reach. He had only his survival vest, containing two pints of water and a couple of snacks.

He reasoned that his best chance for survival was to cross the Red River Valley and work his way to the sparsely populated mountains ninety miles away. But before that, he would have to walk to the river, several miles away, and swim across it. Then he would have to be careful about when he would walk toward the mountains, doing so only at dawn and dusk, and hope to be able to live off the land.

The enemy was searching for him from the start and came within thirty feet of him on his first morning of his attempt to escape. With a two-way radio, Locher tried repeatedly to make contact with one of the other fliers in Linebacker, but with no success. Finally, on June 1, three weeks after he was shot down, a flight of F-4 fighter planes passed directly overhead on their way home from a strike. He called for help on his radio, hoping the crews above had their radio frequencies open.

They did. His call was heard, and within hours, a small search-and-rescue force was on its way from neighboring Thailand. A "Super Jolly" helicopter, piloted by Captain Dale Stovall, started in to rescue Locher, but Stovall was driven back by missiles from MIG fighters. The prevailing attitude that you couldn't be rescued north of the demilitarized zone between North and South Vietnam was beginning to look justified to Locher.

But as John L. Frisbee wrote in *Air Force Magazine,* "Seventh Air Force thought otherwise." More than one hundred planes—fighters, bombers, tankers, and others—fought their way in. Captain Stovall's HH-53 picked up Roger Locher and returned him to safety, proving that yes, it *was* possible to be rescued in that hostile territory.

Frisbee pointed out,

It had been a record-setting show. Captain Locher had eluded capture in enemy territory for 23 days, setting a record for successful evasion in the Vietnam war. Captain Stovall had twice flown his rescue helicopter further into North Vietnam than had been done before, earning him the Air Force Cross. All the principals emerged as heroes. . . .

But there is more to the story. Combat crews who would be flying Linebacker strikes north of the Red River now knew that eluding capture in that inhospitable land and rescue from Hanoi's backyard were indeed possible. That was a good thought to sleep on.

When the enemy finally expressed a willingness to talk about ending the war, Linebacker I was stopped. But Nixon, experienced in diplomacy, was furious when the talks failed to produce an agreement and ordered another extended air offensive—Linebacker II—while adding a significant new element: B-52s bombing near Hanoi.

Nixon was increasingly anxious to force the North Vietnamese back to the negotiating table. It had been eight years since the Gulf of Tonkin incident produced a marked escalation in the war. More Americans were becoming unhappy with the U.S. involvement in that part of the world. Lyndon Johnson, after winning election to a full term as president in a landslide in 1964, felt forced to leave office four years later without seeking a second full term. Public opinion about the war had turned harshly against LBJ and his secretary of defense, Robert McNamara.

Nixon, elected to succeed Johnson in 1968 partly on the basis of his promise that he had a "secret plan" to end the war, won a landslide victory of his own when he ran for reelection in 1972 even though the war was still on. In contrast to Johnson's 1968 fate, Nixon coasted to victory with 61 percent of the vote, to 38 percent for Senator George McGovern. However, Nixon's Republican party suffered major losses in Congress, and speculation rose immediately that the new legislature would come to Washington in January anxious to end the war.

By the end of November, with his second inauguration still almost two months away, Nixon was more determined than ever to negotiate an end to the war, and he wanted to do it through America's superiority in the air. On November 30, he met with his secretary of defense, Melvin Laird, a former congressman, and Admiral William Moorer, the chairman of the Joint Chiefs of Staff, expressing a desire to bomb Hanoi and nearby Haiphong. Laird and Moorer were skeptical about the need for increased bombing and were reluctant to expose the B-52 bombers to capture by the North Vietnamese, giving them an opportunity to examine the electronic systems of the planes and develop ways to combat them.

According to author Marshall Michel in his book *The Eleven Days of Christmas*, Nixon nevertheless ordered the Air Force to increase its flights of B-52 bombers over North Vietnam, including its capital city of Hanoi, to "send a message" to the enemy. The Air Force responded by beginning a series of "special missions" flown by B-52s and lasting for the rest of the year.

The B-52—the Stratofortress—was the right messenger for the job, a long-range heavy bomber that can perform a variety of missions, either atomic or conventional, from altitudes as high as fifty thousand feet—almost ten miles up. Its range is eighty-eight hundred miles, and with in-flight refueling it can fly indefinitely. It is a giant of an airplane—40 feet, 8 inches high and 159 feet, 4 inches long, with a wingspan of 185 feet. It flies at 650 miles an hour under a maximum takeoff weight of 488,000 pounds. It is powered by eight engines. Thanks to advanced technology, the B-52, despite being so much bigger than the World War II bombers, requires a crew of only five, compared to ten for the B-17. When President Nixon sent these giant new bombers into the air war over Vietnam, he was deploying the world's most advanced bomber, one that carried a price tag of $53.4 million per plane.

B-52s had been arriving in Southeast Asia since early in the year, when the buildup began for Linebacker I. In February, B-52s began arriving as reinforcements at Andersen Air Force Base on Guam and U-Tapao Air Base in Thailand. By the beginning of December, just before the start of Linebacker II, 206 of the giant bombers, more than half of the inventory of the Strategic Air Command (SAC), were poised for combat at the two bases. In addition, SAC's arsenal included a force of 172 KC-135 tanker planes to provide in-flight refueling for the long-range B-52s. During Linebacker II, the KC-135s flew 1,312 missions, providing 4,593 midair refuelings for the bombers.

The success of Linebacker II was made possible at least in part by the effectiveness of the command and control structure of the operation. EC-121 planes orbited over Laos and the Gulf of Tonkin, while a Navy ship, *Red Crown,* cruised in the northern part of the Gulf.

Each raid by B-52s was supported heavily by up to 120 fighter planes, increasing the requirement for effective command and control functions. Chris Hobson, author of *Vietnam Air Losses,* pointed out in his 2001 book that "the viability of the B-52 force over Hanoi and Haiphong was still very much an unknown quantity. In the final analysis, SAC's reputation, indeed the reputation of U.S. air power as a whole, depended largely on the men and machines that flew the Linebacker II missions."

Not everyone agreed with Nixon's strategy to bomb North Vietnam to the negotiating table. Marshall Michel, who flew 321 combat missions from 1970 to 1973, including the 1972 bombing of Hanoi, said in his book that "the Joint Chiefs of Staff were not enthusiastic about Nixon's expansion of the war, and Secretary of Defense Laird called the president's reactions to the situation 'wild.' "

Nixon, however, was adamant. He told his national security adviser, Henry Kissinger, "I am absolutely determined to end the war and will take whatever steps are necessary to accomplish this goal . . . I cannot emphasize too strongly that I have determined that we should go for broke. . . ."

Despite having members of his own military establishment question his strategy, Nixon's orders to step up the bombing of North Vietnam seemed to be paying off by the time the 1972 Christmas season was approaching. The raids were having "a major impact on the North Vietnamese people," according to Michel. One North Vietnamese remembered,

The people were frightened and in a panic about the B-52 because word got around about how good they were and the number of bombs they could carry. The people were much more afraid of them than any other aircraft. People were feeling pessimistic about the chances of being able to shoot any of them down, and the government had to work really hard to keep the people's spirits up. The government promised everyone that they would be able to shoot one down, but no one really believed them.

When the Air Force diverted some of the B-52s to bomb other targets in the south to support the ground forces of South Vietnam, Nixon became furious. He told Kissinger and Kissinger's deputy, Major General Alexander Haig, "I want more B-52s sent to Vietnam. I want this order carried out, regardless of how many heads have to roll in carrying it out." He told Kissinger and Haig that "the psychological effect of having 100 more B-52s on the line would be enormous. I either expect this order to be carried out or I want the resignation of the man who failed to carry out the order when it was given."

In the midst of the monsoon season and its terrible flying weather, more B-52s took to the air shortly after Nixon's emphatic order, in what some of the pilots involved were calling "the herd shot 'round the world." General Haig reportedly supported Nixon's emphasis on increased bombing despite the weather conditions. The first Army battalion commander in South Vietnam to use B-52s to support his ground troops, Haig had witnessed the destructive capacity of the big bombers. He also emphasized that the United States was running out of time in seeking an end to the war and could not wait for better weather.

Haig's boss, Kissinger, on the other hand, was less anxious to employ more B-52s. According to Michel, Kissinger felt that the loss of B-52s in air action would give North Vietnam a stronger hand in any peace talks. He was also afraid that civilian casualties would result. Eventually, Kissinger went along with the plan.

Michel fingered Laird instead of any Air Force general as the real culprit in not getting more B-52s to Vietnam soon enough to satisfy Nixon. He said Laird "was pushing hard to get the U.S. out of the war and used his position to try to keep the bombing campaigns as limited as possible."

Michel voiced the opinion that Nixon and Kissinger seemed to want "someone like General Curtis LeMay, a smart, savvy and aggressive combat leader who would have enthusiastically and expertly followed his instructions for a massive bombing campaign—exactly what Lyndon Johnson and Robert McNamara did not want."

On December 14, Nixon issued orders to the Air Force to begin a three-day bombing campaign in "Route Package Six," the Hanoi-Haiphong area, with B-52s and fighter support. The order was later extended into what became an eleven-day operation.

Admiral Moorer notified his new commander of U.S. forces in the Pacific, Admiral Noel Gayler, to begin the series of B-52 bombings on targets in the Hanoi area. The date for the first raid was set for Sunday, December 17. Following the bombing campaign earlier in the year, the new raid was called "Linebacker II."

The Joint Chiefs of Staff sent a message to the Air Force's Strategic Air Command headquarters at Offutt Air Force Base in Omaha, Nebraska, on December 15. It was a list of eight targets in the Hanoi area to be bombed on the first night of Linebacker II—a vehicle repair facility, a railroad yard and repair shop, the Hanoi International Radio stations, and four MIG jet fighter bases. The emphasis was on strategic targets rather than the wholesale leveling of the city. All commanders at Andersen Air Force Base on Guam were briefed about the coming missions on the afternoon of December 16. Later on the same day, it was announced that all U.S. air bases in Southeast Asia would "stand down"—remain on alert—on December 17.

The Joint Chiefs sent their attack message early on the morning of the seventeenth:

You are directed to commence at approximately 1200Z [noon], 18 December 1972, a three-day maxi-

mum effort, repeat, maximum effort, of B-52/TACAIR strikes in the Hanoi-Haiphong area. . . . Objective is maximum destruction of selected targets in the vicinity of Hanoi/Haiphong. Be prepared to extend beyond three days, if necessary.

★ 18 ★

"Unprecedented Massive Bombing Raids"

At five o'clock that afternoon, the preflight briefing for all B-52 aircraft commanders began. Copilot Bill Buckley said the message was clear: "We were going to strike Hanoi in a series of unprecedented massive bombing raids."

Admiral Moorer sent a message to Admiral Gayler on December 18 emphasizing the critical nature of the operation. "Linebacker II offers the last opportunity in Southeast Asia for USAF and USN to clearly demonstrate the full professionalism, skill and cooperation so necessary to achieve the required success in the forthcoming strikes" in North Vietnam, Moorer said. "You will be watched on a real-time basis at the highest levels here in Washington. We are counting on all hands to put forth a maximum, repeat maximum, effort in the conduct of this crucial operation."

At eleven o'clock on the morning of December 18, Colonel James R. McCarthy, commander of the 43rd Strategic Wing, displayed a sense of the theatrical as he began the preflight briefing for the first night of Linebacker II. He said, "Gentlemen, the target for tonight!" Then curtains rolled back and the audience saw a bull's-eye on Hanoi. Captain John Allen said, "All you knew was that you were going 'downtown,' and that you might not be coming home . . . all you were thinking about was, Were you going to make it back or were you not . . . and what about the guy sitting next to you?"

Despite Allen's apprehensions, confidence about the eventual success of the operation ran high. The Air Force pilots and their superiors had been champing at the bit throughout the war to be given a free rein to turn their B-52 giant bombers loose against targets in the north, especially Hanoi, and now President Nixon was giving it to them. Most of them were confident that their raids would be successful and would lead to an early resumption of the peace talks.

Linebacker II was an around-the-clock operation for eleven days and nights, interrupted only for the observance of Christmas Day. Air Force B-52s struck at targets in the Hanoi and Haiphong area in the dark while Navy planes flew diversionary flights on airfields and surface-to-air missile sites. During daylight hours, Air Force planes and Navy fighter planes from no fewer than five aircraft carriers—the *Enterprise, Saratoga, Oriskany, America,* and *Ranger*—continued the pounding, jamming enemy radar in the process. KC-135s, the giant refueling planes of the Air Force, were also a part of the operation.

Snow-01, the giant bomber assigned to John Dalton, took off from U-Tapao at 5:18 P.M. that day as one of twenty-one B-52s headed for Hanoi, preceded by others from Guam, more distant from the target than U-Tapao. One crew member described just how close U-Tapao was to Hanoi: "There was just time enough to say the Lord's Prayer, sing the Air Force Hymn, and recite the twenty-third Psalm. Then we were on the bomb run."

Hanoi, which means "inside the river," sits in the west side of a curve on Red River where Canal de Rapides flows into the Red River. The two channels combine their flows at that point and run into the Gulf of Tonkin. The city is in the center of the Red River Valley delta and is both the nation's capital city and its historical center. It is treated with reverence by the North Vietnamese people. The North Vietnamese leader, Ho Chi Minh, was fond of saying that even if Hanoi should happen to be destroyed, "the Vietnamese people will rebuild it a hundred times, a thousand times more beautiful."

* * *

When the first B-52s came within thirty minutes of Hanoi on the first night, December 18, a "pre-alert" announcement was broadcast over public-address speakers that lined the streets. Fifteen minutes later, sirens began to sound. At this point, members of the general public were expected to head for bomb shelters.

As the B-52s approached their target, Joan Baez, the American folksinger who was an outspoken opponent of U.S. involvement in Vietnam, was sitting in a hotel lobby in Hanoi with other American entertainers as they watched propaganda films about alleged American atrocities. Later she recalled, "The electricity in the building failed, leaving us sitting in the dark." She said everyone "stiffened," with the Vietnamese "speaking rapidly to each other in quiet tones" while the Americans, doing less talking, felt "uneasy."

She said, "I heard a siren coming from a distance, starting at zero base and rising evenly to a solid, high note where it stayed for a second or two and then slid back down through all the notes like a slider. All I could think of was the civilian defense drills we'd had in grammar school." Then one of the Vietnamese officials lit a candle and said calmly, "Please excuse me—alert."

Nguyen Van Phiet, commander of a North Vietnam battalion, said later, "All the radar returns were buried in a jamming curtain of bright, white fog. The screen of the guidance officer and the tracking operators showed many dark green stripes slanted together. . . . After that, hundreds and thousands of bright spots specked the screens. . . ."

In the notorious prisoner-of-war camp called the "Hanoi Hilton," Commander Jim Mulligan of the U.S. Navy began to climb into a sleeping bag, one he had made from North Vietnamese army blankets. He was an A-4 fighter pilot who had been shot down and captured almost seven years earlier. He described the air attack later:

> All of a sudden the wails of the air raid siren echoed through the camp . . . the lights went out and we were

plunged into darkness. I looked out . . . to see if I might catch a glimpse of anything. Suddenly the missiles from the SAM [surface-to-air missiles] sites began to roar off. . . . One, two, three I counted from one side as they climbed heading north. From the southwest I saw more missiles leap skyward heading in the same general direction as the first group. . . . Then all hell broke loose, and I heard the rolling thunder of massive strings of bombs going off in the distance. The earth shook violently and the building reverberated wildly. The sky turned white . . . the rolling thunder of the bombs echoed and reechoed. "It's a B-52 raid . . ." I said to my cellmate. "Pack your bags—we're going home."

Charcoal-01, a B-52 piloted by Lieutenant Colonel Donald Rissi, became the first casualty of Linebacker II. The heavy bomber and its crew from Guam flew in the first wave on the first night. Only seconds away from their objective, they were hit by a surface-to-air missile. Colonel Rissi; his copilot, First Lieutenant Robert Thomas; and their gunner, Master Sergeant Walt Ferguson, were killed. The three other members of the crew—Major Dick Johnson, the radar navigator; Captain Bob Certain, the navigator; and Captain Dick Simpson, the electronic warfare officer—survived the attack but were captured and held as prisoners of war.

The three were released in 1973 as part of Operation Homecoming, the negotiated return of U.S. service members held as POWs. When the plane went down, the status of the plane's copilot, Lieutenant Thomas, was unknown; he was listed as "missing in action, shot down over North Vietnam, 18 December 1972." Six years later, his remains were identified and returned to his family.

A reporter for a French newspaper was on the third floor of the Hoa Binh hotel when that first attack came. Jean Thoraval of Agence France-Presse wrote, "Stretches of sky north and northwest of the city glowed red and white. With each explosion, doors burst open, furniture trembled and bottles fell to the floor. Blasts like immense incandescent mushrooms could be seen. . . ." The reporter described the scene as one resembling a fireworks display. "From time to time," he said, "it was as bright as daylight."

Ed Rock also had a view of the raid. He was the pilot of an F-105 jet fighter. He was serving his second tour in Vietnam, so he had plenty of credentials when it came to describing what he was seeing from his plane. "The thing I remember most," he said, "is the gigantic secondaries. It was beautiful, terrifying, and awe inspiring. I had experienced numerous frustrations my first tour, being assigned to strike dubious targets while being forced to avoid the most lucrative. It was absolutely amazing to see really meaningful targets get wiped out with overwhelming force."

Then a telling question occurred to Rock: "Why couldn't this have been done years before and thus avoided the needless pain and suffering?"

The heaviest raid of the war occurred on the eighth night of the series of missions, December 26, and something called "chaff" was a key reason for its success. *Chaff* refers to tinfoil-like material used in thin, small strips to jam enemy radar scopes by bouncing the radar beams back. It was developed during World War II and had proven effective already in Vietnam during Linebacker I, when no American strike plane was lost in a "chaff corridor."

On the night after Christmas, sixteen U.S. F-4 fighter planes spread a blanket of chaff across the landscape just north of Hanoi. Five minutes later, eight more F-4s did the same thing across the skies north of Haiphong, the strategically important harbor city. The raid involved ten waves of 120 B-52s striking nine different targets. The planes approached both cities from all four directions on the compass, under the protection of a chaff blanket that stretched forty by twenty-three miles over each city.

The official North Vietnamese history of the attacks that night described the effectiveness of the planning for the raid: "The enemy had altered many of his tactics. They also changed the direction of their bombing, changed the flight paths in and out of the bombing area and began to collectively and unceasingly bomb a large number of targets at the same time within a short period."

The history was convincing testimony to the Americans' efficiency in carrying out the raid:

> The enemy sent many groups of B-52s into the area simultaneously. All of the groups arrived at their bombing targets at the same time and this simultaneous attack from many directions caused us many difficulties in focusing our firepower, so we were not able to fire at all of them in time. The enemy split into many groups and many tight formations; they did not stay in the range of our missiles for long.

As copilot Bob Hudson's plane approached its target, the crew heard Nutter Wimbrow, the electronic warfare officer on the plane, say calmly, "We're going to be hit." Then a missile exploded in front of Hudson, who remembered what happened:

> It blew off the radome and the radar. All the windows upstairs were gone. The explosive decompression sucked out everything in the cockpit past my head. The initial explosion killed Bob Morris—I could see part of the hydraulic panel blown through him. I had my left sinus collapsed by the overpressure, my left arm was broken, and I had multiple puncture wounds from glass and debris. I sat there in a daze until the RN (Radar/navigator) called and said we had to get the nose up so we could get the bombs off. I got us centered on the target and we dropped the bombs.

Another missile hit the plane a few seconds later. "We took another missile in the left wing," Hudson said, "and it flipped the aircraft over on its back so I gave the order to bail out. The nav bailed out immediately, and I thought the gunner went, too. Nutter told me he was ejecting and I heard his seat go. The radar navigator said he was ejecting. I looked over at Bob Morris, my best friend. I could see he was dead, and then I, too, stepped over the side."

For Jim Cook, bailing out was proving impossible from his post in the plane's rear turret. As he struggled with straps and handles, the bomber blew up in midair. The force of the explosion blew Cook clear of the plane's wreckage and deposited him on a riverbank in two feet of water. He had come down headfirst. "I hurt all over," he said, "and later I found out both legs had been shattered below the knee, my back had been fractured, and my right shoulder and elbow had been broken. The North Vietnamese found me and interrogated me for twenty-four hours, breaking five ribs in the process."

Three other members of the crew were captured as well.

John Darrell Sherwood, official historian of the U.S. Naval Historical Center in Washington, declared flatly in his book *Fast Movers: Jet Pilots and the Vietnam Experience* that the December 26 raids were the decisive factor in winning the air war over Vietnam:

> The strikes on 26 December 1972 decided the entire air war over North Vietnam: 230 Air Force and Navy aircraft hit a variety of targets, all within a 15-minute window. Only two B-52s went down that day, but the North Vietnamese air defense system was shattered. Their largest missile-assembly facility was destroyed, their ground-based radar early warning and intercept system (GCI) was degraded, and their MIG bases were rendered temporarily unusable. North Vietnam was virtually defenseless against further B-52 attacks, and Hanoi quickly proposed a resumption of peace talks in Paris on 8 January 1973.

Sherwood added that "the air battle was essentially won on 26 December."

Wayne Thompson, chief of analysis at the Air Force History

Support Office in Washington, agreed. In his book *To Hanoi and Back: The USAF and North Vietnam, 1966–1973,* Thompson wrote,

> Linebacker II was by far the heaviest two weeks of bombing in the Hanoi-Haiphong region. All of the massive air power gathered in and near Southeast Asia was focused on this one region. The 200 B-52s based in Thailand and Guam dropped about 15,000 tons of bombs in Route Package Six, and fighters added more than 2,000 tons. . . .

Marshall Michel added his agreement. "Even with two losses," he wrote, "Night Eight's raid was a tremendous success." He concluded, "All indications were that the attack from different directions had befuddled the North Vietnamese defenses."

By the end of Linebacker II, the operation had thrown 729 B-52 sorties at the enemy despite heavy North Vietnamese concentrations of surface-to-air missile sites and anti-aircraft installations, considered some of the most powerful such air defenses in the world. Those enemy emplacements shot down fifteen B-52s. An estimated 15,287 tons of bombs were dropped on thirty-four targets by the B-52s. The Air Force calculated that sixteen hundred military or industrial buildings were destroyed or seriously damaged by the operation. North Vietnam's railroad system had been cut—"interdicted" in military language—in several places, forcing the enemy to move troops and supplies by truck. Some three million gallons of fuel were destroyed.

On January 4, 1973, the week after the smashing success of Linebacker II, Henry Kissinger left for Paris to resume talks toward ending the war, with Nixon saying the North Vietnamese "can't play with us in Paris and prolong the war with immunity from retaliation." On January 23, Kissinger and Le Duc Tho, North Vietnam's chief negotiator, initialed an agreement to stop the fighting. On January 27, it was signed by officials representing the United States, North Vietnam, South Vietnam, and the Vietcong, the Communist guerrilla group in South Vietnam.

The next day, U.S. pilots flew their last air strikes, after 5,226,701 missions since October 1961. At long last, the war was over, thanks in large measure to Linebacker II.

PART 11

Desert Storm

★ 19 ★

The Longest Flight

America began one of its shortest wars with its longest flight.

On the night of January 16, 1991, seven B-52 bombers thundered into the rain and the darkness over Barksdale Air Force Base in Shreveport, Louisiana, carrying fifty-seven members of the 596th Bomb Squadron in the first battle of the Gulf War against Saddam Hussein's Iraq. It was the start of Operation Secret Squirrel, a mission that lasted thirty-five hours round-trip and covered fourteen thousand miles literally around the world, the longest combat mission in the history of military aviation, according to Airman First Class Ryan Hansen of Barksdale's public affairs office in an article in *Aerotech News and Review*.

But why? Why did the United States have to worry about Iraq?

The Gulf War of 1991 had its roots as far back as 1958, when President Eisenhower felt compelled to order a Marine combat team into the Persian Gulf because he feared that a new regime in Iraq posed a threat to the security of that region. The Eisenhower administration was aware that Iraq had kept its eyes on the tiny nation of Kuwait. Three years after Eisenhower's action, Iraq tried to overrun Kuwait, an oil-rich sheikdom, in 1961 but failed, thanks to the presence of a joint Arab-British force.

By 1990, the threat was more ominous than ever, with Iraqi tanks assembling on the border of Kuwait. Saddam Hussein's country was forty billion dollars in debt from its war with Iran in the 1980s, with much of that money owed to Kuwait. Hussein was eager to control access to the Persian Gulf and expand his power and influence. He was in a strong position to cause trouble, flexing his muscles with the fourth largest army in the world, just behind the third-place United States, and the sixth largest air force. Under his command were nine hundred thousand troops and 950 combat airplanes.

With tension growing in that region, the U.S. Air Force issued a white paper on the threat, *Global Reach—Global Power*, in June 1990. The paper warned ominously:

> In the Persian Gulf, our objectives will remain to support friendly states and prevent a hostile power—any hostile power, not necessarily the Soviet Union—from gaining control over the region's oil supplies and lines of communication.

To compound the international situation in that region, talks between Iraq and Kuwait concerning the price of oil reached an impasse by summer. On August 2, 1990, Hussein ordered his army to invade Kuwait. At 2 A.M., three armored Iraqi divisions of Soviet-built tanks rolled across the border into Kuwait. President George H. W. Bush responded on the same day by imposing an economic embargo against Iraq.

Five days later, with Hussein still refusing to remove his troops from Kuwait, President Bush ordered the start of Operation Desert Shield under the command of General Norman Schwarzkopf to liberate Kuwait and force Hussein's army back into Iraq. Twenty-four American F-15 fighter planes soared into the air from Langley Air Force Base in Virginia that day and landed at Dharan the next afternoon after a nonstop flight of fifteen hours, eight thousand miles, and fifteen in-flight refuelings. When they touched down in Saudi Arabia, they were carrying eight missiles and full supplies of ammunition. Immediately on arrival, they were placed on alert. On the same day, two DC-10 commercial airliners from America arrived from Pope Air Force Base in South Carolina with 520 troops of the 82nd Airborne Division.

In his book *Storm Over Iraq: Air Power and the Gulf War,* Richard P. Hallion, the recently retired chief historian of the U.S. Air Force, described the emphasis on American air power from the first planning stages for the war. Hallion wrote,

> Air Force contingency planning began virtually immediately upon the outbreak of the crisis. Colonel John A. Warden III of the Air Staff Plans Directorate assembled a team of twenty experts who, like him, were "true believers"—the kind of airmen who spell *air power* as one word.
>
> They were members of "Checkmate," a special staff in the Air Force's planning operation known for its emphasis on creative and independent planning and analysis in planning combat operations. They carry out their thinking and planning in a crowded basement office area in the Pentagon. On Monday, August 6, on their own initiative, they began planning possible air campaign options for confronting Iraq.

General Schwarzkopf "formally turned to the Air Force," Hallion reported, requesting recommendations on offensive air options from the vice chief of staff, General John M. "Mike" Loh, because the chief of staff, General Michael J. Dugan, was at Hanscom Air Force Base in Massachusetts addressing a meeting of the Air Force Sergeants' Association.

Air Force Colonel Richard T. Reynolds described the conversation in his 1995 book, *Heart of the Storm: The Genesis of the Air Campaign Against Iraq.* In a transatlantic telephone conversation, General Schwarzkopf told General Loh, "You know, we have a decent plan for air/land operations, but I'm thinking of an air campaign, and I don't have any expertise—anybody here who can think in those kinds of terms and look at a broader set of targets or a strategic campaign."

Loh told Schwarzkopf, "We have a cell here that is capable of doing that—that has started talking about that. I will get the support of both TAC and SAC [Tactical Air Command and Strategic Air Command] in helping to flesh that out, and we will start working on that right away and coordinate it with your staff."

Schwarzkopf stressed the urgency facing him:

> I need it fast because he [Saddam Hussein] may launch a chemical Scud [missile] or chemical attack. We can't go out in piecemeal with an air/land battle plan. I have got to hit him at his heart. I need it kind of fast because I may have to attack those kinds of targets deep, that have value to him as a leader, if he decides to launch a plan of attack with Scuds or even with chemical or nuclear weapons. So I need this kind of fast.

Loh got the picture without any trouble. "Okay," he told Schwarzkopf. "I will get back with you. What I need to do is to get a plan going and bring it to you. Give me about a week."

Schwarzkopf was satisfied, saying, "I'm going to call Colin Powell [then the chairman of the Joint Chiefs of Staff] now and tell him that we have talked and that you are working this for me."

Over the next two days, Colonel Warden and his Checkmate colleagues rapidly sketched out a concept for a "focused and intensive air campaign," after General Loh told Warden, "This is the number one project in the Air Force." The Checkmate plan was presented to Schwarzkopf at MacDill Air Force Base in Tampa, Florida, on Friday, August 10.

Hallion said the Checkmate planners called their plan for a war in Iraq "Instant Thunder" because

> its name was intended as a clear signal that any air campaign would be quick, overwhelming and decisive—not a gradualist approach as had been the case with Vietnam's "Rolling Thunder" fifteen years before. Further refined, and with inputs from Navy and Marine representatives, it subsequently formed the basis for what became Desert Storm's first phase.

The plan, Hallion wrote, "won Schwarzkopf's endorsement."

Great Britain joined the cause with twenty-four planes, a number that grew to a force of seventy-three planes of the Royal Air Force. On August 21, Secretary of Defense Dick Cheney announced that the United States had sufficient forces in place in the Mideast to defend Saudi Arabia as part of Operation Desert Shield in the event Hussein decided to try to expand his holdings again.

During that operation and the Gulf War that followed—Operation Desert Storm—32 percent of the Air Force's fleet of C-130 cargo planes was in the Gulf region. In the two operations, they flew almost forty-seven thousand missions, delivering more than three hundred thousand tons of cargo and 209,000 troops.

By the middle of December 1990, eight thousand troops were arriving every day at sixteen different airfields on sixty-five planes, an average of one landing every twenty-two minutes. This air traffic reached a peak of 127 planes a day during Desert Storm. A plane was landing once every twelve minutes.

The American buildup in the Persian Gulf region as the Bush administration prepared for war there was so massive that the airlift flew more "ton miles" in its first six weeks than the entire Berlin Airlift, which lasted sixty-five weeks—ten times as long. Richard Hallion pointed out in his book that the Gulf airlift flew the equivalent of two and a half Berlin Airlifts—more than two hundred thousand people and 210,000 short tons of cargo. During Desert Shield, the buildup before the war, Air Force tankers flew 4,967 missions totaling almost twenty thousand hours. The tankers refueled 14,588 airplanes.

Just before the start of the war, a study by the Army War College warned of difficulties to be expected in fighting Iraq. The study said:

> . . . we do not believe that air power alone will suffice to bring a war with Iraq to an early or decisive conclusion. In the final analysis, ground forces will be required to confront the Iraqi army and either dig or drive it out of Kuwait.

The same study also warned of the possibility of a long and bloody war:

> If we fight Iraq, we should be prepared to defeat it as quickly as possible, since the Iraqi military has shown that it fights well on the defensive. If the Iraqis do not capitulate in the first days of the conflict, we can expect them to "hedgehog." They will wrap themselves around Kuwait and force us to pry them loose—a hideously expensive prospect, in lives as well as in resources.

Richard Hallion reported that Iraq "had a number of disturbing attributes" as the threat of war moved seemingly inevitably toward reality. These attributes included

> a robust, combat-tested army, air force and navy . . . modern airfields with extensive shelter protection, consisting of 24 main operating bases and 30 dispersal bases; excellent redundant command, control and communications; . . . aggressive nuclear, chemical and biological weapons development programs; and a demonstrated chemical warfare capability; approximately 600 Scud-B missiles . . . capable of reaching Riyadh, Dharan, and Tel Aviv, possibly with chemical and biological warfare warheads. . . .

With Hussein bellowing that his Iraqi Army would confront the Americans and their allies with "the mother of all battles," some 844,650 Allied troops were on the ground in the Gulf region, representing sixteen nations. Of the total, 532,000 were Americans. In terms of air power, the nations in the international coalition formed over months by President Bush sent 2,614 planes, 1,990 of which were American.

On November 29, 1990, the United Nations approved Resolution 678, authorizing the use of force to drive Iraq out of Kuwait by force if it had not withdrawn its forces from there by January 15. On January 12, President Bush received the congressional backing he had asked for—a resolution approved by the House and the Senate supporting his plans to force Iraq out of Kuwait and attempt to restore some degree of peace and stability to the region. The votes were supportive but not unanimous: 250–183 in the House and 52–47 in the Senate.

As America stood poised for war again, scenes in its cities seemed like a rerun of newscasts from the Vietnam era. Gatherings of protestors shouted slogans such as "No blood for oil" and "Hell, no, we won't go—we won't fight for Texaco." Others, however, were eager, convinced of the rightness of their cause. One F-16 fighter pilot wrote in his diary:

> Got "The Plan" and my heart soared. I am so damn proud to be part of this! The guys that wrote this plan have put together an incredible air campaign. I was worried that when push came to shove, the right people weren't going to be in the right places where they'd be needed. I am not nearly as apprehensive as before.

In contrast, Professor Michael Walzer of Princeton University's Institute for Advanced Study wrote:

> The U.S. Army and Air Force are pretty much untested: How effectively will they fight? A "quick and easy" war would be a war fought mainly through the air, but is that feasible? Would it even be tried?

The forces of Saddam Hussein were still in Kuwait on January 15, the UN deadline. On that day, President Bush signed a formal directive to his National Security Council authorizing military action against Iraq. Desert Shield suddenly became Desert Storm, and the B-52s, with a full load of deadly new-generation cruise missiles on each plane, soared into the skies over Louisiana in the first minutes of their nonstop trip around the globe. Destination: Baghdad, the capital of Iraq, and other targets throughout that nation.

Information about the mission remained classified for a year after the Gulf War. Ten years later, in January 2001, veterans of the mission relived the experience for Airman First Class Hansen, then a writer in the Public Affairs Office of the 2nd Bomb Wing at Barksdale Air Force Base.

They told him that plans for the mission began almost immediately after Iraq invaded Kuwait five and a half months earlier. Major Blaise Martinick, a navigator on the mission, told Airman Hansen, "There were just two of us briefed into the program initially. Then we eventually briefed in a pilot to help us . . . determine how much air refueling we would need to get over there, do a mission and get back."

Another major, Todd Mathes, an electronic warfare officer on the mission, said, "When we were first called in, we were all under the impression that we were going to be launched fairly quickly. Then it turned out one week went into two weeks, then two weeks went into months. So we started to think it was never going to happen."

One of the aircraft commanders on the mission, Major Marcus Myers, added a description of the intensive preparations that took place with one eye on Hussein's continued presence in Kuwait and the other on the UN deadline. "Week after week, we would study and brief the wing commander on a regular basis," Major Myers said, "but I don't think any of us really thought we were going to do it."

It turned out to be not just the longest bombing mission in the history of the world but also one whose weapons would be the new missiles launched from the air instead of from a warship or an installation on the ground.

These were the new AGM-86C conventional cruise missile, or CALCM, which had been developed in secrecy but had never been tested in combat. More than three dozen of the missiles were stored at Barksdale. While seven B-52 crews were being trained over the autumn months, still unaware of what their mission was going to be, officials at Barksdale received orders to prepare the missiles for launching.

At 3 A.M. on January 16, the alarm rang throughout Barksdale's alert facility:

ALL SIERRA CREWS REPORT TO THE VAULT.

One of the pilots, Steve Kirkpatrick, then a twenty-nine-year-old captain from Fort Worth, Texas, remembered that when they reported to their duty station at Barksdale for this top-secret mission, they were greeted by the local television news media from nearby Shreveport.

Major Martinick recalled the scene: "As we all started filtering in with our flight suits half zipped and so on, there stood the 8th Air Force commander, the squadron commander, and the wing commander, and we realized that this was it."

The 8th Air Force commander, Lieutenant General Ellie G. Shuler, Jr., told the fifty-seven men that their mission was comparable to the one flown by the Doolittle Raiders of almost fifty years before.

Kirkpatrick said, "It really reminded me of something out of an old movie, like in World War II, with the general saying, 'You know some of you guys aren't coming back.' It definitely grabbed our attention." Major Martinick added, "He hammered home that this was the real deal. We were going to go do what we've been trained to do."

Major Mathes pointed out that the crews had to force themselves to remain prepared throughout their months of training because they never knew when "the real deal" might come. "There are always some guys who are caught unaware," he said, "but in our profession you have to have a warrior mentality, and you need to be ready to be called upon to perform your duties."

Three hours later, the crews boarded the seven B-52s and headed around the world, accompanied by their full load of air-launched cruise missiles. When the first Stratofortress took off, it was six thirty-six on the morning of January 16. Kirkpatrick admitted, "It was exciting, yet terrifying at the same time."

As they left the Louisiana pine trees and bayous behind them, the men of Operation Secret Squirrel were taking off against the backdrop of a statement made by Saddam Hussein barely months before: "The United States relies on the Air

Force, and the Air Force has never been the decisive factor in the history of wars."

Hussein's cockiness may have been even greater if he had been aware of something that Richard Hallion commented on later. Hallion said some of the crews on the B-52s were "younger than the planes they were flying."

In the B-52s of the 8th Air Force, the airmen were pinning their hopes on the bomber that had been the Air Force's workhorse attack plane for thirty-seven years, since the first B-52A headed into the skies in 1954. Some 744 B-52s, nicknamed Buffs, were manufactured, with the last one delivered to the Air Force in October 1962.

The first planes of the model still in use, the B-52H, were delivered to the Strategic Air Command in May 1961, during one of the tense periods of the Cold War, when the Soviet Union was making more noises about taking over all of Berlin, by force if necessary—talk that led to the construction of the Berlin Wall three months later.

The B-52 is a giant plane. The plane is capable of flying eighty-eight hundred miles without in-flight refueling. With refueling from KC-135 tankers, the plane can remain aloft indefinitely, limited only by the ability of the bomber's crew members to continue performing their duties. Its crew consists of an aircraft commander, pilot, radar navigator, navigator, and electronic warfare officer.

The B-52's companion plane throughout the around-the-world flight starting that night in Louisiana was the KC-135 tanker, the refueling plane that kept the seven B-52s in the air for their entire trip around the globe. Roughly the same age as the B-52 and manufactured by the same firm—Boeing Company of Seattle—the KC-135 entered Air Force service in 1957. In addition to keeping America's heavy bombers in the air for indefinite periods, the plane also provides other capabilities. It is used by the Strategic Air Command as a flying command post. One such plane is always on alert, ready to take off and control U.S. bombers and missiles if communications and control systems on the ground are knocked out. The planes can also be used for special reconnaissance purposes.

Although not as large as the B-52, the KC-135 is nevertheless a sizable aircraft—136 feet long, 41 feet high, a wingspan of 130 feet, 10 inches, and a speed of 530 miles an hour when flying at 30,000 feet, with the capacity to climb to 50,000 feet. It is flown by a pilot, copilot, navigator, and boom operator, who controls the probe extending from the tanker to the plane being refueled. Like the B-52, the tanker is both heavy and expensive, with a maximum takeoff weight of 322,500 pounds and a price tag of $39.6 million each.

★ 20 ★

"The Coalition Was
at War"

As the airmen took off on the first night of Desert Storm, one of those left behind on the ground held up a sign saying GOOD HUNTING. Major Myers said, "Even though they weren't sure of what we were doing, they kind of had an idea."

The tension rose as the journey unfolded and the planes neared their targets in Iraq. "There were times when things were very calm," Martinick remembered, "but when we got into areas of potential threat, your sense of awareness obviously becomes a little more heightened."

Kirkpatrick agreed. He told Airman Hansen, "The danger of the mission was getting through international airspace and going through countries that may not want you there." A year later, in an interview for this book, Kirkpatrick, who is now a lieutenant colonel and commander of the 93rd Bomb Squadron at Barksdale, said the long flight toward the target was "not too exciting"—until the planes neared their targets in Iraq. The flight over the Mediterranean region was "the most exciting" because they were flying over unfriendly nations. On at least two occasions, he added, with Tomahawk missiles from Navy warships also speeding through the sky, planes narrowly missed midair collisions. At another point in the mission, a plane believed to be from Libya "did a barrel roll" around the formation, Kirkpatrick said, "but our gunners were ready."

The planes of Secret Squirrel flew over the Mediterranean Sea and the Red Sea and finally across the vast stretches of the Arabian Desert while the crew members kept their fingers crossed that they would not be spotted by the planes, ships, or installations of other nations. "The Soviet Navy knew we were there because they were lighting us up [making radar contact] pretty good," Mathes said, "but we had to actually see a missile in the air before we could react."

Martinick added, "All we could do was sit on our hands. We stuck with our flight plan."

Even when launch time for the missiles was almost on them, some of the crew members remained unconvinced that "the real deal" was actually going to happen. "I don't think any of us really thought we were going to do it," Myers said. "We thought Saddam would pull out and it wouldn't happen, but he didn't."

Then the planes turned toward different parts of Iraq, where the night was clear, and launched their deadly accurate missiles, thirty-five of them. Kirkpatrick said, "We literally launched the first weapons of Desert Storm." Their targets were eight "high-value" communications stations, power plants, and transmission facilities in Iraq.

Richard Hallion reported that "in the first four hours of the air war, nearly 400 Allied strike aircraft from the coalition stormed across Iraq, supported by hundreds of others over the Gulf region and over the fleet at sea. Altogether, in that first night, 668 aircraft attacked Iraq, 530 from the Air Force (79%). . . ." Ninety Navy and Marine planes also participated, plus twenty-four from Great Britain and twelve each from France and Saudi Arabia as part of President Bush's international coalition of military forces. In the first day of the war, thirteen hundred combat missions were flown by American pilots and the airmen of the coalition countries.

Martinick remembered having mixed feelings as the missiles were launched. "There was a moment of excitement in launching it," he said, "but then there's also a moment of remorse, because what we're doing could and most probably will cause death. And that is something that everyone has to think of and has in their mind."

They didn't know it, but back home the men were making a different kind of history. Operation Secret Squirrel was the first major bombing raid ever televised live in the homes of the people of one of the warring nations. It was dinnertime in America's Eastern Time Zone, and millions watched in openmouthed amazement, shock, and uncertainty as members of their Air Force fought a war against another nation, live and in color. They saw and heard the reports from CNN's Bernard Shaw and Peter Arnett and other correspondents on other networks and cable systems.

Air attacks were taking place all over Iraq at the same time that night. No fewer than 160 tankers were in the air to refuel the heavy bombers, staying out of range of Iraq's early-warning radar system. Ten all-black stealth fighters loaded with laser-guided bombs weighing two thousand pounds each were cleared for takeoff from Saudi Arabia near the Yemen border. At other bases across Saudi Arabia and other friendly nations in the region of the Persian Gulf, hundreds of other planes took off, in Hallion's words, "amid the thunder of afterburners, forming up, unlit and silent, moving toward the tankers and Iraq."

The planes came from land and sea. Aircraft carriers in the Red Sea and the lower Persian Gulf sent dozens of fighter planes into the air war to protect the American fleet in that part of the world and hit additional targets. Two cruisers and a battleship fired the opening rounds of 106 Tomahawk missiles that were launched against Iraq on that same day.

Hallion pointed out, "Air Force and Navy cruise-missile launches held particular significance, for, unlike manned aircraft, the little missiles could not be recalled. Once these missiles left their launch carriers or fell away from their B-52 mother ships, there was no turning back: The coalition was at war."

Pilots flew below Iraq's radar screens to escape detection, but at least one airman was aware that he and his colleagues could be spotted through old-fashioned techniques, too—means that were considerably less than state-of-the-art. He said, "We could see cars driving down the highways and [were] thinking, *That guy could stop and telephone somebody 150 miles away.*"

Iraq's gunners and trackers at surface-to-air missile sites didn't know where the incoming strikes were coming from or where they were headed. Richard Hallion pointed out that some of their destinations must have been obvious to the Iraqis—especially Scud missile sites—but otherwise the nation's defenders were reduced to the position of "blindfolded boxers, lashing out with potentially lethal force at opponents they could not yet see." He added, "Indeed, no airplanes or missiles were yet over Baghdad."

The seven B-52 Buffs from Barksdale Air Force Base, each armed with five missiles, arrived over their launch points "within fractions of a second" of the planned launch time, according to the mission commander, Lieutenant Colonel Jay Beard—fifteen hours after leaving Louisiana. They launched thirty-five missiles across the desert toward their targets, Hussein's command and control positions in and around Baghdad. An analysis after the war revealed that thirty-one of the missiles hit their targets, a success rate of almost 90 percent.

Kirkpatrick, who was getting his first taste of combat, lost one engine of his plane to "oil starvation"—one of the main worries before and during the mission because of its length. He made it back to Louisiana on seven engines.

Pilots could see the results of the flak from Baghdad a hundred miles away. One Navy attack pilot said, "It was an overwhelming amount. It spread over an enormous area of part of western Iraq. It looked like if you can imagine the fireworks display at Disney World, and you multiply Disney World by a hundred. It's just a continued sparkling effect of white flashes that range in height from the surface to three to four thousand feet."

Hallion wrote,

> By the time dawn broke the morning of January 17, Iraq was well on the way to losing the war, thanks to the

coalition's strategic air campaign. . . . The previous night's attacks separated Saddam Hussein and his leadership from each other and, more important, from their military forces. It drove his regime underground, where they no longer could control events or react to Allied initiatives. . . . Indeed, the major damage occurred in the first ten minutes. Minutes after H-hour, the lights went out in Baghdad, and did not come on again until well after the ceasefire. . . . Eventually, by the end of the second week, with even backup communications systems disrupted, Saddam Hussein was reduced to sending orders from Baghdad to Kuwait by messenger; the trip took at least 48 hours.

Colonel Kirkpatrick says today, "We took the eyes and ears out of the enemy."

The dreaded Iraqi Scud missiles became less of a threat in a hurry. As a result of the bombing raids on Scud sites, the number of Scud launches, which averaged five a day for the first ten days of the war, averaged only one for the last thirty-three days.

During the forty-three days of the war, the coalition's air campaign flew 109,876 missions, 2,555 a day. More than twenty-seven thousand were aimed at Scud sites, airfields, air defenses, electrical power plants, biological and chemical weapons installations, headquarters buildings, and facilities involving communications, oil refining, and the Iraqi Army itself.

With all of their pinpoint successes, the bombing raids and missile launches by the U.S. planes and those of the other coalition forces were just as impressive for what they did *not* hit. Michael Kelly, reporting for *The New Republic* magazine, was in Baghdad on the first night of the war. On the next morning, he saw smoke pouring from Iraq's Ministry of Defense after it had been hit. "The hospital next to it, though, was untouched," he said, "and so were the homes crowded around it." This represented another significant feature of American air power—its ability to strike strategic military targets with surgical precision while avoiding the kind of devastation to civilian population centers that typified every air war until Vietnam.

John Warden has drawn an impressive comparison between the accuracy of aerial bombing in the Gulf War and the accuracy of U.S. bombers in World War II. In his book *The Air Campaign*, Colonel Warden wrote,

> To put this in perspective, if you want to hit something about a third the size of a football field and you want a 90 per cent probability of at least one bomb falling into the described area, you must drop over nine thousand bombs. In WWII terms, that meant flying a thousand B-17 sorties and putting about ten thousand men at risk over the target. Because of the relative inaccuracy of weapons, it was necessary to attack large complexes instead of the important parts of them. Likewise, it was necessary to group large numbers of airplanes together for two reasons: First, they had to leave sufficient mass to penetrate enemy defenses, and second, it was necessary to drop a very large number of bombs in order to have any chance of hitting anything.

In contrast, Warden said,

> If our tools in the Iraq case had been similar to those available in World War II, we would have been compelled to attack Iraq serially and we would have started with some small part of its defense system. If we were very lucky, after a long period of time, we might have been able to start the reduction of the key inner rings, but that would have been far into the future. Likewise, it would have been chancy; Iraq in the summer of 1990 had perhaps the most modern air defense system in the world.

Warden pointed to a sophisticated information system, stealth bombers, unmanned missiles, and "most important of all, we had bombs that had a very high probability of hitting that against which they were aimed. Precision has changed the face of warfare."

Going back to his World War II illustration, Warden noted that to reach the same goal of a 90 percent probability of hitting a target a third the size of a football field, "we could confidently dispatch one F-117 stealth fighter manned by one pilot who would drop one of his two bombs."

Warden also pointed out in his book that the bombing in the Gulf War was much more crippling to the enemy than the bombs dropped in World War II:

> In World War II, conventional bombing seemed to do a lot of damage, and indeed it leveled entire cities. Despite the apparent damage, however, vital functions continued in many cases. In 1945 Berlin, for example, the telephone and teletype systems continued to work until the very end, as did the water system and even much of the electrical system. This was a city that from the air looked badly hurt. The reason for this anomaly is simple: The important things tend to be small and the odds are good that they won't be hit directly. . . .
>
> Contrast 1945 Berlin with 1991 Baghdad: Within minutes of the start of the war, electricity is off in Baghdad and does not return until after the war's end, and the ability to communicate plummets.
>
> When the electricity in a country goes off, it immediately puts a strain on almost every activity in a country and forces the occupants to expend energy to find alternatives. Thus, by shutting down the electrical system, with relatively little effort, we were able to affect almost everything and everyone in most of Iraq.

Reporter Milton Viorst wrote in the *New Yorker* three months later:

> I found Iraqis, on the whole, remarkably tolerant of the allied bombs that had destroyed homes or killed civilians. They referred to them as "mistakes"—conceding, in effect, that American pilots had occasionally missed their aim, but had not deliberately sought out civilian targets.

CNN's Peter Arnett found the same attitude among the Iraqis to whom he spoke. "After the first few days," he said, "the Iraqis were not afraid of our bombs. They knew we were only going after military targets."

For the men of Secret Squirrel, the military enemy wasn't the only problem. The long flight back home to Louisiana was made even longer by severe weather, including strong headwinds. "The anticipation was gone," Mathes said, "and so was our tailwind, so it was really longer physically and mentally."

Kirkpatrick remembered another major concern—in-flight refueling. "The biggest thing was the refueling," he told Hansen. "It was a real workout on the boom for forty-five minutes to an hour of continuous refueling."

Once back at Barksdale, after flying around the world nonstop and launching a war, the crew members were debriefed and then allowed to rest. But they were not allowed to talk. They were ordered to keep all information about the operation secret, a prohibition that lasted into 1992 to protect the secrecy of the new missiles. There was something else noticeable about their return, too, something that Kirkpatrick remembered in his 2002 interview for this book: Because of the secrecy surrounding the mission, there was no celebration, no crowd to greet the returning warriors.

"It was tough to not talk about it," Myers said. "People knew we were doing something, but they didn't know we were doing a CALCM [missile] strike." Kirkpatrick maintained his secrecy even where his wife was concerned: "My wife wanted to know, 'Where have you been?' But I couldn't say anything. I just told her I couldn't talk about it." Twenty-four hours after landing safely back at Barksdale, Kirkpatrick was in the skies again, flying his B-52 to Spain to be ready for additional missions over Iraq.

A year later, the secret classification was lifted and the crew members were able to tell their story. "I am proud to be associated with it," Mathes has said today. "It was something special and unique, and I was proud to do my part."

Kirkpatrick expressed the same feelings. "The guys who were involved with it still talk about it," he noted. "It's a common bond." Martinick added, "It was a mission that anyone who was ever involved with it will never forget. To have an impact like that on the opening stages of a conflict or war is truly amazing."

Each member of each B-52 crew was awarded the Air Medal. Airman Hansen wrote that the awards were bestowed "for superb airmanship and demonstration of the Air Force's philosophy of 'Global Reach, Global Power.' "

Technical Sergeant Shawn Bohannon, the historian for the 2nd Bomb Wing, said, "Historically, this remains an important mission for the Air Force. This was the first time a unit from the continental United States took off, struck a target halfway around the world and returned back to its origin. Operation Secret Squirrel was the ultimate demonstration of the flexible, expeditionary capability of American air power."

Public support for the American raids was strong back home. The *New York Times* said in an editorial that Hussein "could not have missed, or misunderstood, the messages that the rest of the world has sent him repeatedly since his troops devoured Kuwait last August. He surely cannot have missed the message delivered last night by the waves of bombers and missiles."

An Air Force Fact Sheet issued in May 1991, said, "Within ten days of offensive operations, air sorties reached the 10,000 mark. The coalition's intensive air power had crippled or destroyed Iraq's nuclear, biological and chemical weapons development programs, its air defenses, its offensive air and ballistic missile capability, and its internal state control mechanisms."

The U.S. Air Force continued to lead the aerial assault. By February 25, according to the Air Force Fact Sheet, "air power's rain of explosives had forced thousands upon thousands of Iraqi soldiers to abandon their stockpiles of equipment, weapons and ammunition and surrender. Air power had done its job. Two days later—February 27—the Iraqi military was scattered and defeated." The war had lasted one month and eleven days and ended in an overwhelming victory for the Allies, the international coalition formed by President Bush and led by the U.S. Air Force. For President Bush, the smashing victory achieved through the air held special meaning. He was a Navy fighter pilot who had flown in combat in the Pacific in World War II.

The might of the Air Force in the war against Iraq stands out in the numbers compiled after the war:

- More than fifty-five thousand U.S. Air Force personnel were in the region during the war.
- Civil engineers of the Air Force constructed more than five thousand tents, built buildings totaling more than three hundred thousand square feet, and laid more than 1.6 million square feet of concrete and asphalt during Desert Shield and Desert Storm.
- During the two operations, the Air Force deployed 256 KC-135 tankers and forty-six KC-10 tankers to the Persian Gulf. The tankers refueled every type of airplane—fighters, bombers, cargo planes, and airborne warning and control system (AWACS) planes. The Air Force reported that so much fuel was used during in-flight refueling it would fill the gas tank of every private, commercial, and publicly owned automobile in Texas and Oklahoma.

In March, two months after the war ended, Secretary of Defense Dick Cheney was asked why the coalition forces, led by the powerful weapons and well-trained men of the U.S. armed forces, had been able to win such a smashing victory, and in record time. Cheney pointed to the power and size of the Iraqi fighting machine, saying, "This was a force that was very successful against Iran, a force that had fought an eight-year battle with Iran. It was well equipped with Soviet equipment. It was not a backward force by any means." Then he added, in a significant elaboration:

> It was crushed, I think, by the air campaign, and the way in which we went about the campaign meant that when we finally did have to move our ground forces in,

and we sort of kicked in the door, they collapsed fairly rapidly.

John Warden was more blunt in *The Air Campaign:* "The Iraqis lost air superiority in the first minutes of the war—and were doomed thereafter." Then he added emphatically, "No one can afford to lose air superiority!"

That same "air superiority" was dominant again twelve years later in what is now being called "Gulf War II," America's war in the spring of 2003 to oust Saddam Hussein from his ruthless dictatorship in Iraq and his involvement in worldwide terrorism. While not producing massive missions involving so many planes that they blocked out the sun on the ground below, which happened on occasion in World War II, U.S. Air Force crews flew about 40 percent of the combat sorties and delivered two-thirds of the munitions tonnage. The remainder was divided among the U.S. Navy and Marine Corps, the Royal Air Force, and the Royal Australian Air Force.

On the second day of the war, U.S. Secretary of Defense Donald Rumsfeld met with reporters at the Pentagon and elaborated on the subject of precision bombing by U.S. pilots. Speaking bluntly, he said:

> Just before coming down, after the air campaign began in earnest, I saw some of the images on television, and I heard various commentators expansively comparing what's taking place in Iraq today to some of the more famous bombing campaigns of World War II.
>
> There is no comparison.
>
> The weapons that are being used today have a degree of precision that no one ever dreamt of in a prior conflict. They didn't exist. And it's not a handful of weapons. It's the overwhelming majority of the weapons that have that precision.

Only five days after the start of the war, Rumsfeld sounded much like one of his predecessors in the job, Dick Cheney. Rumsfeld told reporters, "We've got total dominance of the air."

Rumsfeld had ample justification for making such an emphatic statement. In three weeks, Robert S. Dudney, editor in chief of *Air Force Magazine,* reported, U.S. planes and those of other nations in the international coalition fighting the war dropped 15,000 guided bombs and launched 750 cruise missiles. At one point, American pilots were flying roughly 300 strikes a day, 80 percent of them in direct support of ground forces. "In one week," Dudney said, "coalition pilots destroyed one thousand Iraqi tanks and reduced the strength of Republican guard divisions (the elite arm of the Iraqi fighting force) by fifty percent or more—sometimes much more."

A three-star general of the U.S. Air Force, T. Michael "Buzz" Moseley, commanded the Combined Forces Air Component. On April 5, with the war only two weeks old, Moseley told reporters, "Our sensors show that the preponderance of the Republican Guard divisions that were outside of Baghdad are now dead."

In those thousands of sorties, American aviation history was made. Captain Jennifer Wilson became the first woman pilot to fly a B-2 stealth bomber on a combat mission. On April 1, she flew a B-2 over Iraq with the 393rd Expeditionary Bomb Squadron. It was not Captain Wilson's first combat flight. She had already flown B-1B combat missions during Operation Allied Force over Kosovo in 1999.

On one of the lingering questions of the war, the fate of Saddam Hussein, General Moseley told reporters on April 5, "I don't know whether he's still alive, but I suspect his quality of life is not as good as it was two weeks ago."

Then General Moseley needed only nineteen words to describe American air power in Gulf War II:

> I find it interesting when folks say we're softening them up. We're not softening them up. We're killing them.

Midway through the war, Columnist George Will wrote in *Newsweek* magazine, "Air power by itself recently won a sort of war— the 1999 no-casualty campaign, conducted from 15,000 feet, to stop Serbia's depredations in Kosovo. However, air power alone will never supplant ground power. As has been said, no one surrenders to an airplane. But today's air dominance vastly simplifies the tasks of ground forces because they cannot be threatened from the air, and enemy ground forces cannot concentrate."

The spokesman for the Central Command, Brigadier General Vincent Brooks of the U.S. Army, talked at a press briefing on March 31 about the absence of the enemy's air force from the skies over Iraq and the influence of American air power on the outcome of Gulf War II:

If they fly, they die. It's as simple as that.

Epilogue: History's Heroes

★

"He who does not learn from history," Voltaire once told us, "is condemned to repeat it."

One thing we learned from the history of aviation in the twentieth century and continue to learn today is that the human race's determination to protect its freedom is equaled only by its resourcefulness in inventing the means to do so. The airplane is the most dramatic example of that determination and resourcefulness.

When the twentieth century arrived, there were no self-powered airplanes. By the end of that century, individuals and nations had perfected and flown the Wright brothers' first plane, sleek commercial airliners, and the most sophisticated weapons of aerial warfare. In 1900, only a few of the most farsighted visionaries predicted that human beings and nations would one day be dueling in the sky and dropping bombs on cities, wiping them out in a single raid and even with a single bomb.

Yet that is the short but dazzling history of military aviation, with the United States Air Force as its most dramatic example. From Aeroplane No. 1 to today's stealth bombers, with the B-17s, B-25s, B-29s, and a long parade of others, each more deadly and far reaching than the one before, nations and their aviators have developed faster and more powerful weapons of the air to protect us against those who would use similar air weapons to threaten our freedom and our lives.

Some of the chapters in this book tell of the most primitive times, the horse-and-buggy stage of aviation, from those first days when men cranked up the engines of their planes by hand and dropped their bombs by leaning out the side of their single-engine aircraft—when the term "bombers" would have been an exaggeration. Other chapters tell of the dramatic and destructive bombing missions over Europe and Japan in World War II as American airmen flew and fought to protect Americans and our allies from enemy attacks. Still others tell of the devastating raids in Korea, Vietnam, and the Gulf Wars, and of the classic humanitarian aid when Air Force planes were used to save the people of Berlin from starvation during one of the Cold War's most dangerous showdowns.

Today, in another century, with still more powerful airplanes and more destructive bombs, the planes of the world's leading nations and the men and women who fly them continue to write stirring chapters in the fast-paced history of military aviation. These members of the U.S. Air Force are in the forefront of these heroes, as these pages attest.

While they continue to serve as they fly at supersonic speeds and undreamed-of heights, today's Air Force pilots and crews can draw inspiration, as all Americans can, from the deeds and the sacrifices of the men on these pages. From their early flying machines to today's stealth bombers, they have protected us and kept us free during grave threats of war and uncertain years of peace, including the U.S. bombing missions over Bosnia and Kosovo to protect the Muslim population during the civil wars in those countries. Others have gone beyond their jet planes and into space shuttles like the Challenger and the Columbia where, like those in combat before them, they have given the last full measure of devotion.

Today, in a new century and a new millennium, these Americans occupy positions of particular prominence among freedom's bravest heroes.

Bibliography

American Battle Monuments Commission. *American Armies and Battlefields in Europe: A History, Guide and Reference Book.* Washington, D.C.: U.S. Government Printing Office, 1938.

Boyne, Walter J. "The St. Mihiel Salient." *Air Force Magazine,* February 2000.

Correll, John T. "The Decision That Launched the *Enola Gay.*" *Air Force Magazine,* April 1994.

———. *Revisionism Gone Wrong: Analysis of the* Enola Gay *Controversy, March 1994–December 1996.* Arlington, Va.: The Air Force Association, 1994.

———. *Revisionism Gone Wrong: Analysis of the* Enola Gay *Controversy, Part II.* Arlington, Va.: The Air Force Association, 2002.

Foulois, Benjamin D., and C. V. Glines. *From the Wright Brothers to the Astronauts.* New York: Arno Press, 1980.

Frisbee, John L. "Big Week: Day One." *Air Force Magazine,* August 1995.

———. "A Bridge Downtown." *Air Force Magazine,* January 1992.

———. "Into the Mouth of Hell." *Air Force Magazine,* September 1988.

———. "A Place Called the Doumer Bridge." *Air Force Magazine,* February 1988.

———. "In the Beginning . . ." *Air Force Magazine,* June 1984.

———. "When Push Came to Shove." *Air Force Magazine,* December 1983.

———. "A Good Thought to Sleep On." *Air Force Magazine,* March 1982.

———. *"Question Mark* 'Refuelers' Honored." *Air Force Magazine,* July 1976.

Futrell, Robert Frank. *The United States Air Force in Korea, 1950–1953.* Washington, D.C.: Center for Air Force History, 1983.

Gilbert, Bill. *They Also Served: Baseball and the Home Front, 1941–1945.* New York: Crown Publishers, 1992.

Glines, C. V. "In Pursuit of Pancho Villa." *Air Force Magazine,* February 1991.

———. "Flying the Hump." *Air Force Magazine,* March 1991.

———. *The Doolittle Raid: America's Daring First Strike Against Japan.* Atglen, Penn.: Schiffer Military/Aviation History, 1991.

Hallion, Richard P. *Storm Over Iraq: Air Power and the Gulf War.* Washington, D.C., and London: Smithsonian Institution Press, 1992.

Hobson, Chris. *Vietnam Air Losses: United States Air Force, Navy and Marine Corps Fixed-Wing Aircraft Losses in South-east Asia, 1961–1973.* Hinckley, U.K.: Midland Publishing, 2001.

Hoyt, Brigadier General Ross G. Hoyt. "Reflections of an Early Refueler." *Air Force Magazine,* January 1974.

Hughes, Thomas Alexander. *Over Lord: General Pete Quesada and the Triumph of Tactical Air Power in World War II.* New York: The Free Press, 1995.

Lawrence, Bill. *Six Presidents, Too Many Wars.* New York: Saturday Review Press, 1972.

McCullough, David G., editor. *The American Heritage Picture History of World War II, Volumes I and II.* New York: American Heritage Publishing Co., 1966.

McCullough, David G. *Truman.* New York: Simon & Schuster, 1992.

Michel, Marshall L. III. *The Eleven Days of Christmas.* San Francisco: Encounter Books, 2002.

Miller, Roger G. *To Save a City: The Berlin Airlift, 1948–1949.* Honolulu: University Press of the Pacific, 2002.

Reynolds, Colonel Richard T. *Heart of the Storm: The Genesis of the Air Campaign Against Iraq.* Maxwell Air Force Base, Montgomery, Ala.: Air University Press, 1995.

Sherwood, John Darrell. *Officers in Flight Suits: The Story of Air Force Fighter Pilots in the Korean War.* New York: New York University Press, 1996.

Sherwood, John Darrell. *Fast Movers: America's Jet Pilots and the Vietnam Experience.* New York: The Free Press, 1999.

Spencer, Otha C. *Flying the Hump: Memories of an Air War.* College Station: Texas A&M University Press, 1992.

Stenfels, Major Robert W., and Frank Way. *Burning Hitler's Black Gold.* Laguna Beach, Calif.: self-published, 2002.

Thompson, Wayne. *To Hanoi and Back: The USAF and North Vietnam, 1966–1973.* Washington, D.C.: Smithsonian Institution Press, 2000.

Tibbets, Paul W. *Return of the* Enola Gay. Columbus, Ohio: Mid Coast Markering, 1998.

Truman, Margaret, editor. *Where the Buck Stops.* New York: Warner Books, 1989.

U.S. Air Force Fact Sheet 91-03, Special Edition. *Airpower in Operation Desert Storm.* Washington, D.C.: U.S. Air Force, 1991.

Warden, Colonel John A. III. *The Air Campaign.* Lincoln, Neb.: toExcel Press, 2000.

Index